CW01650244

Units 1/2

Recording and Accounting for Cash and Credit Transactions

Study Pack

Foundation (NVQ Level 2)

Published August 1999 by Financial Training, 10–14 White Lion Street, London N1 9PE

ISBN 1 85179 774 2

This text has been published by Financial Training, one of the leading providers of training in accountancy and finance. Although it is aimed at students on the Education and Training Scheme of the Association of Accounting Technicians (AAT) it is not published or approved directly by the AAT. Any queries on the Education and Training Scheme and AAT Administration should be addressed to Student Services at AAT, 154 Clerkenwell Road, London EC1R 5AD (0171 837 8600), or emailed to studentsupport@aat.org.uk.

Publisher's note

Financial Training study materials are distributed in the UK and overseas by Stanley Thornes (Publishers) Limited. It is another company within the Wolters Kluwer group and can be contacted at Stanley Thornes, Ellenborough House, Wellington Street, Cheltenham GL50 1YD. Telephone: 01242–228 888. Fax: 01242–221 914.

We are grateful to the Association of Accounting Technicians for kind permission to reproduce tasks from the central assessments.

Contents

Chapter 6 Legal relationship of buyer and seller

Chapter 7 Trading on credit terms

Chapter 8 Maintaining the sales day book

Chapter 9 Maintaining the debtors' ledger

Central Assessment Pack

Introduction

Units 1 and 2 at the Foundation level of AAT are assessed by both Devolved and Central Assessment.

Central Assessment

The only Central Assessment at the Foundation level is a three hour paper covering both Unit 1 Recording and accounting for cash transactions and Unit 2 Recording and accounting for credit transactions. As the assessment covers both units, you should not attempt it until you believe you are competent in all aspects of both units. There are two Central Assessment sittings each year, in June and December. You must register with the AAT in advance if you want to attend a particular sitting! For more details, contact your Approved Assessment Centre (AAC).

Format of the Central Assessment

A typical format has emerged over the last few sittings as follows. Please note that you must complete all tasks.

Section 1: Processing exercise

A test of double-entry principles, requiring you to post individual transactions from the cash book and petty cash book into the creditors' and debtors' ledgers and totals into the nominal ledger accounts, prepare debtors' and creditors' ledger listings, reconcile the control accounts, close off the nominal ledger accounts and prepare a trial balance.

You will normally be given outline nominal ledger accounts and a proforma trial balance.

Section 2: Short answer questions

Around 20 short answer questions, possibly related to the scenario in Section 1 covering topics such as accounting principles, purpose of business documents, contract law.

In most cases you will put a ring around your chosen answer or write in the gaps shown.

Section 3: Communicating accounting information

Two communications exercises requiring you to prepare business communications (eg, letters, memoranda), based on a given scenario and including a certain element of technical knowledge (for example, dealing with cheques referred to drawer).

You will normally be provided with the relevant business stationery (pre-printed memoranda, letter-headed writing paper).

Common problems with this central assessment

The assessor has made the following comments.

General

- Candidates should be aware that central assessments are primarily concerned with testing knowledge and understanding of the relevant standards of competence. It is also important to appreciate that the various tasks set within the assessment are all compulsory. In order to demonstrate competence, it is therefore necessary for candidates to be in a position to answer questions from *any* or *all* of the standards (these are listed at the end of this Introduction).
- Of the various accounts required, candidates appeared to find the control accounts most difficult to handle.
- Some candidates did not fully understand the purpose of the day books in providing totals for posting to the various accounts and instead posted each individual transaction separately.
- The full names of accounts should be used ... and candidates should thus avoid abbreviations.
- A common difficulty related to the treatment of VAT within a system of double-entry. Without a sound grasp of the basic principles of VAT, it becomes impossible to demonstrate competence in Section 1 of the assessment.

Other candidates unfortunately continue to show gaps in their knowledge, particularly concerning banking and the law of contract.

Comments regarding Section 3

- The communication should be appropriate in terms of content and format. For example, it is not appropriate to threaten withdrawing credit facilities for a valued customer.
- The communication should be complete and thus contain all the necessary information needed by the recipient.
- The communication should be clear to the person receiving the letter or memorandum.
- It is important to read the requirements for each task carefully to ensure that all points are covered within the communication.
- It is difficult to demonstrate competence unless the communication is complete, appropriate to the situation and coherent.

Other

- Those who were unfortunately not successful often appeared to need further practice in answering the type of tasks set in central assessments and to be aware of the full range of standards at this level.

- Candidates with a sound knowledge of the standards were able to achieve very high marks in this section (Section 2).

- Well prepared candidates were once again able to achieve full marks for this section (Section 1).

What the assessor is looking for

Your objective is to prove that you are competent in the unit(s) being assessed. You must therefore aim for an extremely high standard of presentation.

How to tackle the central assessment

- Always read all the instructions carefully before starting.

  In Section 2 you are required to put a **ring** around your chosen answer and this is the only acceptable method of answering. Do not tick your chosen answer or cross out the others as this can lead to confusion and loss of marks.

- Work through the paper in the order set.

  You may discover that some of the tasks in Section 2 relate to aspects of Section 1.

- Allocate your time sensibly between the tasks, although time-pressure should not be a problem if you are well-prepared.

- Work methodically through the bookkeeping exercise.

  You must aim to get all of this exercise correct if you are to be assessed as competent.

- If you have problems with one of the short answer questions, leave it and return to it later.

  Never leave a gap.

- Plan your approach to the communications exercises carefully.

  Read all the information carefully. Make sure you understand what you are required to do and what the aim of the communication is. Remember that in most cases you are writing to someone with limited or no knowledge of accounting, so you must explain any accounting terms.

- Ensure your answer is legible and neat.

  You will gain few marks if the assessor cannot read or follow your answer.

Devolved assessment

Devolved assessment for the AAT qualification involves submitting evidence to show the assessor that you are competent at certain tasks. To achieve competence in a particular Unit, you must prove that all the performance criteria which make up the Unit have been satisfied. The performance criteria for Units 1 and 2 are listed at the end of this introduction.

Preparing an accounting portfolio for devolved assessment

Your accounting portfolio will be a collection of evidence which you have gathered together to demonstrate to the assessor that you are competent.

It may consist of:

- evidence of prior learning and experience
- current workplace evidence
- simulations.

Before you start to accumulate evidence for your accounting portfolio, it is important to decide which of the above three types of evidence will be used.

Note. Your portfolio may comprise a single type of evidence eg all current workplace evidence or all simulations, or a mixture of the three types.

To help you decide, use the following suggested approach.

1 Review the performance criteria to identify any criteria covered by previous experience. If you find there are certain activities which you have already performed in the workplace, your existing work can be used in your portfolio.

2 The remaining criteria should then be split into two; one set to be covered by current/future workplace evidence and the other set out to be covered by simulations. Deciding which type of evidence will be appropriate is not always an easy task. If in doubt, you should speak to your manager and ask "Am I likely to get experience in these areas in the workplace?" Your manager may be able to arrange for you to broaden your work experience if necessary. If this isn't possible, you may attempt simulations provided by your AAC to plug any gaps in your portfolio.

Once you have identified what might be included, the best approach is to gather evidence gradually over a period of time. Many people find it easiest to keep a file at work into which they put a copy of each piece of evidence as it arises. You will also need to allocate some time to actually compiling the portfolio.

Essentially, your portfolio will be a collection of documents, selected by you which you feel are sufficient to demonstrate your competence in the performance criteria.

Most of these documents will probably be photocopies of actual pieces of work completed as part of your work, as part of a work placement or as a simulation. You may also sometimes include evidence of other qualifications if you feel they are relevant. Check their relevance with your AAC first.

Each piece of evidence must be accompanied by a completed *commentary sheet* which you will find in your *Student Record Book.* Do not forget that the accounting portfolio also provides evidence of your communications skills which are seen as an important part of all assessments at all stages.

Simulations

What will the simulation cover?

Most simulations will cover either complete units or selected elements. Where you only require a simulation to cover certain performance criteria, you may find that your AAC still requires you to sit a simulation covering a complete element or unit as it may not be possible to assess those performance criteria out of context.

A typical simulation covering all the Unit 1 elements would require you to carry out accounting tasks as well as prepare a short business communication, such as replying to a letter or preparing a memorandum.

How much preparation is required?

You must be confident that you are competent in all the relevant performance criteria before attempting the simulation. You should attempt (or revise) the *practice simulation* in this Study Pack.

There is no pass mark for simulations: you are either assessed as *competent* or *not yet competent.* This means that you should aim to complete every task with complete accuracy. In fact, a few minor errors may be allowed, but this can only be decided by the assessor.

How long will it last?

There is no set time period for a simulation, although most take between three and four hours to complete. The aim is not to put you under unrealistic time-pressure, but to ensure that you can complete tasks in a reasonable period of time.

What is the assessor looking for?

While preparing for simulation, it is worth considering what the assessor is looking for. Remember that the assessor will assess you as either *competent* or *not yet competent.* To give you an indication of the general level required, ask yourself whether your supervisor/manager would be satisfied with a particular piece of work if you submitted it for review. Remember that the simulation is meant to simulate real work tasks, so the same standards must apply.

If we consider a typical simulation for Unit 1 *Recording and accounting for cash transactions*, the assessor will be looking for evidence of good presentation skills, completeness, good communication skills, accuracy and technical knowledge.

Good presentation skills

All work should be neat and well presented, as if it were real work. You should use black ink or biro. Pencil is not acceptable, neither is correcting fluid (eg Tipp-Ex). Cross out any errors neatly and clearly. Always use a ruler for underlining.

Completeness

All tasks should be complete (for example, columns totalled). Unlike in other forms of test, you cannot decide to leave out part of an exercise and still hope to be successful.

Good communication skills

Communication skills are fundamentally important in all the assessments for all stages. You are expected to show a good standard of English, including correct spelling and correct use of accounting terms.

Accuracy

All calculations must be completed accurately (for example, the calculation of the tax on a salary). All documents completed (for example, cheques) must be accurate. All accounting entries must be correct.

All discrepancies and exceptions must be identified and dealt with correctly. At Foundation stage, this normally means referring them to someone at supervisor level.

Technical knowledge

Any explanations given – for example, how VAT works – must be accurate.

Contents of the accounting portfolio

Let us now look at specific examples of evidence which you could include either in your Unit 1 or Unit 2 portfolio.

The following items might be found in a candidate's portfolio. Note that it might not be necessary to include all of these types of evidence, neither is this an all-inclusive list of possible evidence.

- Photocopies of the candidate's diary of accounting work undertaken, highlighting tasks relating to cash and petty cash or dealing with credit transactions.
- A description of an unusual transaction (unidentified CHAPS payment) and the steps taken by the candidate to identify the payment.
- A flowchart drawn by the candidate showing the procedures for accounting for petty cash, plus a written description prepared by the candidate of internal controls over petty cash.
- A selection of letters and memoranda prepared by the candidate, each accompanied by a short written description of the circumstances of their preparation and clearly covering the complete range statement.
- Extracts from the organisation's procedures manual concerning the security arrangements for the handling of cash and cheques, plus a description prepared by the candidate describing their involvement in those procedures.
- Photocopies of bank reconciliations prepared by the candidate, accompanied by a short description of the procedures carried out.

- A copy of a report prepared by a working party on the feasibility of using BACS payments accompanied by a description of the candidate's involvement.

- A copy of a memorandum sent by the candidate to her supervisor concerning a bank error identified on the bank statement, plus a list, prepared by the candidate, of other possible unusual items or discrepancies which might be found within the bank reconciliation.

- A description of a special project undertaken which involved supplying information for a specific purpose.

- A copy of a memorandum sent by the candidate to her supervisor concerning problems with supplying information before the required deadline, accompanied by a longer description of the circumstances.

- A signed statement prepared by the candidate and signed by a supervisor, detailing the work carried out in their employment.

- A copy of a certificate from another accounting administration qualification (completed six months earlier) and a copy of the syllabus which includes recording and accounting for petty cash or credit transactions, accompanied by a short description prepared by the candidate explaining the relevance to the standards.

- A simulation covering any performance criteria not already covered by workplace evidence.

Notice that the candidate should make the relevance of each of the items to their experience clear, for example by including a description of their involvement or of the actual procedures carried out.

A note about confidentiality

You may have concerns about submitting copies of confidential documents as part of your accounting portfolio. In all cases, you are advised to seek permission from your employer and to remove as appropriate (with liquid paper) any sensitive information.

If there are further problems of confidentiality, you should consider submitting detailed descriptions of actual work undertaken, signed by your employer, or evidence generated by completing the activities within this Study Pack.

If in doubt, you should always discuss the best method of assessment for you with your AAC.

Format and presentation

You are advised to use a lever arch file as the volume of documentation may be considerable.

Presentation is an important part of your accounting portfolio. All documents should be neat and tidy, with careful indexing and cross-referencing. A checklist is given below which you may find useful to ensure that your accounting portfolio contains the basic information required for assessment.

The assessment process for Devolved Assessment

Your accounting portfolio will be assessed against the standards. In most cases, the assessment process will involve a short interview.

There are two possible outcomes of the process: you will be assessed as either *competent* or *not yet competent*. In the case of the latter, you will receive feedback as to where improvements need to be made within your accounting portfolio and invited to re-submit it at a later date.

(*Note.* Grades are not awarded for accounting portfolios.)

Accounting portfolio completion checklist

Before you submit your portfolio for assessment, ask yourself the following questions.

- Are your name, address, AAT registration number, AAC number and the identity of the units attempted clearly shown on the file?
- Have all documents been numbered?
- Have you included a list of all the documents within the portfolio?
- Have you supplied a list of all the performance criteria for this unit, cross-referenced to the relevant evidence?
- Have all the performance criteria been covered by the evidence included within the portfolio?
- Does each piece of work have a completed commentary sheet attached?
- Does the portfolio contain a signed statement (or statements) from your supervisor/manager that your contribution to each piece of work has been accurately recorded and that permission has been given to include certain documents?
- Does each piece of work have a clear title and show the date of its preparation?
- Are the commentaries neatly and clearly presented?
- Is it clear, in every case, exactly what your contribution was to the piece of work?
- Is it clear how each piece of work demonstrates your competence in the particular performance criteria?

If you answer *No* to any of these questions, then you should not submit your portfolio without supplying this additional detail.

Overall competence in Unit 1 and Unit 2

To achieve competence in Unit 1 and Unit 2, you must achieve competence in both the Devolved and the Central Assessments. There is no requirement to complete one before the other, and if competence is demonstrated in one, you keep credit for that one whether or not you are competent in the other.

Using the Study Pack

Whatever your previous experience, you are encouraged to work through the Study Pack, paying attention to the areas which are most relevant to you. Here is a short explanation of the aim of each aspect of this Study Pack and the areas in which they are relevant. This will help you decide how best to approach your studies.

- **Study Pack Chapters 1–14.** These contain study material, examples and questions (with answers in Chapter 15) on a particular topic to help you to learn the required techniques. Performance criteria covered are identified at the beginning of each chapter, as is a list of what you should actually be able to do once you have completed your studies of the chapter. There is also a summary at the end.

- **Study Pack Chapter 16 Practice Simulations.** These are comparable in difficulty with the devolved assessments that you will eventually have to complete. Both have full answers.

- **Study Pack Chapter 17 Practice Central Assessment.** This formed the Specimen Central Assessment distributed by the AAT when the Standards were last revised in 1998, and so represents a fair example of what you will have to face. Full answers are provided.

- **Central Assessment Pack Chapters 1–14.** These contain additional questions, most of which come from recent Central Assessments set by the AAT. All have full answers (Chapter 16).

- **Central Assessment Pack Chapter 15.** This contains two large-scale processing exercises, both with full answers.

- **Central Assessment Pack Chapter 17 Mock Central Assessment.** This is the December 1998 actual paper, for you to try as far as possible under timed conditions. Full answers are provided.

You should try to make sure that you attempt all questions and central assessments in the Study Pack without looking at the answers. It is only by doing this that you get full value from the Study Pack. By peeking the only person you are cheating is yourself!

Central Assessment Pack

The Financial Training Company also publishes a *Central Assessment Pack* designed to give you additional practice towards the *cash and credit* central assessment. As well as containing new exercises of the sort featured in the real central assessments, it also contains brief revision notes of all major topics.

Performance criteria for Unit 1

Recording and accounting for cash transactions

Element 1: Record and bank monies received

Performance criteria

(i) Monies are banked in accordance with the organisation's policies, regulations, procedures and timescales.

(ii) Incoming monies are checked against relevant supporting documentation.

(iii) Cash is correctly counted and correct change given where applicable.

(iv) Monies received are correctly and legibly recorded.

(v) Written receipts are correctly issued where required.

(vi) Totals and balances are correctly calculated.

(vii) Paying-in documents are correctly prepared and reconciled to relevant records.

(viii) Documentation is correctly filed.

(ix) Cash handling, security and confidentiality procedures are followed.

(x) Discrepancies, unusual features or queries are identified and either resolved or referred to the appropriate person.

Element 2: Make and record payments

Performance criteria

(i) Payments are made and recorded in accordance with the organisation's policies, regulations, procedures and timescales.

(ii) Payments are properly authorised.

(iii) Cheques are prepared correctly and are signed by designated person(s) prior to despatch.

(iv) Standing orders and other inter-bank transfers are correctly documented.

(v) Remittance advices are correctly prepared and despatched with payments.

(vi) Totals and balances are correctly calculated and checked against documentation.

(vii) Available cash discounts are identified and deducted.

(viii) Documentation is correctly filed.

(ix) Safety and security procedures for the handling of cash and cheques are followed.

(x) Discrepancies, unusual features or queries are identified and either resolved or referred to the appropriate person.

Element 3: Maintaining petty cash records

Performance criteria

(i) Transactions are accurately recorded and analysed to the correct expenditure heads.

(ii) Cash withdrawals from the main cash account are accurately recorded.

(iii) Claims are properly authorised, are within prescribed limits and are supported by adequate evidence.

(iv) Totals and balances are correctly calculated.

(v) The balance of cash in hand is reconciled with the petty cash records at appropriate intervals.

(vi) Documentation is correctly filed.

(vii) Analysed totals of petty cash expenditure are transferred to the correct ledger accounts.

(viii) Cash handling, security and confidentiality procedures are followed.

(ix) Any discrepancies, unusual or queries are identified and either resolved or referred to the appropriate person.

Element 4: Account for cash and bank transactions

Performance criteria

(i) Entries in the cash book are accurately transferred to correct ledger accounts.

(ii) Bank reconciliation statements are accurately prepared and are presented within specified timescales.

(iii) Recorded transactions are supported by properly authorised primary documentation.

(iv) Details for the relevant primary documentation are recorded in the cash book and analysed accurately.

(v) Totals and balances are correctly calculated.

(vi) Security and confidentiality procedures are followed.

(vii) The organisation's policies, regulations, procedures and timescales are observed.

(viii) Any discrepancies, unusual features or queries are identified and either resolved or referred to the appropriate person.

Performance criteria for Unit 2

Recording and accounting for credit transactions

Element 1: Process documents relating to goods and services supplied on credit

Performance criteria

(i) Invoices and credit notes are correctly authorised and coded, and despatched to customers

(ii) The calculations on invoices and credit notes, including discounts and VAT, are correct.

(iii) Invoices and credit notes are correctly entered as primary accounting records in a form acceptable to the organisation.

(iv) The analysis and totalling of the primary record is completed accurately.

(v) Documentation is correctly filed.

(vi) The organisation's policies, regulations, procedures and timescales are observed.

(vii) Discrepancies, unusual features or queries are identified and either resolved or referred to the appropriate person.

Element 2: Process documents relating to goods and services received on credit

Performance criteria

(i) Suppliers' invoices and credit notes are correctly checked against ordering documentation and evidence that goods/services have been received.

(ii) Suppliers' invoices and credit notes are correctly coded.

(iii) Calculations on suppliers' invoices and credit notes are correct.

(iv) Documents are correctly entered as primary accounting records in a form acceptable to the organisation.

(v) Documentation is correctly filed.

(vi) The organisation's policies, regulations, procedures and timescales are observed.

(vii) Discrepancies, unusual features or queries are identified and either resolved or referred to the appropriate person.

Element 3: Account for goods and services supplied on credit

Performance criteria

(i) Entries in the primary records are correctly transferred to the correct ledger accounts.

(ii) Adjustments involving debtors' accounts are properly authorised and documented, and are correctly transferred to the correct ledger accounts.

(iii) The control account in the general ledger is reconciled with the total of balances in the sales (debtors') ledger.

(iv) Where required, statements of account are sent to debtors promptly.

(v) The organisation's policies, regulations, procedures and timescales are observed.

(vi) Discrepancies, unusual features or queries are identified and either resolved or referred to the appropriate person.

(vii) Communications with debtors regarding accounts are handled promptly, courteously and effectively.

Element 4: Account for goods and services received on credit

Performance criteria

(i) Entries in the primary records are correctly transferred to the correct ledger accounts.

(ii) Adjustments involving creditors' accounts are properly authorised and documented, and are correctly transferred to the correct ledger accounts.

(iii) The control account in the general ledger is reconciled with the total of balances in the purchases (creditors') ledger.

(iv) The organisation's policies, regulations, procedures and timescales are observed.

(v) Discrepancies, unusual features or queries are identified and either resolved or referred to the appropriate person.

(vi) Communications with creditors regarding accounts are handled promptly, courteously and effectively.

FTC Training Centres

Birmingham 1st floor Centre City Tower 7 Hill Street Birmingham B5 4UA Tel: 0121 644 4747	*Leicester* 3rd Floor Beckville House 66 London Road Leicester LE2 0QD Tel: 0116 285 6767	*Manchester* 6th Floor St James Building Oxford Street Manchester M1 6FQ Tel: 0161 233 2018	*Wokingham* Swift House Market Place Wokingham RG40 1AP Tel: 0118 977 4922
Cardiff 5th floor Market Chambers 5-7 St Mary's Street Cardiff CF1 2AT Tel: 01222 388 067	*Liverpool* 3rd Floor Coopers Building Church Street Liverpool L1 3AA Tel: 0151 708 8839	*Newcastle* Provincial House Northumberland Street Newcastle upon Tyne NE1 7DQ Tel: 0191 232 9365	*Hong Kong* 24th Floor Wyndham Place 44 Wyndham Street Central Hong Kong Tel: (852) 2526 3686
Glasgow 91 Mitchell Street Glasgow G1 3LN Tel: 0141 248 8080	*London (AAT, ACCA, CIMA)* Chapter House 18–20 Crucifix Lane London SE1 3SW Tel: 0171 407 5000	*Nottingham* 3rd Floor Alan House 5 Clumber Street Nottingham NG1 3ED Tel: 0115 853 3600	*Kuala Lumpur* 1st Floor Wisma Alma 2-4 Jalan Manau 50460 Kuala Lumpur Malaysia Tel: (603) 274 8884
Hull Suite R The Shirethorn Centre Prospect Street Hull HU2 8PX Tel: 01482 620578	*London – ACA* 10-14 White Lion Street London N1 9PD Tel: 0171 837 0700	*Sheffield* Pegasus House 463a Glossop Road Sheffield S10 2QD Tel: 0114 266 9265	*Mauritius* Coopers & Lybrand Training Centre 3rd Floor, Astor Court George Guidert Port Louis Mauritius Tel: (230) 208 7945
Leeds 49 St Paul's Street Leeds LS1 2TE Tel: 0113 388 9320	*London – Financial Markets* New London House 6 London Street London EC3R 7LQ Tel: 0171 265 1011	*Southampton* 32 Castle Way Southampton SO14 2AW Tel: 01703 220852	*Singapore* 107A Sophia Road Singapore 228 172 Tel: (65) 333 1877

THE FINANCIAL TRAINING COMPANY

AAT DIVISION

E Mail: aat@financial-training.com

http://www.financial-training.com

A MEMBER OF THE WOLTERS KLUWER PROFESSIONAL TRAINING GROUP

Financial Accounting

Financial statements

The objective of financial accounting is to provide financial information about a business. This information is given in a set of financial statements (or accounts), which consists of two principal statements:

- The **profit and loss account**. This is a summary of the business's transactions for a given period.

- The **balance sheet**. This is a statement of the financial position of the business at a given date (usually the end of the period covered by the profit and loss account).

The basic principles

- **First principle**: Dual effect

  The first basic principle which governs all aspects of book-keeping and accounts is that:

  Every transaction has two effects, not just one.

  Imagine a shopkeeper buying and selling goods. When he **buys** goods, he has more stock **and** less cash.

  Or, alternatively, if he doesn't pay for them immediately, he has more stock **and** an amount owed to his supplier.

  When he **sells** goods he has less stock **and** more cash, or less stock **and** an amount owed to him by his customers, if **they** don't pay immediately.

- **Second principle**: The accounting equation

  Net assets = Owner's funds is the ultimate statement of what is often called the **accounting equation**, but we must first define our terms and build this equation up by means of an example.

Let us look at the position of a sole trader.

Definition of terms

- **Net assets** means the total of a business's assets less the total of its liabilities.

- An **asset** is something **owned** by a business, available for use in the business.

- A **liability** is an amount **owed** by the business, ie an obligation to pay money at some future date.

The term **owner's funds** represents the total amount which the business **owes to its owner**. This consists of:

		Capital	ie the amount which the owner has invested in the business.
	Plus	**Profits**	ie amounts generated by the business.
or	**minus**	**Losses**	ie amounts lost by the business.
	minus	**Drawings**	ie amounts taken out of the business by the owner for his personal use.

Note. Remember that it is essential to realise the distinction between a business and its owner, even where the owner trades entirely on his own. We shall be writing up the books of a business, and preparing its accounts, **from the business's point of view**, not the owner's.

The layouts of the trading and profit and loss account and the balance sheet are shown below.

Proforma trading and profit and loss account

Trading and profit and loss account of Stanley for the year ended 31 December

	£	£
Sales		X
Cost of goods sold		
Stock, at cost on 1 January (opening stock)	X	
Add: Purchases of goods	X	
	—	
	X	
Less: Stock, at cost on 31 December (closing stock)	(X)	
	—	
		(X)
		—
Gross profit	X	
Sundry income		
Discounts received	X	
Commission received	X	
Rent received	X	
	—	
		X
		—
c/f		X

	£	£
Less other expenses b/f		X
Rent	X	
Rates	X	
Lighting and heating	X	
Telephone	X	
Postage	X	
Insurance	X	
Stationery	X	
Office salaries	X	
Depreciation	X	
Accountancy and audit fees	X	
Bank charges and interest	X	
Bad and doubtful debts	X	
Delivery costs	X	
Van running expenses	X	
Advertising	X	
Discounts allowed	X	
	—	
		(X)
		—
		X
		—

Explanations

- The **trading** account discloses the **gross profit** generated by the business by comparing sales with the cost of the sales. A shopkeeper, for example, will purchase for resale items from various suppliers (wholesalers); by adding a profit margin to this cost, the selling price of the goods will be computed, and this margin is the **gross profit**.

- Cost of goods sold is calculated by taking the cost of the goods **available for sale** during the year or period (ie opening stock plus purchases), and deducting the cost of the goods which **were** unsold. Sales and cost of goods sold relate to the **same** number of units.

- The **profit and loss account** shows other items of income and expenditure earned or incurred by the business, in order to arrive at **net profit**.

Proforma balance sheet

Balance sheet at 31 December

	Cost	*Depreciation*	
	£	£	£
Fixed assets			
Freehold factory	X	X	X
Machinery	X	X	X
Motor vehicles	X	X	X
	—	—	—
	X	X	X
	—	—	
Current assets			
Stocks		X	
Debtors		X	
Prepayments		X	
Cash at bank		X	
Cash in hand		X	
		—	
		X	
Current liabilities			
Trade creditors	X		
Accrued charges	X		
	—		
		(X)	
		—	
Net current assets			X
			—
			X
Long-term liabilities			
12% loan			(X)
			—
			X
			—
Capital at 1 January			X
Profit for the year			X
			—
			X
Less: Drawings			(X)
			—
			X
			—

Explanations

- **Fixed assets:** Assets bought for use within the business with a view to earning profits, but not for resale. They are normally valued at cost less accumulated depreciation.

- **Current assets:** those in which the business deals (eg stocks of goods for resale); they should not be valued at a figure greater than their net realisable value. Net realisable value is the amount that an asset could be sold for, less any selling costs.

- **Current liabilities:** Amounts owed by the business, payable within one year.

- **Net current assets:** Funds of the business available for day-to-day transactions. This can also be called working capital.

- **Long-term liabilities:** Funds provided for the business on a medium to long-term basis by an individual or organisation (eg a bank) other than the owner.

Within these main headings the following items should be noted.

- **Fixed assets**

  Depreciation is an amount charged in the accounts to write off the cost of an asset over its useful life.

- **Current assets**

  Debtors are people who owe amounts to the business.

  Prepayments are items paid by the company before the balance sheet date but relating to a subsequent period.

- **Current liabilities**

  Trade creditors are those suppliers to whom the business owes money.

  Accrued charges are amounts owed by the business, but not yet paid, for other expenses at the date of the balance sheet.

Revenue and capital expenditure

Only **revenue** expenditure (eg the payment of rent) is deducted as an expense in the profit and loss account whereas **capital** expenditure (eg the purchase of a motor car) is not.

Revenue expenditure

Revenue expenditure is expenditure incurred in:

- the acquisition of assets required for conversion into cash (ie goods for resale);

- the manufacturing, selling and distribution of goods and the day-to-day administration of the business; and

- the maintenance of the revenue-earning capacity of the fixed assets (ie repairs, etc).

Remember, the amount of revenue expenditure charged against the profits for a year is the amount **incurred** for the period irrespective of whether cash has been paid or not. Similarly, all sales made during the period under review will be included in the trading account even though all the cash may not have been received. This is the **accruals concept**.

Capital expenditure

Capital expenditure is expenditure incurred in:

- the acquisition of fixed assets required for use in the business and not for resale;
- the alteration or improvement of assets for the purpose of increasing their revenue earning capacity.

Because the benefit is spread over a considerable period of time, capital expenditure is not immediately charged to the profit and loss account.

Ledger accounting

Introduction

The purpose of preparing ledger accounts is to summarise similar transactions to help with the preparation of the profit and loss account and balance sheet.

Debits and credits

Each ledger account has two sides. By convention the left-hand side is called the **debit** side and the right-hand side the **credit** side.

Ledger account

A **debit entry** represents:	A **credit entry** represents:
◆ an increase in the value of an asset;	◆ a reduction in the value of an asset;
◆ a reduction in the value of a liability;	◆ an increase in the value of a liability;
◆ an item of expenditure; or	◆ an item of income; or
◆ a drawing.	◆ an item of capital.

For every debit entry there must be a credit entry.

Layout of ledger account

Title of account

Debit (Dr)			*Credit (Cr)*		
Date	*Narrative*	*Amount*	*Date*	*Narrative*	*Amount*
		£			£

Example

Percy started business on 1 January by paying £20,000 into a business bank account. He then spent £500 on a second-hand van, £1,000 on stock and took £50 cash for his own use. On 2 January he bought goods on credit costing £500 and made sales on credit of £2,000.

Record these transactions in the relevant ledger accounts.

Cash

Date			£	*Date*			£
1 Jan	Capital	(1)	20,000	1 Jan	Van	(2)	500
					Purchases	(3)	1,000
					Drawings	(4)	50

Capital

Date			£	*Date*			£
				1 Jan	Cash	(1)	20,000

Van

Date			£	*Date*			£
1 Jan	Cash	(2)	500				

Purchases

Date			£	*Date*			£
1 Jan	Cash	(3)	1,000				
2 Jan	Creditors	(5)	500				

Drawings

Date			£	*Date*			£
1 Jan	Cash	(4)	50				

Creditors

Date			£	*Date*			£
				2 Jan	Purchases	(5)	500

Sales

Date			£	*Date*			£
				2 Jan	Debtors	(6)	2,000

Debtors

Date			£	*Date*			£
2 Jan	Sales	(6)	2,000				

Item 1

Debit (Dr) Cash £20,000

The business has £20,000 more cash.

Credit (Cr) Capital £20,000

The business now owes the owner £20,000. Capital is the amount owed by the business to its owner.

Item 2

Dr Van £500

The business now has a van costing £500.

Cr Cash £500

The business has £500 less cash.

Item 3

Dr Purchases £1,000

The business has made purchases of stock costing £1,000. You may have used a stock account but this would be wrong.

Cr Cash £1,000

The business has £1,000 less cash.

Item 4

Dr	Drawings	£50

The proprietor has made drawings of £50. You may have debited the capital account as the amount that the business owes the owner has fallen by £50. Use of the drawings account achieves this as well as providing more detailed information.

Cr	Cash	£50

The business has £50 less cash.

Item 5

Dr	Purchases	£500

The business has made purchases of stock costing £500.

Cr	Creditors	£500

The business owes its suppliers £500.

Item 6

Dr	Debtors	£2,000

The business now has debtors who owe £2,000.

Cr	Sales	£2,000

The business has made sales of £2,000.

Balancing a ledger account

If we need to know how much capital Percy's business has we need only look at the capital account to find that it is £20,000.

If we wanted to know how much cash it has then the answer is not immediately apparent. We have to strike a balance in the cash account.

Method

- Add up the debits (£20,000)
- Add up the credits (£1,550)

If the debits exceed the credits – the excess is a **debit balance**.

If the credits exceed the debits – the excess is a **credit balance**.

This would be shown in the ledger as:

Date		£	Date		£
1 Jan	Capital	20,000	1 Jan	Van	500
				Purchases	1,000
				Drawings	50
		20,000			1,550
				balance c/f	18,450
	balance b/f	18,450			20,000

(The abbreviations c/f and b/f refer to balances **carried forward** at the end of an accounting period and **brought forward** at the beginning of the next period. The abbreviations c/d and b/d – carried down and brought down – are also used.)

Now we can see that Percy's business has £18,450 in cash.

Note . This 'cash' is actually a bank balance. You will quickly become used to bank balances being referred to as cash.

The trial balance

Introduction

The trial balance is a list showing the balance on each ledger account.

Illustration

	Debit	*Credit*
	£	£
Sales		5,000
Opening stock	100	
Purchases	3,000	
Rent	200	
Car	3,000	
Debtors	100	
Creditors		1,400
	6,400	6,400

Note that the trial balance contains a figure for **opening stock** not closing stock.

The trial balance is produced immediately after the double-entry has been completed and balances extracted on the accounts. If the total of the debits equals the total of the credits, the double entry system has probably operated correctly.

Reasons for extracting a trial balance

- **To ensure that the double-entry has been completed.** Note however, that there are some types of error that will not be picked up merely by extracting a trial balance.

- **A first stage in the preparation of the financial statements.**

Errors identified by extracting a trial balance

- **Single entry** – The debit entry may have been made correctly but the associated credit entry has been overlooked. The result will be that the total of the debits will exceed the total of the credits.

- **Casting error** – An account or the trial balance may have been added up wrongly. In this case, the trial balance will not balance.

- **Transposition error** – An amount of £7,532 may have been incorrectly written as £7,352. If one such error has occurred, the difference on the trial balance will be divisible by 9.

- **Extraction error** – An account may be correct in the ledger but has been copied out wrongly (or not at all) onto the trial balance.

Errors not identified by extracting a trial balance

- Errors of original entry – Where the original figure is incorrectly entered in both parts of the double-entry, then the trial balance will still balance.

  For example: a sale of £50 is recorded in the books as £500.

- Compensating errors – Quite simply, where one error is compensated exactly by another in the opposite direction. Again, the trial balance will still balance.

- **Errors of commission** – Here, the double-entry is completed in the wrong accounts, though in the right **type** of account.

  For example: a £50 payment for rates is debited to the wages account and credited to cash. The double-entry is complete and so the trial balance will balance, but the wrong account has been debited.

- **Errors of principle** – Similar to errors of commission, but using the wrong type of account.

  For example, a £50 payment for rates (an expense) is debited to a fixed asset account and credited to cash. The double-entry is complete and the trial balance will balance, but fixed assets are overstated and expenses understated.

Questions

Question 1 (AAT CA D94)

Mary Chang has decided that some of the offices are looking rather shabby. She arranges for the walls to be redecorated and for the purchase of some new office furniture.

(a) Is the cost of the redecoration capital or revenue expenditure?

(b) Is the cost of the new office furniture capital or revenue expenditure?

Question 2 (AAT CA D93)

Music World Limited are considering purchasing a new computerised accounting system. Would the following be capital or revenue expenditure?

(a) The purchase of computer hardware.

(b) The purchase of accounting software.

(c) The training of accounting staff to use the new system.

Question 3 (AAT CA J94)

Classify the following ledger accounts according to whether they represent asset, liability, expense or revenue:

(a) Stock

(b) Rent received

(c) Heat, light and water

(d) Bank overdraft

Question 4

(a) Show by means of ledger accounts how the following transactions would be recorded in the books of Bertie Dooks, a seller of second-hand books:

(i) Paid in cash £5,000 as capital.

(ii) Took the lease of a stall and paid six months' rent. The yearly rental was £300.

(iii) Purchased on credit from J Fox books at cost of £275.

(iv) Spent £140 cash on the purchase of other books from W Smith.

(v) Paid an odd-job man £25 to paint the exterior of the stall and repair a broken lock.

(vi) Put an advertisement in the local paper at a cost of £2.

(vii) Sold three volumes containing *The Complete Works of William Shakespeare* to an American for £35 cash.

(viii) Sold a similar set on credit to a local schoolmaster for £3.

(ix) Paid J Fox £175 on account for the amount due to him.

(x) Received £1 from the schoolmaster.

(xi) Purchased cleaning materials at a cost of £2 and paid £3 to a cleaner.

(xii) Took £5 from the business to pay for his own groceries.

(b) Balance the various accounts and insert the correct balances.

Question 5

What type of balance would you expect to find in the following ledger accounts (debit or credit)? What does it represent?

(a) Cash in hand

(b) Overdraft

(c) Value added tax

(d) Capital

(e) Debtors

CHAPTER 1

Money and Legal Tender

Objectives

The objectives of this chapter are to outline the different forms of money and to introduce the concept of legal tender.

The importance of money to a business

A business cannot survive without money!

Although its aim is to make money for its owners, it also needs money to be able to run properly.

Day to day, a simple business, such as a sweet shop, needs money so it can:

- buy things to sell to its customers;
- pay wages;
- pay bills (eg electricity, telephone).

But where does that money come from? Most of it will come from the sales it makes to its customers. It is therefore very important that **sums of money received** from customers and **paid** to third parties are:

- **recorded** accurately and as soon as possible

to give management accurate information on money available to the business.

Money received must also be:

- **banked** as soon as possible

so that the business can make use of that money to make payments.

Money effectively goes round in a 'cycle' within a business:

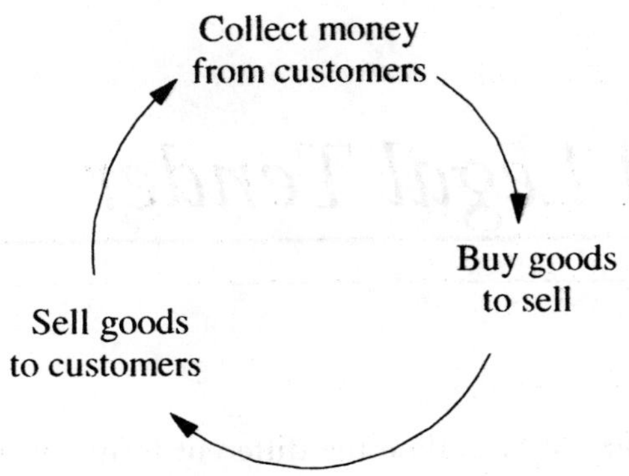

The business also needs money for longer-term uses, for instance buying premises or motor vehicles for use by the business.

The money used for these items will tend to come from:

- the owners of the business;
- the banks.

Money in its many forms. Money may be held by a business in two forms. These are:

- cash;
- bank accounts.

Cash

Notes and coins

The amount of cash held will tend to be low because of the risk of theft. It is convenient to hold cash for various purposes including giving change and buying small items.

Every business must have at least one bank account. Only money belonging to that business will be kept in its individual bank account.

It will normally be a current account opened with one of the high-street banks (eg Natwest, Barclays, Lloyds, Midland, TSB).

If the business has a lot of money it may also have a deposit account.

Current account

The current account (or cheque account) is used by those who want to be able to use the money in it at any time, without restriction.

Deposit account

Money left in a deposit account earns interest at a rate set by the bank. The interest is added to the balance in the account regularly (eg every six or twelve months). There are some restrictions on using the money, ie you must give the bank advance warning if you want to use it.

Bank accounts are a safer method of keeping money.

For each account a bank statement will be sent regularly by the bank, for instance every month. The account holder can usually decide how often the statements are sent.

Bank statement

A statement showing how money has gone into or left a bank account, and the amount of money held in that account at a certain date. There is a standard format with a few variations between banks.

FINANCIAL BANK plc CONFIDENTIAL

You can bank on us!

10 Yorkshire Street, *Account* CURRENT *Sheet No.* 103
Headingley
Leeds LS1 1QT MISS ELIZABETH DERBY
Telephone: 0113 633061

19T5 *Statement date* 31 July 19T5 *Account Number* 34786695

Date	*Details*		*Withdrawals (£)*	*Deposits (£)*	*Balance (£)*
28 JUN	*Balance from sheet no.* **102**				2670.91
1 JUL	000354		7.95		
	SECURITY INSURANCE	DD	10.15		
	LEEDS BRIGATE	AC	50.00		
	NWWA	DD	13.03		2589.78
2 JUL	SUPERSAVER	CP	12.63		2577.15
5 JUL	000349		40.00		2537.15
8 JUL	000348		18.80		2518.35
11 JUL	SURE BULDING SOCIETY	DD	327.74		
	000346		29.80		
	DEPOSIT ACCOUNT	TR	250.00		1910.81
14 JUL	ENGLISH GAS	SO	12.50		1898.31
17 JUL	000355		30.95		1867.36
20 JUL	ENGLISH ELECTRICITY	SO	5.00		1862.36
22 JUL	000356		50.00		1812.36
25 JUL	000351		11.29		1801.07
29 JUL	000352		5.29		
	000350		50.00		
	PAYROLL			340.99	2086.77
30 JUL	000358		26.51		
	Balance to Sheet no. **104**				2060.26

SO Standing order DD Direct debit CP Card purchase AC Automated cash OD Overdrawn TR Transfer

Money may be paid into the bank account free of charge in any branch of that particular bank. Other banks may charge a small fee.

The money paid in can be:

- cash;
- cheques;
- postal orders.

The amounts to be paid in must be summarised on a paying-in slip.

Paying–in slip

A summary of details of money paid into a bank account. There is a standard format with a few variations between banks.

To be retained by receiving bank

For the credit of TRADING COMPANY LIMITED

Cheques etc for collection to be included in total credit of £ 295.69 paid in 15/9 19X3

	£	brought forward	£	brought forward	£
SJ Smith	59.26				
RS Hayes	73.80				
S Bates	15.73				
Carried forward	£148.79	carried forward	£	Total cheques etc	£

Date 15/9/X3

Cashier's stamp and initials

56 – 28 – 48

FINANCIAL BANK PLC

EXETER HIGH STREET

Credit Trading Company Limited

£50 Notes	100	00
£20 Notes	40	00
£10 Notes		
£5 Notes		
£1 Coins	5	00
50p	1	00
20p		
Silver		90
Bronze		
Total Cash	146	90
Cheques, POs etc	148	79
TOTAL £	295	69

Fee

No Chqs

Paid in by J Vorlott

Address/Ref No. ______

Methods of payment

There are lots of different methods of making a payment. Let us look at just a few to begin with.

- **Cash**: Notes issued by the Bank of England are legal tender (ie the law says they are an acceptable method of payment) in England only.

- **Postal orders** This is a method of payment used when it would be unsafe to send cash, which might be stolen. You can buy them at any Post Office. They are available at set values between 25 pence and £20. Postage stamps added to the face of the postal order make up non-standard values. They have a standard format.

  They can normally be exchanged for cash at a Post Office or bank, or paid into a bank account.

- **Cheques.** These are used to make a payment using money from a bank account. They are an **order** to a bank to pay a third party using money held in that account. Cheques have a standard format with a few variations between banks.

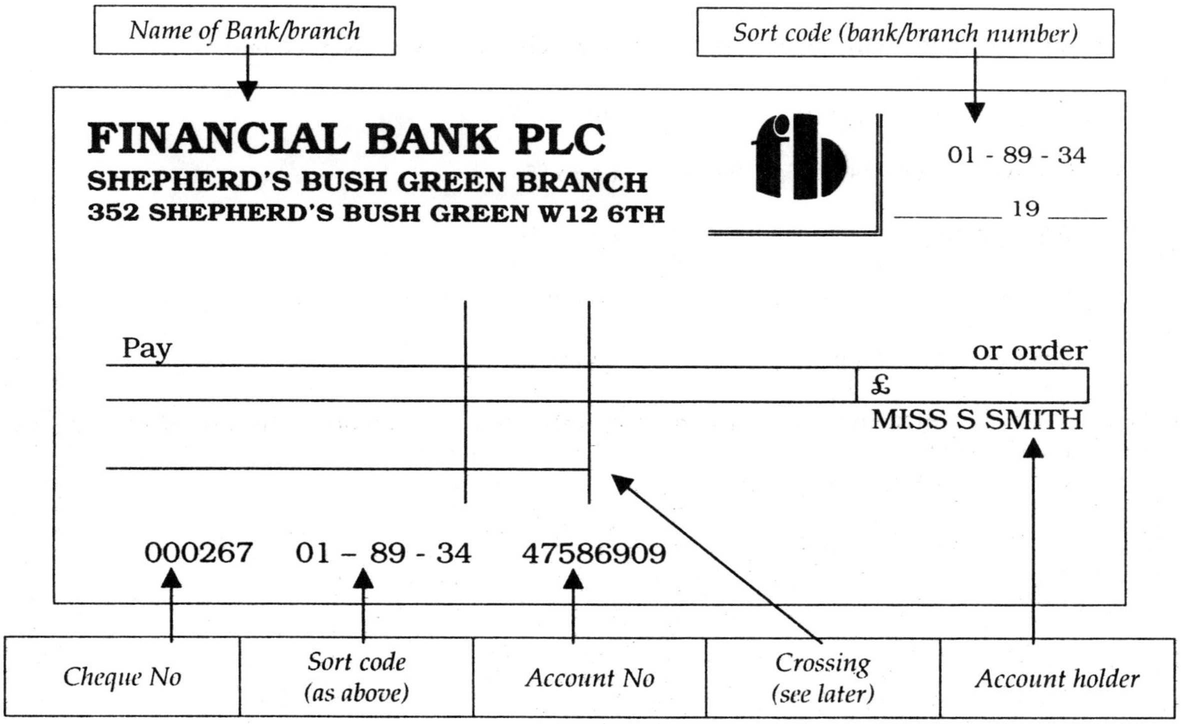

Legal tender

Let us look further at the idea of legal tender.

Money can be defined as follows.

- **Money.** Anything which is generally acceptable as a method of settling a debt.

However, legal tender is something slightly different.

- **Legal tender.** Any method of payment which must be accepted by law in settlement of a debt.

The importance of this is that a £5 note is legal tender and therefore must be accepted as payment of a £5 debt. A cheque for £5 is not legal tender and therefore does not have to be accepted for a debt of £5.

In addition, the exact money must be given or the seller can refuse to accept it, eg. a £5 note offered to pay for a newspaper can be refused by the newsagent.

There are also limits to the amount of currency which can be used as payment:

Bronze coins (ie 1p, 2p)	–	up to 20p
Cupro-nickel coins (ie. 5p, 10p)	–	up to £5
20p, 50p coins	–	up to £10
£1 coins	–	no limit
Bank of England notes	–	no limit

We can say that £1 coins and banknotes are **unlimited** legal tender, whereas other coins are **limited** legal tender.

Questions

1

Examine the bank statement for Miss Derby again, then answer the questions below.

(a) What was the bank balance on 22 July 19T5?

(b) At which branch of the bank is the customer's account held?

2

You have received the following cash from customers. You must:

(a) total the cash received and

(b) complete the paying-in slip.

£20	notes	–	3
£10	notes	–	2
£5	notes	–	3
£1	coins	–	28
50p	coins	–	15
20p	coins	–	17
10p	coins	–	35
5p	coins	–	12
2p	coins	–	18
1p	coins	–	23

There is a paying slip for you to complete on the next page.

To be retained by receiving bank

For the credit of ____

Cheques etc for collection to be included in total credit of £ ________ paid in ________ 19___

	£	brought forward	£	brought forward	£
Carried forward		carried forward	£	Total cheques etc	£

Date ________________

Cashier's stamp and initials

56 – 28 – 48

FINANCIAL BANK PLC

EXETER HIGH STREET

Credit Trading Company Limited

Fee	No Chqs

Paid in by ____________

Address/Ref No. ______

£50 Notes		
£20 Notes		
£10 Notes		
£5 Notes		
£1 Coins		
50p		
20p		
Silver		
Bronze		
Total Cash		
Cheques, POs etc		
TOTAL £		

3 (AAT CA D93)

The following receipt was obtained on 30 November for cash paid in at the bank.

Notes	£50		
	£20	1,600	00
	£10	400	00
	£5		
Coins	£1		
	50p		
	20p		
	silver		
	bronze		
Cash		2,000	00
Cheques			
	£	2,000	00

How many notes were paid into the bank?

1,600 / 80 / 400 / 2,000 / 120

4

You wish to pay £28.34 by cheque to S Greenwood & Company Limited.

Today's date is 26 June 19X3. Here is the cheque to complete.

FINANCIAL BANK PLC
SHEPHERD'S BUSH GREEN BRANCH
352 SHEPHERD'S BUSH GREEN W12 6TH

01 - 89 - 34

_____ 19 _____

Pay ______________________________ or order

£

MISS S SMITH

000267 01 – 89 – 34 47586909

5

Nigel wants to pay his bus fare of 28p. He has the following coins in his pocket.

Value	*Number of coins*
100p	2
50p	3
10p	1
2p	10
1p	8

How can he pay this fare with exact legal tender, using as many of the bronze coins as possible?

6

Define 'money'.

Summary

Cash

- Notes and coins
- Risk of theft
- Can be used as method of payment
- Can be used to buy postal orders (another method of payment)

Bank account

- Current account
- Day-to-day use
- Deposit account – long-term use
- More secure than keeping cash
- Bank statement received regularly
- Can pay-in cash, cheques or postal orders
- Can make payments from current account to third parties using cheques

Legal tender

- Methods of payment which must be accepted according to the law
- Coins and banknotes are unlimited legal tender in England
- Other coins are limited legal tender in England

CHAPTER 2

Receiving Money in a Retail Business

Objectives

This chapter covers the following performance criteria.

- Monies are banked in accordance with organisation's policies, procedures and timescales.
- Incoming monies are checked against relevant supporting documentation.
- Cash is correctly counted and correct change given where applicable.
- Monies received are correctly and legibly recorded.
- Written receipts are correctly issued where required.
- Totals and balances are correctly calculated.
- Paying-in documents are correctly prepared and reconciled to relevant records.
- Cash handling, security and confidentiality procedures are followed.

Accepting cheques

If a cheque is accepted as payment from an individual rather than a business, then it must be accompanied by a cheque guarantee card.

Cheque guarantee card

- For a £50 cheque guarantee card, this card guarantees that a cheque for up to £50 will be paid by the bank, regardless of the amount of money in that account.
- Only one £50 cheque for each transaction is allowed.
- The cheque must not exceed £50, or the bank can refuse to pay anything.
- Some cards guarantee cheques for higher amounts than £50.

In accepting a cheque accompanied by a cheque guarantee card the acceptor must ensure the following.

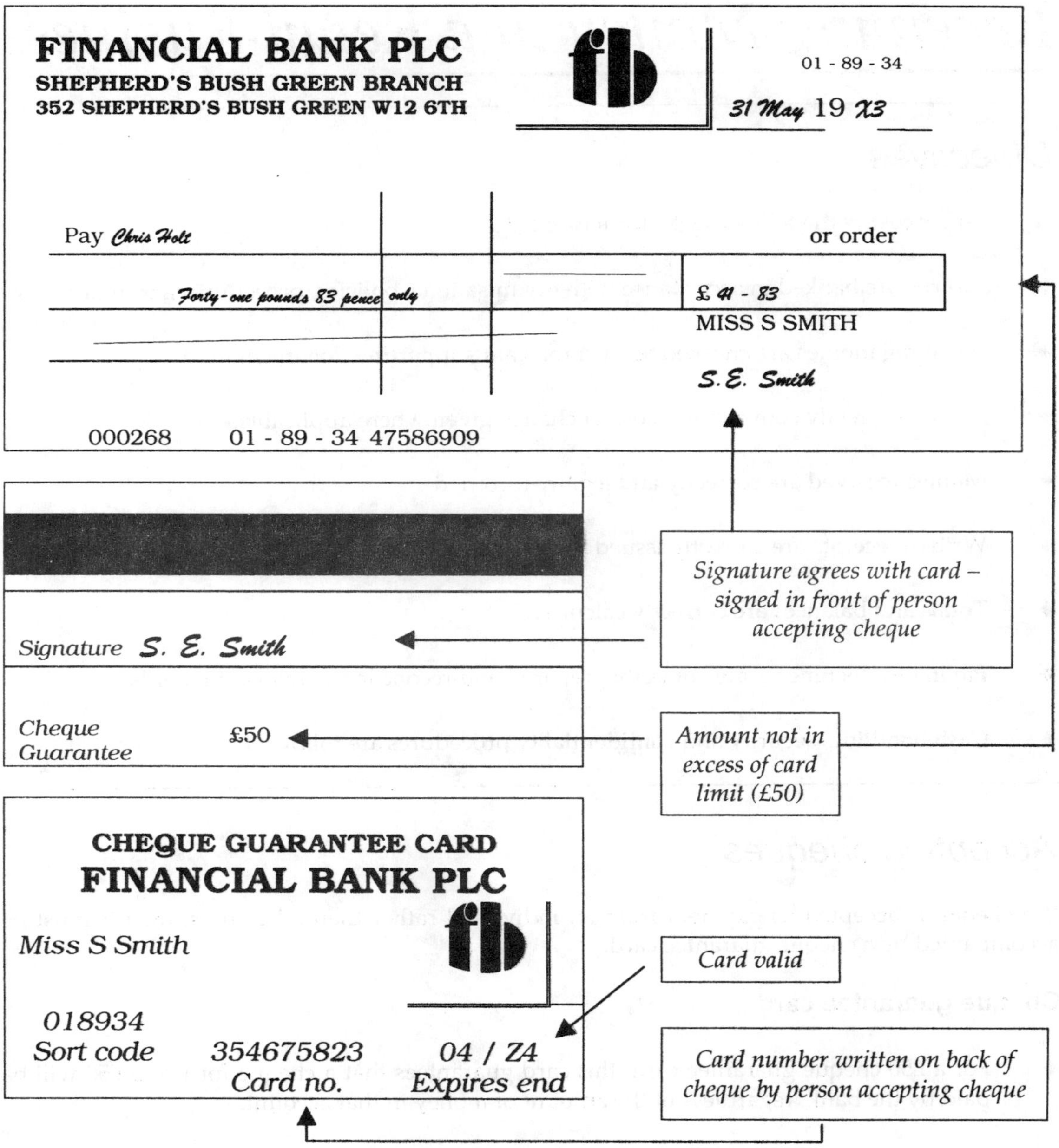

Note: Cheques from companies cannot be guaranteed by cheque guarantee card.

If the retailer is suspicious in any way he should contact the bank which has issued the card.

Summary of checks

Card

- Card is valid (start and expiry date)
- Signature agrees with signature on cheque
- Details agree with the cheque (eg account number, sort code)

Cheque

- Correct date.
- Amount does not exceed the amount on the cheque guarantee card
- Amount in both words and figures
- Cheque signed in presence of person accepting it
- Cheque guarantee card number written on back by person accepting it
- Only one cheque for the purchase

A different form of payment

Certain businesses accept payment by credit card. These businesses include:

- shops and supermarkets;
- restaurants;
- petrol filling stations;
- hotels;
- theatres;
- cinemas;
- railway station ticket offices.

Credit cards

Cards issued by the credit card companies which allow customers to make purchases (without using cash or cheques) at certain shops, hotels, etc.

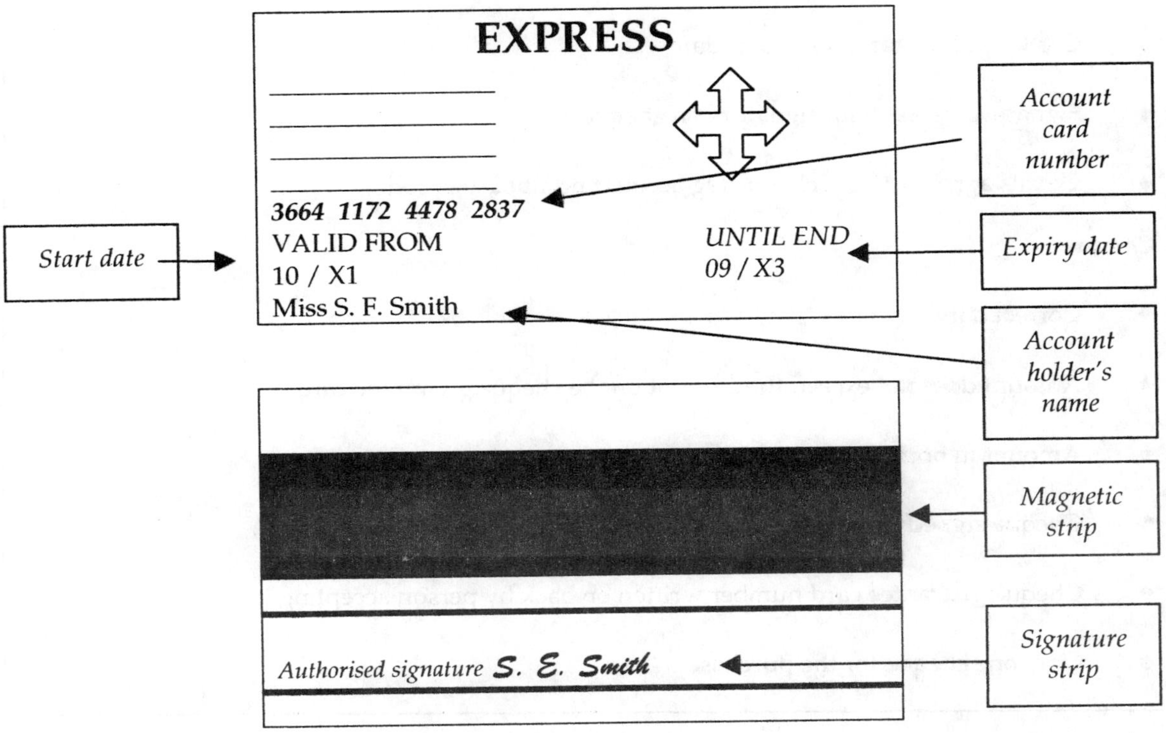

An individual opens an account with one of the credit card companies (eg, Access, Visa) by filling in and posting off an application form. If accepted, the individual will receive a credit card.

This credit card can then be used in places which accept that particular card (they normally display a sign). The payment is recorded on a credit card sales voucher.

Once a month, the credit cardholder receives a statement detailing how much he has 'spent' which is the amount he owes the credit card company.

The cardholder has a choice of:

- paying a minimum balance (set by the credit card company dependent upon the amount owed);
- paying off more than the minimum but less than the total balance outstanding;
- paying off the total balance outstanding.

Payment can be:

- by post;
- at a bank using a bank giro credit slip;
- by regular monthly direct debit (minimum balance only).

If the cardholder does not pay off the total balance within 25 days of receiving the statement, he will have to pay interest on the unpaid amount. The interest charged by credit card companies tends to be higher than that charged by the banks.

The limit for the amount which can be owed at any time is set by the credit card company.

Accepting credit cards

Businesses which make direct sales to the public are generally known as retailers. If a retailer is to be able to accept payment by credit cards, he or she must have the agreement of the credit card company to be allowed to accept payment by that particular credit card.

In return for this service the credit card company will normally charge a commission on each payment using that card.

To complete a sale the retailer needs the following.

- **Imprinter** – A machine which transfers the cardholder's and the retailer's details onto a credit card voucher.
- **Credit cards sales voucher** – Voucher recording details of retailer, customer and sale. Normally three or four copies. At least one copy for each of customer, retailer and bank/credit card company. Vouchers have a standard format with variations between credit card companies.
- **Cardholder's card**
- **A pen.**

3664 1172 4478 2837 **EXPRESS** 10/X1 09/X3

CARDHOLDER COPY

Miss S. E. Smith
048 9133
CHESTERS
BOLTON

DAY		MONTH		YEAR		DEPT	SALES NO	INITIALS
0	8	0	8	X	2	020	115	ANO

DESCRIPTION	AMOUNT	
Books	26	95
Books Token	10	00

CARDHOLDER'S SIGNATURE
S. E. Smith

AUTHORISATION CODE

TOTAL POUNDS PENCE 36 : 95

Cardholder's Declaration: I promise to pay the total amount shown as payable together with any charges thereon subject in the rules of issue.

SALES VOUCHER

Please keep this copy for your records

Why are credit cards popular?

They are popular with the customer because:

- there is no need to carry cash (this is safer and more convenient);
- the items bought can be taken away immediately;
- payments can be spread out;
- free credit is given – there is no need to pay until the account statement is received and the customer then has 25 days to make his payment;
- permanent access to credit is allowed – as soon as the customer repays some of his account he can make further purchases again up to his credit limit. (This is known as revolving credit.)

They are popular with the retailer because:

- vouchers paid into the bank are immediately credited to the retailer's account;
- they allow sales for a value in excess of £50 to be made with more security;
- they increase sales.

Using a cash register

Most retailers will have a till, or cash register.

The cash register has three main purposes:

- It is a secure container for cash and cheques within the shop.
- It records takings.
- It issues receipts.

Receipt

```
CITY TAKE AWAY

VAT: 583 9985 11

  03.07.X1                  0144 01

  15 : 10


Sandw             £1.65

Can               £0.45

Sweet             £0.85

Total             £2.95

Cash              £5.00

Chng              £2.05
```

As well as printing the receipt, the cash register also keeps a record of sales on a till roll within the cash register. These till rolls are kept to provide accounting information.

At the end of each day an X-reading is taken. This gives the total sales so far for the week. By taking this reading at the end of each day the daily takings can be calculated.

At the end of the week a Z-reading is taken which gives the total for the week and sets the cumulative total back to zero.

Look out for different types of cash register used by different businesses. In particular look at the equipment used by supermarkets (eg bar-code scanners) and fast food outlets (eg complex key pads recording each item individually).

Banking credit card vouchers

Credit card sales vouchers and refund vouchers are paid into a bank.

These are summarised on a retail voucher summary and the total (only) is included on a normal bank paying-in slip.

- **Retail voucher summary** – Slip completed by retailer when banking credit card vouchers. Normally has four copies: two for retailer's records and two for bank.

The retailer must complete the back as well as the front of the summary.

Please do not pin or staple this voucher as this will affect the machine processing

All sales vouchers must be deposited within three banking days of the dates shown on them.

If you are submitting more than 26 vouchers please enclose a separate listing.

If a voucher contravenes the terms of the retailer agreement then the amount shown on the voucher may be charged back to your bank account, either direct or via your paying in branch.

Similarly, if the total amount shown on the Retail Voucher Summary does not balance with our total of vouchers, the difference will be credited (or debited) to your bank account.

	£	p
1		
2		
3		
4		
5		
6		
7		
8		
9		
10		
11		
12		
13		
14		
15		
16		
17		
18		
19		
20		
21		
22		
23		
24		
25		
26		
SALES VOUCHERS TOTAL		

	£	p
1		
2		
3		
4		
5		
6		
7		
REFUND VOUCHERS		

EXPRESS

PLEASE WRITE FIRMLY WITH A BALLPOINT PEN

RETAIL VOUCHER SUMMARY

RETAILER NAME

DAY		MONTH		YEAR		RETAILERS NUMBER

NO OF VOUCHERS		AMOUNT	
SALES VOUCHERS			
REFUND VOUCHERS			

AUTHORISATION CODE	TOTAL POUNDS	PENCE
	:	

VOUCHERS ARE ACCEPTED SUBJECT TO VERIFICATION AND TO TERMS AND CONDITIONS OF THE MERCHANT AGREEMENT

KEEP COPIES 1 & 2 AND REMIT COPIES 3 & 4 WITH YOUR SALES VOUCHERS

PLEASE COMPLETE THIS SUMMARY QUOTING YOUR CURRENT RETAILER NUMBER

RETAILER COPY

RETAILER COPY 1

EXPRESS

PLEASE WRITE FIRMLY WITH A BALLPOINT PEN

RETAIL VOUCHER SUMMARY

RETAILER NAME

SPORTS CHAIN Ltd

DAY		MONTH		YEAR		RETAILERS NUMBER
0	2	1	2	X	4	9099001

NO OF VOUCHERS		AMOUNT	
SALES VOUCHERS	7	293	31
REFUND VOUCHERS	3	121	25

AUTHORISATION CODE	TOTAL POUNDS	PENCE
	172 :	06

VOUCHERS ARE ACCEPTED SUBJECT TO VERIFICATION AND TO TERMS AND CONDITIONS OF THE MERCHANT AGREEMENT

KEEP COPIES 1 & 2 AND REMIT COPIES 3 & 4 WITH YOUR SALES VOUCHERS

PLEASE COMPLETE THIS SUMMARY QUOTING YOUR CURRENT RETAILER NUMBER

RETAILER COPY

RETAILER COPY 1

Each month Head Office receives a statement from the credit company showing the value of vouchers paid in and the commission charged by the credit card company.

Summary of procedures

On retail summary voucher:

- enter retailer's name and number;
- enter date;
- list sales vouchers and refund vouchers;
- calculate total for sales and total for refunds;
- record totals on face of retail summary voucher;
- calculate net amount.

For an amount payable to the retailer:

- complete a paying-in slip for that amount.

For an amount to be paid by the retailer:

- write out a cheque.

Take to the bank:

- retail summary voucher;
- paying-in slip or cheque;
- bank's copies of sales and refund vouchers.

Maintaining a float

A retail business needs to have enough notes and coins, particularly of small denominations (ie, value), to give its customers change.

Each time the cash is banked, a float made up of different notes and coins is kept back to use at the start of the next day to give change.

The float is set at a fixed amount (eg £50), made up of a particular combination of notes and coins.

Security over cash takings

Cash is an asset which is vulnerable to theft. For this reason, security procedures are very important.

At the end of each day, cash takings for that day can be calculated using the X readings on the cash register. The total cash receipts per the cash register should be reconciled with the actual cash received and any discrepancies investigated. (Some cash registers record details such as the person making the sale, the time of the sale and whether the customer paid by cash, cheque, credit card or debit card. These details can help in the reconciliation process.) The reconciliation should take into account any changes to the float or any money taken from the till for any reason (for example, some businesses may pay sundry expenses directly from takings).

Segregation of duties is important here. The sales assistants should not be responsible for counting or recording the cash takings. Cash should be counted in the presence of the sales assistant as theft is less likely to happen at this stage if two people are involved.

Physical control over cash is vital. Access to the cash registers and to the keys which operate them should be limited. Staff should be made aware of the importance of safeguarding cash. The float should be kept in the safe overnight and transferred to the cash register just before the shop opens. All cash takings (other than the float) should be banked promptly (see Chapter 2).

Using the nightsafe

The nightsafe is a service offered by most of the high street banks. A small annual fee is charged.

The nightsafe is used by shops and businesses who wish to bank their takings after the banks have closed, and do not want to keep takings in their safe over night. Only cash and cheques can be deposited in this way.

The nightsafe is sited on an outside wall of the branch of the bank.

The bank supplies a leather pouch in which the takings are placed, and a key to open the nightsafe. The nightsafe is opened with the key and the pouch placed in the container inside. The pouch is then released from the container into the nightsafe itself only once the nightsafe has been closed again.

Users of the nightsafe are advised to open it again to check that the pouch has dropped out of sight.

Both copies of the paying-in slip are put in the pouch. The customer's copy is stamped and returned with the empty pouch on the next working day.

Other forms of payment

Some businesses may accept other forms of payment, including the following.

- **Savings stamps** – These are accepted as payment for certain bills, by the Post Office to pay for TV licences and by British Telecom to pay telephone bills.

- **Gift vouchers** – Many retail stores sell these which can then be exchanged for goods from one of their branches (eg Marks and Spencer). The use of the gift vouchers tends to be restricted to that one retail business.

- **Book tokens** – These are more flexible as they can be exchanged for goods at most bookshops.

- **Luncheon vouchers** – These are only accepted by certain shops as payment for food.

Generally, none of the above can be reconverted into cash.

The items above must be identified separately amongst takings recorded on remittance lists.

Making refunds

Customers may sometimes return goods and ask for a refund. The customer has certain rights under the Sales of Goods Act.

The customer has a legal right to receive a refund only in the following cases:

- The items bought are faulty (eg electrical goods which do not work).
- The items bought are not as described (eg a tin marked 'peaches' actually contains sardines).
- The items bought are not of satisfactory quality. This means they are not fit for their usual purpose. This may only become obvious once the items have been used for that purpose (eg underwear which still contains chemicals used in the manufacturing process and which make the underwear unwearable).
- The items bought are not fit for the particular purpose. This means that the customer must have told the retailer of the specific purpose, or made it clear through his actions (eg the customer wishes to use a particular type of paint to paint the outside of his house).
- The retailer agrees, at the time of the sale, that the goods can be returned, even if they are perfect. (This is the policy of Marks and Spencer and certain other retailers.)

Note that contracts of sale are between the buyer and the seller, not the buyer and the manufacturer. The customer is entitled to a refund if any of the above conditions apply, regardless of whether a fault (for example) is the responsibility of the manufacturer.

The customer does not, by law, have to produce his receipt to get a refund in the above cases. A retailer cannot insist on a receipt as a proof of purchase. A receipt makes the refund more straightforward and many retailers therefore encourage their customers to keep their receipts. Otherwise the retailer must accept the customer's word that he paid for the goods.

In some cases the customer may change his or her mind about the goods, but the retailer has not agreed a refund in advance. The retailer can choose whether or not to accept the goods and make a refund. Some shops allow their customers to return goods but will only issue a credit note for the value of the goods which the customer can then use to buy something else in the same shop or another branch of the same chain.

Credit card

The voucher is imprinted and completed as normal using the customer's card.

It is the sales assistant who signs the refund voucher.

If the original sale was authorised, then the sales assistant must contact the credit card authorisation department immediately with details of the refund.

- **Credit card refund voucher –** Voucher recording details of retailer, customer and refund made.

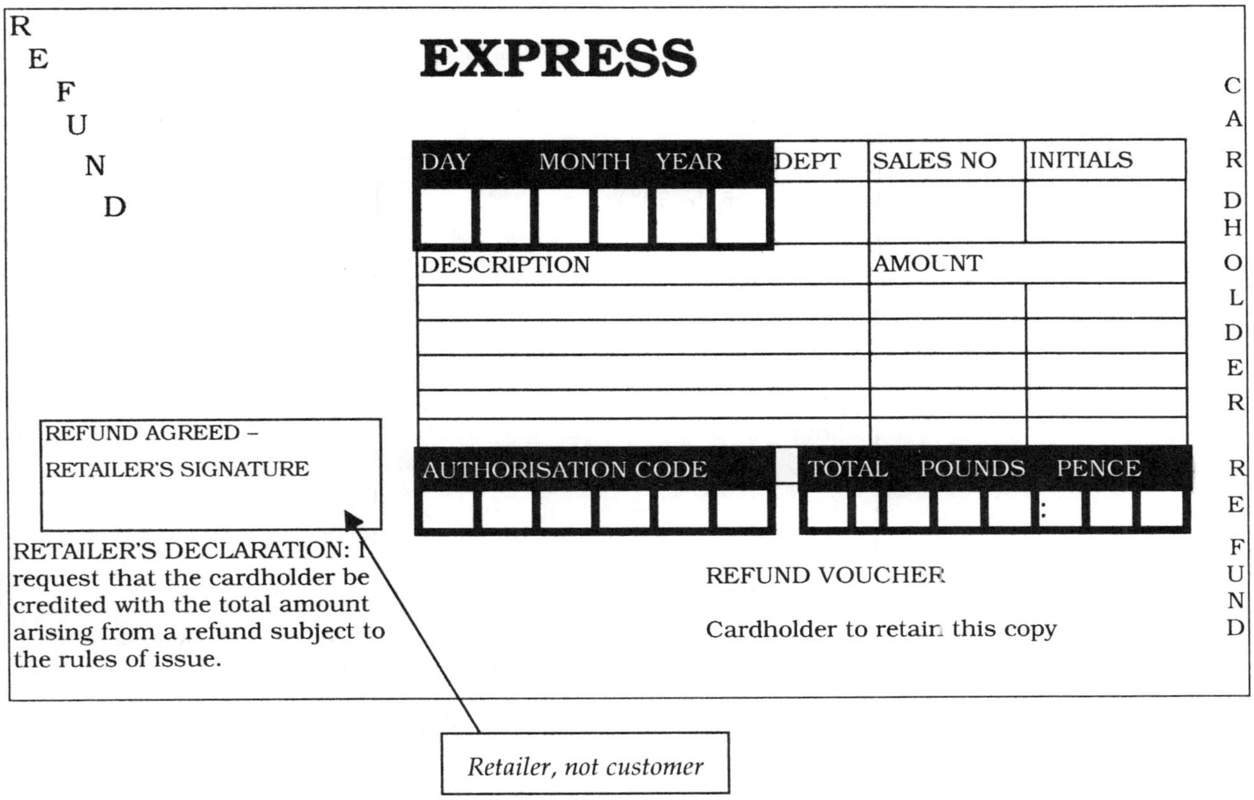

REFUND

EXPRESS

CARDHOLDER REFUND

DAY	MONTH	YEAR	DEPT	SALES NO	INITIALS

DESCRIPTION	AMOUNT	

AUTHORISATION CODE	TOTAL POUNDS	PENCE

REFUND AGREED –
RETAILER'S SIGNATURE

RETAILER'S DECLARATION: I request that the cardholder be credited with the total amount arising from a refund subject to the rules of issue.

REFUND VOUCHER

Cardholder to retain this copy

Retailer, not customer

Computerised credit card payments

Many retail businesses have taken the opportunity offered by the new information technology system EFTPOS to simplify the procedure for accepting payment by credit card.

The retailer installs a terminal which is generally attached to the electronic cash register or is part of the cash register itself.

Watch out for different types of equipment used by retail outlets, particularly filling stations and high street clothes retailers.

The terminal is linked directly to the credit card company's computer at its operations centre by telephone line.

The exact format of the credit card sales voucher depends upon equipment used, but it will normally have only two copies. The cardholder signs at least one of the copies which is returned to the retailer for the retailer's records. The other copy is for the cardholder's records.

```
1900 2359
CASA ITALIA PIZZERIA
05/07/X1   21:58
Express: 2554006633579400

TOTAL    £15.80

Auth code: 54662
THANK YOU
SIGN BELOW
Please debit my account as
shown

 -----------------
```

No banking of the vouchers need be done by the retailer because all transactions are immediately transferred electronically by the terminal via the telephone line.

The terminal automatically performs any authorisation procedures by contacting the computer at the operation centre.

What is EFTPOS?

Electronic Funds Transfer at Point of Sale (EFTPOS) is a relatively new system which uses advanced information technology.

- **EFTPOS** – A national scheme which links terminals in shops and supermarkets with the processing department of banks, building societies and credit card companies.

The system is very flexible because it allows almost any type of credit card or debit card (see below) to be accepted by one system.

Example of EFTPOS

- Janet is a 27 year old nurse from South Wales. She has gone into a petrol filling station on the M3 and filled her car with petrol.
- She wishes to pay by credit card. The filling station is linked up to the EFTPOS system.
- Janet's credit card is an Access card. The filling station's bank is Lloyds Bank in Gravesend, Kent.
- Janet produces her card at the cash desk (point of sale).
- The sales assistant swipes the card through a card reader on a terminal attached to the cash register.
- The sales assistant enters the amount of the purchase into the cash register.

- The information on the magnetic strip on the card is read by the retailer's terminal. A coded message (scrambled for security) is sent by telephone line to the central EFTPOS processing centre. This includes details of the amount. The card details are recorded and the request is sent to Access for authorisation by telephone line.

- The Access processing computer checks certain details.

- In this case, the Access processing computer authorises the purchase and updates its records. It notifies the central EFTPOS processing centre of the authorisation.

- The central EFTPOS processing centre transmits the authorisation to the retailer's terminal.

- A two-part credit card sales voucher is printed out and signed by Janet.

- The sales assistant checks Janet's signature against the signature on the card.

- The cash register also prints a receipt.

- After authorisation, the central EFTPOS processing centre sends details of the purchase to Lloyds Bank where the money is transferred into the filling station's account

- The sales assistant gives Janet her card, her copy of the credit card sales voucher and her receipt.

This has all taken a matter of minutes. The authorisation process is much quicker than the manual procedure.

More plastic money

Debit cards

During the last few years debit cards have become increasingly popular. They are not the same as credit cards because no credit is given to the cardholder.

- **Debit cards** – The debit card is a method of making payments direct from a bank account without having to write a cheque or produce a cheque guarantee card.

The payments are made by the customer using the EFTPOS technology described above. Payments made appear on the customer's bank statement alongside any other payments made by cheque, standing order, direct debit, etc.

Shop credit cards (or storecards)

In addition to the credit card companies set up by the banks whose cards are accepted by a wide variety of businesses, several major retailers now offer their own credit card service to customers.

These cards can only be used within branches of that shop (eg Marks and Spencer chargecard) or branches of shops within the same group (eg Burton, Principles, Debenhams and Dorothy Perkins are all within the same group).

The credit card operation might either be run by a company set up specially by the retailer for that purpose (eg Marks and Spencer chargecard) or by a company whose business is to provide a credit card service for a number of retailers.

Recording money received

All money held, in any form, must be carefully looked after as there is a high risk of it being stolen. This applies even to cheques and postal orders.

The risk of cash being stolen is particularly high just after it has been received. This is because the details of the receipt have not yet been recorded in the business's books.

In a credit business, money is normally received by post. Incoming mail should be opened by at least two people working together. If this is not possible, the mail should not always be opened by the same person. In a small business, the proprietor or another responsible person will probably deal with incoming mail.

All cash received should be listed on a **remittance list** (sometimes known as a **cheques received list**). The list should give details of:

- the customer;
- the invoice numbers to which the payment relates (if known);
- the amount paid; and
- any discount allowed.

The list should be totalled and signed.

Security over money held

After money received has been listed on a **remittance list** or **other documentation**, it should always be kept in a safe until it can be banked.

The safe should be kept locked at all times. Only those people who need to use the safe should know the combination to unlock it.

Cash, cheques and postal orders should be banked regularly. Most organisations have a policy of banking receipts at set intervals, usually daily.

The person banking the money should never go to the bank alone. For security purposes, different people, routes and times should be used for banking procedures.

Using remittance advices

When a business issues an invoice to a customer, the invoice will often have a detachable slip. This slip is called a **remittance advice**.

- **Invoice** –Note showing quantity of goods/services provided and amount payable by customer.

- **Remittance advice** –A slip returned by the customer when paying an invoice so as to identify what the payment is for.

When receiving cheques from a customer it is vital to ensure that the correct amount has been paid. This can be done by agreeing the amount of the cheque to the details on the remittance advice or to the invoices themselves.

Offering cash discounts

Occasionally a business will offer **credit** customers cash or settlement discounts to encourage customers to pay more quickly.

- **Cash or settlement discounts** – A reduction in the price charged if the customer pays within a certain period of time.

These discounts will tend to be expressed as a percentage, eg 2.5% discount if the customer pays within 30 days.

These discounts must be checked and recorded when the payment is received. Discounts allowed are normally recorded on the remittance list.

Paying money into the bank

In Chapter 1, we looked at the preparation of the paying-in slip.

Most businesses bank receipts daily. Each day, a paying-in slip is prepared. The total on the paying-in slip must agree to the total on the remittance list.

At the bank the cashier checks that the total of the cheques and cash paid in agree to the total on the paying-in slip.

Questions

1 (AAT CA D93)

(a) On the face of it, would the cheque below be accepted for payment if it were now presented to the National Bank plc?

(b) Give two reasons for your answer.

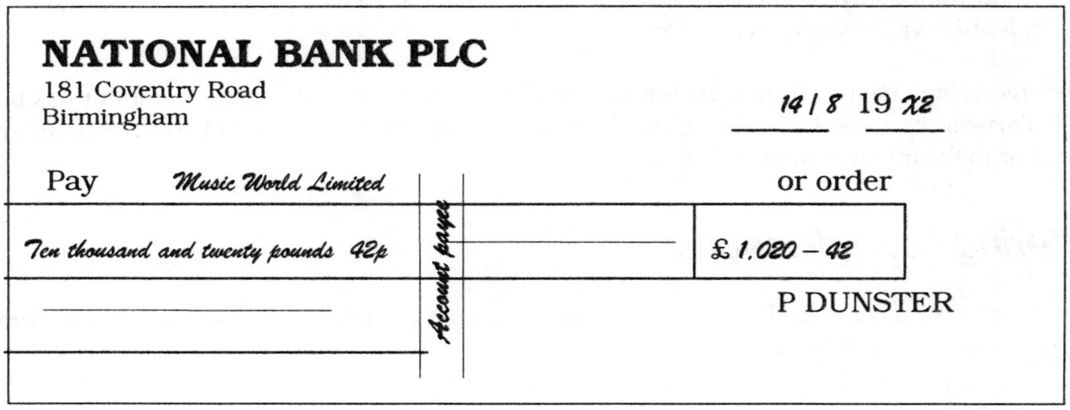

NATIONAL BANK PLC
181 Coventry Road
Birmingham

14 / 8 19 X2

Pay *Music World Limited* or order

Ten thousand and twenty pounds 42p

Account payee

£ *1,020 – 42*

P DUNSTER

2 (AAT CA D94)

List **three** checks that should be carried out specifically relating to the receipt of a cheque from a customer when the cheque is supported by a cheque guarantee card.

3 (AAT CA D93)

A credit card is used in conjunction with a cheque to guarantee payment up to a specified sum.

True / False

4 (AAT CA J93)

List **three** checks that should be made when accepting a credit card in payment for goods.

5 (AAT CA D94)

A customer wishes to purchase £320 of clothes from the shop using a credit card for payment. The floor limit set by the credit card company is £100.

(a) Is it possible that the transaction can still go ahead despite the floor limit?

(b) Briefly explain the reason for your answer.

6 (AAT CA D94)

The cashiers employed by Chang Fashions Limited each have an electronic cash register. It is important for the company to ensure that the cashiers do not keep any of the cash handed over by the customers for themselves. Briefly describe what you consider should happen at the end of each day's trading as a system of control.

7 (AAT CA J92)

A small number of sales are made each day to members of the public for cash. This occasionally means that the company receives sizeable sums of money after the bank has closed for the day. What service generally offered by banks would ensure that the cash is kept securely overnight?

8 (AAT CA D94)

A customer has come into the shop with a pair of jeans bought three days earlier. She complains that the zip is broken and she demands a refund. The cashier refuses and points to a sign on the wall which states: 'Goods bought in this shop will not be exchanged and refunds will not be made'.

(a) Would it appear that the customer is entitled to a refund? Yes / No

(b) Briefly explain the reason for your answer.

9 (AAT CA J93)

During May, a customer had purchased, by cheque, a portable colour television for £235 inclusive of VAT. She returned the next day complaining that, although the sound worked, there was no picture and demanded a cash refund. The sales assistant who spoke to her refused and said that, as it appeared to be a manufacturing fault, she would have to contact the manufacturer for a replacement or refund.

(a) Was the sales assistant legally justified in refusing to give a refund? Yes / No

(b) Briefly give a reason for your answer.

(c) If a cash refund had been given, what double-entry would have been passed?

10 (AAT CA D94)

Debit cards allow customers to use funds held in their bank accounts to make payments without the need to issue cheques.

True / False

11 (AAT CA D94)

A remittance advice is a document sent by a supplier to a customer to advise the customer that goods ordered have been sent off to the customer.

True / False

12 (AAT CA J94)

Cash discounts are normally available only to customers who pay immediately in cash.

True / False

13 (AAT CA D93)

Music World Limited has received two quotes for the same product from two different suppliers. One has offered a price of £150 less a 10% trade discount, the other a price of £150 less a 10% cash discount. Which appears to be the better offer or are the two offers exactly the same?

The trade discount / The cash discount / The offers are the same

Briefly explain your answer.

14 (AAT CA D92)

Payment has recently been received from a valued new customer, Allied Hairdressers Limited of Chichester, in respect of their first order for supplies.

The conditions of payment applying to the order were Hairdressing Supplies' normal ones of 2.5% cash discount if paid within ten days of the receipt of the invoice, otherwise payment in full must be made by the end of the month following the date of the invoice.

However, the customer had paid five weeks after the date of the invoice but had still deducted cash discount. Enquiries revealed that they had received the invoice two days after it was posted to them.

Marjorie Thistlethwaite, the accountant, agreed that the company should not press for payment of the discount and has asked you to draft a tactful letter to confirm this but to remind the customer of the agreed conditions of payment.

Summary

Cheques from individuals

- Must be accompanied by cheque guarantee card

Cannot accept more than one £50 cheque for each transaction

Credit cards

- Widely accepted
- Convenient form of payment
- Gives access to continuous credit
- Gives flexibility of repayment to account-holder
- Popular with retailers

Cash registers

- Used to store money during shop opening hours
- Record takings.
- Issue receipts

Banking credit card vouchers

- Summarise sales vouchers and refund vouchers on retail voucher summary
- Total sales and refunds
- Deduct refunds from sales
- If sales exceed refunds, complete paying-in slip for net amount
- If refunds exceed sales, write cheque for net amount

Float

- Cash kept in the cash register to use as change
- Fixed amount used every day

Nightsafe

- Service offered by banks so that account-holders do not have to keep large amounts of money overnight in their own safes.

Value added tax

- Full VAT receipts to be issued by all businesses, except:
  - retailers
  - filling stations
  - savings stamps.

Other forms of payment

- Gift vouchers
- Book tokens
- Luncheon vouchers
- Of very limited use
- Cannot normally be converted into cash

Refunds

- Retailer must make refund if:
  - goods are faulty
  - goods are not as described
  - goods are not of merchantable quality
  - goods not fit for the specific purpose
  - retailer agreed in advance .
- Customer does not require receipt in above circumstances.
- Refund vouchers completed for credit card refunds:
  - signed by sales assistant;
  - must be authorised if original sale was authorised.
- If customer only changes his mind about perfect goods, retailer does not have to make a refund

Computerised credit card payments

- Made using EFTPOS technology
- Direct link between retailer's terminal and credit card company
- Authorisation performed electronically

EFTPOS

- Flexible system
- Accepts credit or debit cards

Other types of cards

- Debit cards
- Store cards

Security over money held

- Use safe for money kept on the premises
- Keep safe locked
- Restrict knowledge of the combination
- Bank money received regularly
- Do not go to bank alone

Using remittance advices

- Used for credit customers
- Slip sent out by the supplier
- Returned by the customer with the payment
- Supplier uses them to identify invoice paid

Cash discounts

- Discounts offered to credit customers to encourage them to pay more quickly

CHAPTER 3

Making Payments to Credit Suppliers

Objectives

This chapter covers the following performance criteria.

- Payments are made and recorded in accordance with the organisation's policies, regulations, procedures and timescales.
- Payments are properly authorised.
- Cheques are prepared correctly and are signed by designated person(s) prior to despatch.
- Remittance advices are correctly prepared and despatched with payments.
- Totals and balances are correctly calculated and checked against documentation.
- Available cash discounts are identified and deducted.
- Safety and security procedures for the handling of cash and cheques are followed.

Authorising payments

Businesses normally make payments by cheque. Payments by cheque are more likely to reach the correct person or business than payments by cash. We shall look at the reasons for this in a later chapter.

A business must make a payment only if there is authorised documentation to show that the payment is genuine. Authorised documentation might include:

- an invoice which has been signed or stamped by a responsible official;
- a cheque requisition form;
- a signed payroll document;
- a memo from a responsible official.

Cheques are normally prepared by the cashier. We looked at the preparation of cheques in Chapter 1. The cashier should ensure that the amount of the cheque agrees to the authorised documentation. Many businesses pay their suppliers monthly, in response to suppliers' statements. This means that one cheque may cover several invoices. In this case, the cashier must ensure that the total amount of the cheque has been correctly calculated.

The number of cheque signatories (ie people who can sign cheques) must be restricted. The business must complete a form (known as the **bank mandate**) which shows who can sign cheques. The form includes sample signatures of all cheque signatories.

In large organisations, several people may be authorised to sign cheques and two signatures are normally required on cheques over a certain limit (set by the business). Typically, individuals will be authorised to sign cheques up to a limit which depends on their level of seniority. The bank must be made aware of any limits or other restrictions on the signing of cheques.

The cashier is not normally a cheque signatory. This is because fraud and errors are less likely if the cheque is checked and signed by someone other than the person who prepared it. This is called **segregation of duties**. Segregation of duties is an important **control** and can be used in many different operations within a business. You will see many other examples of it. (You have already seen that cheques should not be banked by the same person who opens the mail.)

A business must keep cheque books under lock and key, preferably in a safe. The cashier must use the cheques in strict order and keep any incorrectly completed cheques. These cheques must be cancelled on their face so that they cannot be used.

Some businesses which regularly need to make a large number of payments use computerised cheques. The business's computer prints the cheque details. Some computers also print the signature. This means that security procedures over computerised cheques must be very strict.

Completing remittance advices

A business will complete remittance advices and return them with the cheque payments. Some businesses use the remittance advice provided by the supplier. Others prefer to prepare their own. Both types help the supplier to identify the invoices which are being paid.

Businesses which pay by computer cheque usually send their own remittance advice which is printed by the computer at the same time as the cheque.

Taking cash discounts

If the business pays an invoice within a certain period of time it may receive a cash or settlement discount.

The discount must be calculated and deducted from the payment.

Value added tax – an introduction

The operation of VAT

The standard rate of VAT is 17.5%, although certain items are 'zero rated' with VAT at 0%; 8% is levied on domestic fuel and power.

VAT is a tax levied on **consumer** expenditure, yet it is levied at each stage in the production and distribution chain. Most businesses (being **taxable persons** as defined later) avoid having to treat VAT as an expense as they may deduct the VAT they have paid on their purchases **(input tax)** from the VAT they charge to customers on their sales (**output tax**) and pay only the difference to HM Customs and Excise.

Example

Leaving aside, for now, the accounting entries, let us examine a simple illustration. We will assume a standard rate of 17.5%, and follow one article, a wooden table, through the production and distribution chain.

- A private individual cuts down a tree and sells it to a timber mill for £10.

  Tax effect – none. The individual is not a 'taxable person'.

- The timber mill saws the log and sells the timber to a furniture manufacturer for £100 + VAT.

  Tax effect – Being a taxable person, the mill is obliged to charge its customers VAT at 17.5% on the selling price (output tax). There is no input tax available for offset.

  Cash effect – It has paid out £10 for the log, which would be charged as an expense to trading and profit and loss account, and has collected £117.50 from the customer (or has a debtor for this sum). Of this, £17.50 has to be remitted to HM Customs and Excise, and therefore only £100 would be recognised as sales in the trading and profit and loss account.

- The manufacturer makes a table from the wood, and sells this to a retailer for £400 + VAT.

  Tax effect – The manufacturer is obliged to charge VAT at 17.5% on the selling price (ie £70), but in this instance would be allowed to set off, against this output tax, the input tax of £17.50 charged on the purchase of wood from the mill.

  Cash effect – Tax of £52.50 is remitted to HM Customs and Excise (output less input tax – £70 less £17.50). £400 is recognised as sales and £100 as purchases in the accounts.

- The retailer sells the table to a private customer for a tax inclusive price of £1,000.

  Tax effect – Included within the £1,000 retail price is an element of output tax $\left(1{,}000 \times \frac{17\frac{1}{2}}{117\frac{1}{2}}\right)$ of £149.

  Against this output tax may be set off the input tax of £70 charged on the purchase from the manufacturer.

  Cash effect – £79 (£149 – £70) is remitted to HM Customs and Excise. Purchases would be shown in the books at £400 and sales at £851.

- **The private customer** – VAT is a tax levied on consumer expenditure and the chain ends here. The customer is not a taxable person, and cannot recover the tax paid.

  You will note that everybody else has passed the VAT on and, though the customer has paid his £149 to the retailer, HM Customs and Excise has received its tax by contributions from each link in the chain, as shown below:

	£
Timber mill	17.50
Manufacturer	52.50
Retailer	79.00
	149.00

Tax definitions

A basic definition of the charge to VAT

VAT is charged on the **taxable supply of goods and services** in the United Kingdom by a **taxable person** in the course of a business carried on by him.

Taxable supply of goods and services

Taxable supply is the supply of all items except those which are **exempt.** Examples of exempt items are as follows.

- Certain land and buildings, where sold, leased or hired
- Insurance
- Post Office postal services
- Betting, gaming and lotteries

Input tax cannot be reclaimed where a trader makes exempt supplies.

There are two rates of VAT on taxable supplies. Some items are 'zero-rated' (similar to *exempt* except that input tax can be reclaimed as exempt supplies are outside the scope of VAT) and others are rated at 17.5%. Examples of 'zero-rated' supplies follows.

- Water and certain types of food
- Books and newspapers
- Drugs and medicines
- Children's clothing and footwear

VAT on some items is non-deductible. This means that VAT on any purchases of these items cannot be deducted from the amount of tax payable to Customs and Excise. The business has to bear the VAT as an expense.

Non-deductible items include:

- motor cars
- business entertaining.

Taxable person

A taxable person is any individual, partnership, company, etc. who intends to make taxable supplies and is liable to register.

A person is liable to register if the value of his taxable supplies exceeds a specified amount in a 12-month period. Most companies and partnerships and many sole traders are liable to register.

Price structure

	£
Selling price including VAT, or **gross** of VAT	117.5
VAT	17.5
Price exclusive of VAT, or **net** of VAT	100.0

eg Selling price = £2,350

VAT = $\frac{17.5}{117.5} \times 2{,}350$	350
Price exclusive of VAT = $\frac{100}{117.5} \times 2{,}350$	2,000
	2,350

The effect of value added tax

If a business is registered for value added tax (VAT), it must issue its invoices in a specific form.

A full VAT invoice must include the following information.

- name, address and VAT registration
- number of supplier
- an identifying number
- date of sale
- name and address of customer
- nature of transaction (eg sale)
- description and quantity of goods or services
- for each item
  - VAT rate
  - amount payable excluding VAT (in sterling)

- total amount payable excluding VAT (in sterling)
- the amount of VAT chargeable at each rate
- total amount of VAT payable
- amount payable including VAT (in sterling).

Retailers

A retailer only needs to issue a VAT invoice if the customer requests it. If the sales value is less than £100 (including VAT), a less detailed VAT invoice can be issued.

The less detailed receipt would show:

- name and address and VAT registration number of retailer;
- date of sale;
- description of goods;
- rate of VAT;
- date of supply;
- total amount payable including VAT.

This less detailed receipt can only include items on which VAT is charged at standard rate.

Filling stations

Filling stations can also issue slightly different receipts, but you do not need to know about this in detail.

To calculate cash (or settlement) discount with VAT

Invoices should show the VAT payable as 17.5% of the discounted price. The amount paid by the customer is either:

(a) taking discount – discounted amount (excluding VAT) plus discounted VAT; or

(b) not taking discount – full amount (excluding VAT) plus discounted VAT.

Note. The amount of VAT paid is always based on the discounted amount.

Example

Invoice shows:

	£
20 items @ £5 each	100.00
VAT @ 17.5%	17.15
Total	117.15

A 2% discount is offered for settlement within 30 days.

The VAT is calculated as:

(100 × 98%) × 17.5%; or

(100 – (100 × 2%)) × 17.5%.

The amount paid by the customer is either of the following:

(a) *Taking discount*

	£
Discounted amount	98.00
Discounted VAT	17.15
Total	115.15

(b) *Not taking discount*

	£
Full amount	100.00
Discounted VAT	17.15
Total	117.15

The difference between (a) and (b) is £2, the cash discount on £100.

Questions

1 (AAT CA J93)

Joan Brookes is concerned that the business could lose money if fraudulent cheques were issued and signed by somebody in the accounts department with access to the cheque book. You suggest to her that segregation of duties should be introduced as a form of internal control.

Explain briefly the meaning of the term and purpose of segregation of duties.

2

You have received the following invoices from suppliers (which are not registered for value added tax) which offer settlement discounts. You must calculate the discount offered and decide whether or not you can take the discount if you send a cheque today. Today is 21 June 19X9.

	Supplier	*Invoice date*	*Amount*	*Discount terms*	
(a)	ABC Fencing	22 May 19X9	£239.50	2½%	30 days
(b)	Brown & Black	15 June 19X9	£458.63	1½%	28 days
(c)	Peter's Wood Products	10 June 19X9	£168.00	2%	14 days
(d)	SJ Lever	15 May 19X9	£391.48	2%	30 days
(e)	A J Bennett	1 June 19X9	£56.91	2½%	14 days

3 (AAT CA D93)

Music World Limited purchases 80 CDs at £7.50 each plus VAT. These are then all sold to a customer for a total of £846 inclusive of VAT. What sum will be owing to HM Customs and Excise in respect of this purchase and sale?

4 (AAT CA J93)

Businesses making exempt and zero-rated supplies do not charge VAT to their customers. Only one of these two types of supply can offset input VAT and this is: an exempt supply / a zero-rated supply?

5 (AAT CA J94)

For the quarter ended 31 March 1994, sales amounted to £1,821,250 inclusive of VAT. On 31 March the balance of the VAT account was £26,250 credit. Calculate the total of the vatable purchases made during the quarter inclusive of VAT.

6

What information is missing from the following full VAT invoice?

Invoice **68553**

A.J. Broom & Company Limited.

59 Parkway, Manchester M2 6EG

J Hardy Construction,
Poplar Works,
Poplar Street,
Oldham OL4 6QB

Tel: 0161 560 3392
Fax: 0161 560 5322

Tax Point: 23 August 19X3

Code	Supply	Description	Quantity	VAT rate	Unit price £	Amount (£) exclusive of VAT
950 BB3	Sale	Cotswold Bricks	3	17.50%	300.00	900.00
159 504	Sale	Roof Tiles – Red	5	17.50%	195.50	977.50
874 KL5	Sale	Brick Tiles	1	17.50%	56.65	56.65
To		AT				1,934.15
VAT at 17.5%						338.48
Total amount payable						**2,272.63**

7 (AAT CA D92)

The following letter has been received from Mr Petersley, the sales manager. You have been asked to draft a letter to Mr Petersley describing sufficient of the VAT system to explain why VAT is excluded from the bonus calculation.

Draft a suitable reply.

HAIRDRESSING SUPPLIES LIMITED
(Sales Division)

Park Road, Guildford, Surrey GU1 1AA

27 March 19X2

Marjorie Thistlethwaite
Accountant
Head Office
Hairdressing Supplies Limited
Station Road
Dorking
Surrey GU10 1ZZ

Dear Marjorie

Sales commission scheme

You will be aware that company salesmen have been paid a 10% sales bonus on the gross profit on their sales since 1 February.

I have just discovered, however, that the sales figure does not include VAT which of course we quote to customers and is part of the payment made by them.

As the company is allowed to retain most of this tax, is it not a little unfair that it is omitted in the bonus calculation?

Best wishes.

Yours sincerely

Fred

F Petersley
Sales Manager

Summary

Making payments

- Payment by cheque is the safest method of payment
- Restrict number of signatories
- Decide upon two signatures for larger amounts
- Authorise cheques
- Keep blank cheques in safe
- Use cheques in order
- Keep and cancel incorrectly written cheques

Remittance advices

- Prepare remittance advice sent by supplier; or send own computer-printed remittance advice

Cash discounts

- Deduct from payment if valid
- If VAT is included on invoice, discount is on amount excluding VAT only

CHAPTER 4

Banks and their Customers

Objectives

This chapter addresses the following performance criterion.

- Standing orders and other inter-bank transfers are correctly documented.

The objectives of this chapter are to introduce you to the rights and duties of banks and their customers.

Who is the customer?

When can a business or individual be regarded as being a **customer** of a bank?

Customer of a bank – A person or organisation:

- with a current account or similar arrangement with the bank, and who has banked there for any length of time (however short); or
- who has agreed to open an account.

The relationship between the bank and the customer

The relationship between the bank and the customer can be described in three ways:

- debtor/creditor;
- principal/agent;
- bailor/bailee.

All of these are recognised by the law.

Debtor/creditor relationship

This is the basic bank/customer relationship. It arises out of the fact that the bank holds money which belongs to the customer. The money has to be repaid at some time, and therefore from the bank's point of view, the customer is the **creditor** (ie the bank owes money).

From the customer's point of view the bank is the debtor (ie owes the money to them).

However, when the customer borrows money from the bank the relationship is reversed.

For the bank the customer is the **debtor** and for the customer the bank is the **creditor**.

Note

The usual meanings of debit and credit in double-entry bookkeeping in the context of cash are:

debit – increase in cash balance;

credit – decrease in cash balance.

On a bank statement these meanings are reversed as the statement is prepared from the bank's point of view, that is:

Debit	Increase in a debtor (eg increase in overdraft)
or	Decrease in a creditor (eg decrease in cash balance)
Credit	Decrease in a debtor (eg decrease in overdraft)
or	Increase in creditor (eg increase in cash balance)

The law states that if the bank holds the customer's money, it is up to the customer to ask for the money back. This is unusual, because normally the onus is on the person who owes the money to repay it.

The bank agrees to receive money and collect payment for cheques on the customer's account.

The bank can only close the customer's account with reasonable notice.

The customer must be careful when writing cheques so as not to mislead the bank or make forgery easy.

The customer's request for repayment must be in writing (eg a cheque).

Principal/agent relationship

An agent is someone who works for a principal and makes contracts on his behalf. An agent in law is not just someone who calls himself an agent, eg travel agent, estate agent, but anybody who makes contracts on behalf of other people.

A principal is the person who tells the agent what he wants him to do on his behalf.

Example

When someone (the principal) books a holiday through a travel agent (the agent) he asks the travel agent to deal directly with the tour operator on his behalf.

The principal/agent relationship between the customer and the bank arises when the bank deals with a third party on behalf of the customer.

Example

When the bank obtains payment of a cheque paid into the customer's account, the bank is acting as agent in collecting payment from the third party's bank.

Bailor/bailee relationship

One of the bank's services is to receive valuables (eg gold, jewellery, documents) to hold on behalf of the customer. When the bank is holding these valuables in safe custody the bank must take reasonable care of the items.

A **bailor** is the person who gives the property to a bailee (eg the bank) for safe keeping.

The **bailee** receives that property and must look after it in a careful and professional manner.

Rights of the bank

The law gives the bank various rights which it can exercise in its dealings with the customer or third parties on behalf of the customer.

A bank has the right to:

- charge reasonable amounts for its services (eg arranging loans, providing a current or cheque account) and interest on loans and overdrafts;
- reclaim losses from a customer who has overdrawn his account;
- be repaid on demand with any overdrawn balance;
- exercise a **lien** over the customer's property in the bank's possession, eg cheques paid in by the customer – this does not include items held in safety deposit boxes;

Lien – The right to keep goods as payment for a debt.

- use the customer's money in any way it wishes (ie lend it to whoever it chooses) provided it pays any cheques written by the customer;
- expect the customer to use reasonable care when writing out cheques – eg the customer should not leave parts of the cheque blank (eg the figures for the amount payable) because this would make fraud by another person very easy.

Duties of the bank

The bank also has certain duties, ie things it must do because of the law or for other reasons.

The bank has a number of duties, as follows.

- To pay the cheques which the customer writes, provided:
  - they are correctly completed;
  - there is money in the account, or an overdraft has been agreed;
  - the bank does not know that the customer is dead, bankrupt or mentally incapacitated;

- the bank is not aware of any legal reason why they should not pay (eg it knows the cheque to be lost or stolen);
- the drawer's signature has not been forged.

◆ To follow any express mandate, such as a standing order.

◆ Not to reveal the customer's details, unless:

- the law requires it. – this would normally only be when the courts ask the bank to do so (eg at a tax fraud trial);
- it would be in the public interest to do so (eg the customer was trading with the enemy, or the customer was involved in drug trafficking) – this is a very difficult area; the bank would always take legal advice before going to the authorities;
- it is in the interest of the bank (eg when taking a customer to court to get a loan repaid);
- the customer has agreed either verbally or in writing, or by his actions.

◆ To give the customer reasonable notice that it wishes to close the customer's account. This is to give the customer sufficient time to make other arrangements.

◆ To provide bank statements regularly and to provide details of the balance on the account if asked.

The bank should keep an accurate record of the customer's account.

It is not the customer's responsibility to check the bank statements or tell the bank about any errors. This means that the bank must be careful not to make any mistakes.

◆ To accept the cash and cheques paid in by the customer and credit the customer's account.

◆ To repay the customer's money when the customer asks in writing during banking hours at the branch where the account is held or another agreed branch.

◆ To tell the customer immediately of any possible forgery of the customer's signature.

◆ To exercise proper care and skill. This is particularly important because it is required by law. The law believes that there is a fiduciary relationship between the bank and the customer (ie the customer trusts the bank and the bank must therefore act in an appropriate way).

Duties of the customer

The customer has a duty to use reasonable care when writing cheques to stop the cheque being altered as part of a fraud.

He or she also has a duty to tell the bank of any forgery of his signature of which he or she is aware.

The customer does **not** have a duty to check the accuracy of his bank statement.

Services offered

The high-street banks offer their customers a wide range of services.

These services fall into four broad categories: deposit-taking, money transfer, advances and other services.

Deposit-taking

This basically means looking after the money which the customer gives to the bank.

This may be in a **current account** where the customer wants to be able to write cheques and have instant access to that money. Recently banks have introduced interest schemes offering (low) rates of interest on current account funds.

The customer's money may also be in a **deposit account** where it will earn interest, but access to the money is restricted. Banks sometimes market deposit accounts under 'brand' names, such as 'savings account' or 'high interest'.

Money transfer

This area of activity includes:

- paying **cheques** written by customers (ie transferring money from the customer's account to another person's account);
- transferring money from the customer's account by **standing order**, **direct debit** or **BACS**;
- allowing customers to withdraw cash through **cash dispensers** (also known as ATMs – Automatic Teller Machines);
- providing the customer with additional payment methods through **credit cards** and **debit cards**;
- collecting payment for the customer for **cheques paid-in**;
- accepting transfers from other accounts into the customer's account by **standing order**, **direct debit**, **BACS** and **bank giro credit**.

Advances

This is the bank's term for lending money to customers.

Banks lend money in the short-term through:

- **overdraft facilities**, ie allowing the customer to overspend on their current account up to a certain limit;
- providing **credit cards** to customers as an additional source of credit;

or long-term:

- **loans** for specific purposes (eg to buy a car);
- **mortgages** which are a long-term loan (usually 25 years) to buy property – the mortgages are secured on the property (ie if the loan is not repaid, the bank can sell the property to get its money back);
- **business loans** made to all types of businesses (these will also normally be secured loans).

Other services

These include:

- supplying or exchanging **foreign currency**;
- **safe deposit boxes**;
- **nightsafes**;

and a whole range of other services which were previously only offered by other types of organisation, but which, owing to changes in the law in the mid-eighties and the increase in competition are now offered by the banks. These include:

- investment advice;
- share dealing (ie acting as a stockbroker for customers);
- advice on wills;
- insurance.

Getting payment for the customer

When a customer (ie someone who has an account with the bank) pays into his or her branch a cheque which he or she has received from another person, the customer is asking the branch to obtain payment from the other person's bank account and credit it to (ie pay it into) his or her bank account.

The branch has a duty to:

- credit the customer's account with the value of the cheques presented by the customer;
- collect the money from the third party;
- credit the money to the correct account.

Paying in cash and cheques

We have already seen the preparation of the paying-in slip.

The individual who is paying in takes the cash, cheques and paying in book to the bank and hands them to the cashier behind the counter.

The cashier:

- agrees the items to be paid in against the information on the paying-in slip;
- checks the other details on the paying-in slip (eg date, payee);
- stamps both copies;
- removes the bank's copy (the top copy);
- returns the paying-in book.

Cash which is paid into the bank must be bagged up by the customer before taking it to the bank.

Different coins must be put in separate plastic bags (supplied by the bank) up to certain values decided on by the bank (eg £5 worth of 50 pence pieces).

This helps speed up the process of paying-in cash at the bank. The bank will then recount the cash, either by weighing it or using a money-counting machine.

Any cash paid in will be credited direct to the business's account when the branch records all of the transactions for the day.

Cheques paid in are sorted and put through the clearing system.

How the clearing system works

The major banks have developed a system known as the **clearing system** which is the method by which the banks exchange cheques.

Some of the banks currently involved in this system are:

- Barclays
- Co-op
- Lloyds
- HSBC
- National Girobank
- National Westminster

- Royal Bank of Scotland
- TSB.

The whole process of clearing cheques takes three working days.

Day 1

The branch of the bank (the collecting bank) will have received cheques paid-in by customers written by third parties who have their accounts at:

- other clearing banks;
- other branches of the same bank.

At the end of the day these cheques are:

- sorted by the bank;
- stamped with details of the branch/bank;
- processed through a machine which puts the amount payable onto the bottom of the cheque in code.

The cheques are then sent by courier to the bank's own clearing department.

Day 2

The bank's clearing department receives cheques from all its branches. It will now:

- sort the cheques by bank;
- take other banks' cheques to the Central Clearing House;
- send the cheques relating to its own branches to those branches without sending them to the clearing house (this is **inter-branch clearing**).

The clearing house arranges for all the banks involved to attend to 'swap' cheques and to arrange for any differences in the values of cheques swapped to be paid on the following day.

The clearing departments of the banks then receive the cheques which have been written by their customers. Each department will:

- sort the cheques by branch using a machine which reads the code on each cheque;
- record the cheque information into the bank computer (to debit customers' accounts by the amounts paid on the cheques);
- send the paid cheques to the paying customers' branches.

Day 3

Each branch receives the cheques written by its own customers. The branch has to check that the cheque is valid and to return any cheques that cannot be paid.

Any cheques which cannot be paid are sent by first class post to the branch that collected them (shown by the stamp placed on the cheque on day 1).

Clearing debts

The clearing process results in banks owing money to each other.

Each clearing bank maintains an account with the Bank of England. These accounts are known as **operational balances**. These balances are used to settle the debts which arise between the banks in the course of clearing.

Cheques which are written by an account holder at the same branch do not leave the branch.

Cheques which are written by an account holder of a different branch of the same bank go from the bank's own clearing department to the other branch.

More about cheques

Let us consider cheques again:

Cheque – An unconditional order in writing signed by the drawer, requiring a bank to pay on demand a sum certain in money to a named person or to the bearer.

1	**Unconditional**	Payment cannot depend upon the outcome of events, eg 'pay Mr Brown £75 provided my salary cheque has been paid into my account'.
2	**Writing**	A cheque must be in writing. Pen, biro, print, or pencil can be used. Details in pencil can, however, be changed easily, and should be avoided. Most banks insist their preprinted cheques be completed in ink.
3	**Signed**	A cheque must be signed by the drawer, that is the person paying the money.
4	**On demand**	It is expected that the cheque will be paid as soon as it is presented to the bank.
5	**A sum certain**	The amount must be definite, in both words and figures.
6	**Named person or bearer**	The cheque must be payable to a named person or to the bearer, ie whoever has the cheque in his or her posChapter. A cheque made out to 'cash' will be treated as payable to bearer.

Problems with cheques

The collecting bank

When the bank accepts a cheque which has been paid in by a customer, the bank must carefully review that cheque. Each item must be considered in turn:

Date

Out of date

A cheque is valid for six months from the date of issue, unless a shorter period is written on the face of the cheque.

For example, a cheque dated on 1 August 19X0 would be out of date if held until 8 February 19X1.

Post-dated

A cheque which is dated later than the day on which it is written cannot be paid in until that later date.

For example, a cheque written on 5 May 19Z1 but dated 10 May 19Z1 could not be paid into a bank account before 10 May 19Z1.

Undated

If a cheque is presented to the payee undated the payee can insert a date. The bank's cashier would normally ask the payee to do this.

If any undated cheques are accidentally accepted by the bank, the date stamp can be used to insert it.

Once a date is entered on a cheque it cannot, however, be altered by the payee.

- **Payee** – The payee's name should be the same as the one shown on the account that the cheque is being paid into.

  If the name is different, then an endorsement is required (see below). If a cheque is presented with no payee's name then it cannot be entered by the customer or by the bank's cashier.

- **Words and figures** – Both words and figures should be completed and should agree.

  If they disagree the cheque should be returned by the bank to the drawer for amendment or for a new cheque to be issued.

  A returned cheque will often be marked R/D or 'Return to drawer'.

- **Signature** – The cheque must be signed, by the drawer.

- **Crossings** – If the cheque has a crossing (two parallel lines on the face of the cheque), it must be paid into a bank account. It cannot be exchanged for cash over the counter. Preprinted cheques carry crossings.

- **Endorsements** – The bank must check that the endorsement is valid.

The paying banker

After a cheque has passed through the clearing system it is sent to the branch of the drawer.

The drawer's bank then has to record the payment against the customer's account.

The paying banker has a legal obligation to pay customers' cheques provided that:

- there is sufficient money in the account, or an overdraft has been agreed;
- the cheque has been completed correctly;
- the bank does not know that the customer is dead, bankrupt or mentally incapacitated.

The bank must *not* pay the cheque if:

- the bank knows the cheque to be lost or stolen;
- the drawer's signature is forged.

The bank must *always* pay a cheque guaranteed by a cheque guarantee card, provided that the payee has observed the rules.

First, the bank must check certain details on the cheque.

Date

Out of date

A cheque is valid for six months from the date of issue, unless a shorter period is written on the face of the cheque.

An out of date cheque must be returned.

Post-dated

A cheque which is dated later than the day on which it is written must be returned.

Undated

The correct date can be inserted.

Payee – The payee's name must be shown on the cheque.

Endorsements – The bank must ensure that any endorsement is consistent with the payee's name.

Crossings – The bank must obey any crossing.

Alterations – Any changes to the details on the cheque must be signed by the drawer.

Drawer's signature – The signature, or signatures, must be present and correct.

Torn cheques – A torn cheque, or one that has been torn into two or more pieces, is invalid, even if the cheque has been mended.

Stopped cheques – A customer has the right to stop a cheque right up until the banker pays it. The customer must write to the bank and give clear details of the payee's name, the cheque's number and the amount payable.

Returning cheques – The paying bank has a time limit if it is returning a cheque, otherwise it may face legal action. Returned cheques are sent back to the collecting bank. The reason for the return is marked on the top left hand corner of the cheque.

Cheque endorsements

The person to whom a cheque is payable may wish to transfer the cheque to a third party. To do this, the payee signs the back of the cheque. This signature is called an endorsement. Which signature? The endorsement signature must, as far as possible, accurately reflect the name of the payee. The endorsement should be the normal signature of the payee. Courtesy titles such as Mr, Mrs, Reverend must not be included before the signature, but they can be included after.

A married woman may add *Mrs* after her name, if she wishes.

If, however, the cheque is payable to her husband's Christian name or initials, the endorsement must include such words as wife of eg:

Actual name	**Payee**	**Endorsement**
Mrs Gill Younge	Mrs T Younge	Gill Younge wife of Tim Younge

Types of endorsement

There are three types of endorsement.

- **Blank or general** – The payee's signature on the back of a cheque makes the cheque payable to the bearer (sometimes known as a 'bearer cheque').

- **Specific** – The payee's signature is followed by the name of the person to whom the cheque is being transferred making the cheque payable to that person.

  For example, Payee D Brett endorsed 'David Brett, pay to L Brown or order'. The words 'or order' mean that this cheque could then be reindorsed by L Brown to another person.

- **Restrictive** – A restrictive endorsement is one which consists of a specific endorsement with a restrictive wording added. The additional wording prevents further transfer of the cheque.

  For example, Payee D Brett endorsed 'David Brett, pay to L Brown only'.

When are endorsements required?

Banks usually ask for endorsements in the following circumstances.

- When cheques written to joint payees are credited to a sole account (ie an account in the name of one of the payees).

  For example, a cheque payable to Mr and Mrs T Younge is paid into the account of Mrs T Younge.

  Mr T Younge must sign the back of the cheque.

- When cheques are cashed over the counter (ie exchanged for cash).
- When 'R' (receipt) is printed on the cheque; for example, a cheque issued by an insurance company to a policyholder who is receiving the benefits of the policy.
- If cheques are negotiated (ie they are used as a form of payment to settle a debt with a third party). Instead of writing another cheque, a cheque received by the payee is endorsed and handed over to a third party.

Endorsements are **not** required when:

- a cheque is paid into the payee's account;
- cheques in favour of a sole payee are credited to a joint account.

Cheque crossings

A crossing is an instruction to the bank of the drawer of the cheque. It consists of two parallel lines on the face of the cheque near the centre. Owing to a change in the law, all cheques provided by banks now have the crossing pre-printed on them.

It is also a warning to the collecting bank not to cash the cheque over the counter.

It means that the cheque must be paid into a bank account. This means that there is much less chance of fraud.

Several types of crossing exist:

- general crossings;
- special crossings.

General crossings

A general crossing consists of two parallel lines with or without the words 'and co', 'and company' or 'not negotiable'.

These cheques must be paid into a bank account (but not necessarily the payee's). They must not be exchanged for cash over the counter.

Not negotiable means that if the cheque is stolen, the person who is in possession of that cheque, even if they accepted it in good faith, is not legally entitled to keep the cheque.

If 'not negotiable' does not appear, then any person who receives the cheque afterwards is entitled to keep it provided they took the cheque:

- in good faith;
- for value (in other words it was not a gift);
- without knowing of the theft.

FINANCIAL BANK PLC
SHEPHERD'S BUSH GREEN BRANCH
352 SHEPHERD'S BUSH GREEN W12 6TH

01 - 89 - 34

____19____

Pay

& Co

or order

£

MISS S SMITH

000267 01 - 89 - 34 47586909

FINANCIAL BANK PLC
SHEPHERD'S BUSH GREEN BRANCH
352 SHEPHERD'S BUSH GREEN W12 6TH

01 - 89 - 34

____19____

Pay

And Company

or order

£

MISS S SMITH

000267 01 - 89 - 34 47586909

FINANCIAL BANK PLC
SHEPHERD'S BUSH GREEN BRANCH
352 SHEPHERD'S BUSH GREEN W12 6TH

01 - 89 - 34

____19____

Pay

Not negotiable

or order

£

MISS S SMITH

000267 01 - 89 - 34 47586909

Special crossings

A special crossing consists of the name of the bank, and sometimes also the name of the branch. This can be with or without parallel lines. The cheque must be paid into the branch or bank mentioned in the crossing.

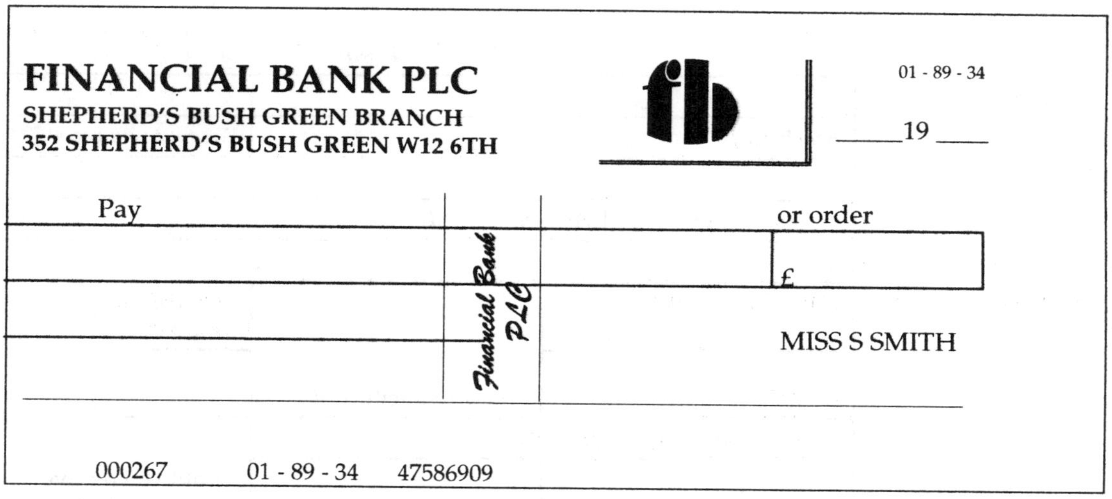

Other instructions

In addition to the crossing there may also be a further instruction. This is the words 'account payee only' or 'account J Smith' or 'account payee'.

This is an instruction to the collecting bank. It is not part of the crossing. It means the cheque can only be paid into the account of the named payee. An endorsement cannot override this instruction.

The same change in the law means that this is also now always pre-printed on the cheque.

Transferring money by different methods

A bank customer can transfer money from his account to another person's account by two other methods which do not involve the cheque clearing system or writing cheques. These are:

- standing orders;
- direct debits.

Standing order –This is an instruction to a customer's bank to make regular payments (usually fixed amounts).

To arrange a standing order all the customer needs to do is sign a **standing order mandate** which authorises the bank to make the payments.

They are ideal for paying regular monthly bills such as insurance premiums. They can also be used to transfer money between a customer's own account, eg transferring surplus money from a current account into a deposit account where it will earn interest.

To **FINANCIAL BANK PLC**

______________ Branch STANDING ORDER MANDATE

Please pay	*Bank*	*Branch title (not address)*	*Sort code number*
Credit	*Beneficiary's name*		*Account number*
the sum of	*Amount in figures* £	*Amount in words*	
commencing	*Date of first payment* now/*	and thereafter every	*Due date & frequency*
until	*Date and amount of last payment*	£	* until you receive further notice from me/us in writing
quoting the reference			and debit my/our account accordingly

Please cancel any previous standing order or direct debit in favour of the named beneficiary above.

Special instructions

Account to be debited	*Account number*

Signature (s) Date ______________

____

____

*Delete if not applicable

Direct debit – An instruction to a customer's bank to allow a **third party** to **debit** (ie collect money from) the customer's account at regular intervals.

Direct debits are better than standing order when either:

- the amount is uncertain;
- or the date of payment is uncertain.

Direct debits are useful for paying items such as membership subscriptions which increase from year to year.

Both direct debits and standing orders continue to be valid until the customer cancels or changes them.

Special forms of payment

Occasionally a customer may wish to use one of the following methods of payment: bills of exchange or banker's drafts.

Bills of exchange – Used mainly today for trade with foreign countries, these were used before cheques were invented.

It is an order to pay a certain sum of money on demand or at a specified future time.

These bills are fairly rare nowadays in inland transactions.

Banker's draft – This is a cheque drawn by a bank itself. It is virtually a banknote issued by that bank.

The banker's draft is often used when a bank's customer needs to pay a large sum of money, eg to buy a house or car.

Because the draft is guaranteed by the bank it is the next best thing to money. In addition, because the seller does not need to wait until the purchaser's cheque has cleared (as would normally be the case to guarantee payment), the purchaser can collect the goods immediately.

Bank giro credit

Another method of transferring money into someone else's bank account is to use a bank giro credit (or credit transfer).

Bank Giro credit – A method of transferring money into someone else's bank account in any bank in the country.

The system is commonly used to pay bills such as electricity, gas, credit cards, telephone.

Many businesses issue the credit transfer slip as part of their bill, or in a book.

The system can also be used to pay wages and salaries to employees. One credit transfer slip is completed for each employee. The credit transfer slips are then forwarded to the bank with a cheque for the total amount payable.

These payments are then cleared through a system (credit clearing) which is similar to the cheque clearing system.

Electronic clearing

To try to reduce the number of pieces of paper used to clear payments using the cheque clearing and giro clearing systems, a further service was introduced in 1968.

This service is known as BACS (Bankers Automated Clearing Services) and is part of the clearing system.

BACS – A method of clearing payments in which transactions are recorded on magnetic tape or discs (rather than on paper). Transactions are then processed at the BACS computer centre instead of through the clearing house.

BACS can be used by banks or by companies which have been allowed to do so by the banks.

BACS is used for:

- standing order payments;
- direct debits;
- salary payments;
- bank giro credits.

The system works as follows.

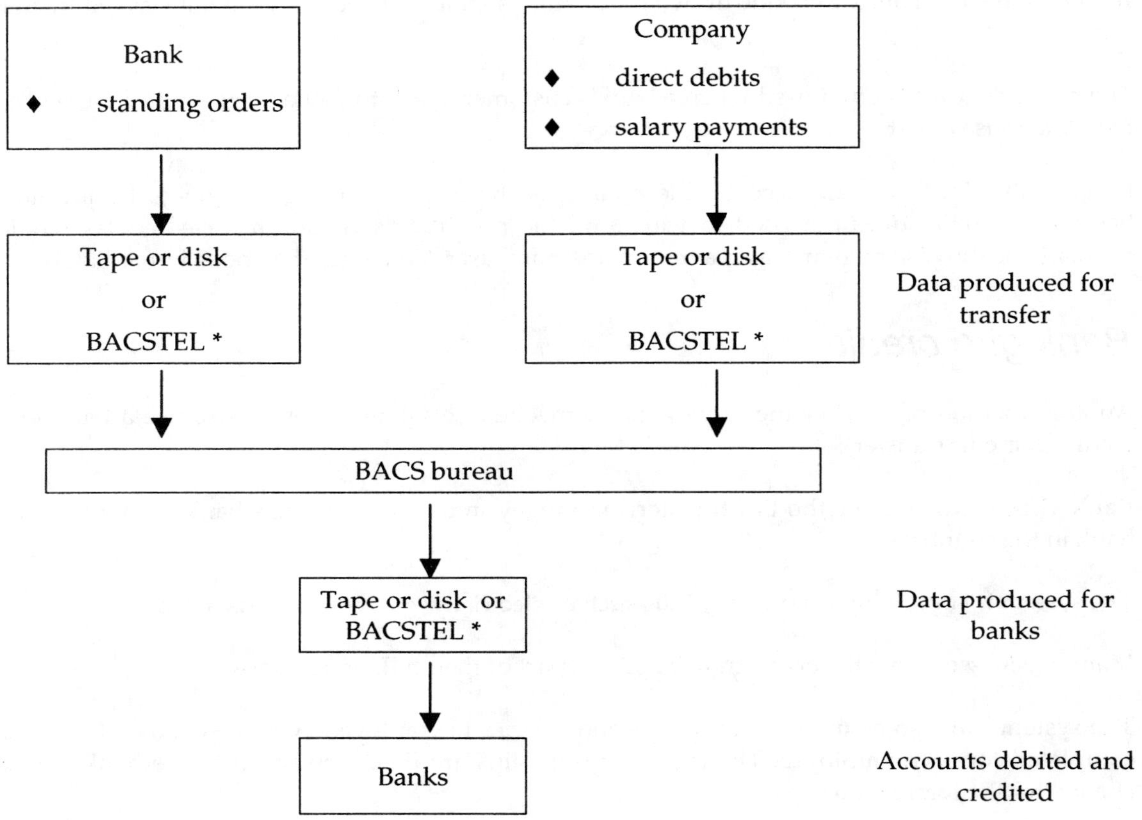

* Transfer by telephone line

Telegraphic transfer or mail transfer may be used for large transactions that need to be processed quickly. These are electronic funds transfers between bank accounts and can be made to foreign bank accounts as well as to accounts within the UK.

To arrange an electronic funds transfer, an business must write to its bank requesting that the payment be made and enclosing details of the bank account to which the payment must be made.

A further service is also available to customers wishing to transfer large sums of money. This is CHAPS (Clearing House Automated Payments System).

CHAPS – Electronic clearing system for large sums. Payments are credited to the payee on same day received.

Questions

1 (AAT CA J92)

Various legal relationships can exist between a bank and a customer. For each of the following, identify the relationship by stating the title given to each of the parties (eg Customer – Mortgagor, Bank – Mortgagee).

(a) Customer deposits a sealed package for bank to hold in safe custody.

(b) Customer has an overdraft with the bank.

(c) Customer instructs the bank to purchase shares on his behalf.

(d) Customer executes a charge over her property in favour of the bank as security for a loan.

2 (AAT CA J93)

A credit balance on a personal account normally denotes a liability. In view of this, explain briefly why when the company has funds in the bank, it should receive a statement showing a credit balance.

3 (AAT CA J94)

MEL Motor Factors Limited's bank statement shows that the company has a credit balance of £4,032 as at 1 June. There is thus a debtor/creditor legal relationship between the company and the bank. In this relationship, which party is the debtor?

Royal Bank Limited / MEL Motor Factors Limited

4 (AAT CA J93)

Midwest Bank Limited had been asked by Future Electrical Limited to arrange the property insurance on all of its buildings. What in this case is the banker customer relationship?

Principal–Agent / Mortgagor–Mortgagee

5 (AAT CA J94)

On 15 June, MEL Motor Factors Limited receives a bank statement dated 14 June. Although the bank is not in the habit of making mistakes, the following two items appear to be errors:

(a) Cheque No. 409662 for £240.62 was debited to the account on 12 June. You are unable to trace a cheque book containing this number and you are also unable to find an amount for £240.62 in the cash book.

(b) A standing order for £471.50 payable to Western Finance, reference P/T000654NL, was debited to the account on 10 June. The standing order mandate given to the bank indicated that the 12 monthly payments for this amount were to commence on 10 July.

Draft a letter to the manager of the Royal Bank Limited, 18 Preston Road, Manchester, MM9 0BU. This should draw the manager's attention to the two payments, request correcting entries and ask for the manager to contact Cathy Payne (the accountant) if there are any problems relating to either issue. The letter is to be signed by Cathy Payne.

6 (AAT CA J94)

Martin wants to be able to buy goods and services without the need for cash or a cheque book. He would also like to have some flexibility in the period of time taken to pay for each of his purchases from, say, a few days to several months. Which service available from the banks would appear to be the most appropriate for this purpose?

7 (AAT CA J93)

During the day Barclays Bank accepted £10 million of Lloyds' cheques and Lloyds Bank accepted £12 million of Barclays' cheques. Both banks use the banker's clearing house where the cheques are exchanged.

(a) What settlement should now take place between the two banks?

(b) How does the settlement take place?

8 (AAT CA J92)

The following bank statement is received from the company's bankers, National Bank plc

National Bank plc

Allsports Limited – Statement of account

Account No. 80439561 — Statement date: 15 June 19X2

Date	*Details*	*Debits*	*Credits*	*Balance*
5 June	Balance forward			10,822 o/d
8 June	606218	23		
8 June	Sundry credit		46	10,799 o/d
9 June	606219	387		
9 June	Direct debit	86		
9 June	Standing order	131		11,403 o/d
10 June	Bank giro credit		249	
10 June	606221	1,181		
10 June	606224	346		12,681 o/d
15 June	Dividend		81	12,600 o/d
16 June	Bank charges	286		12,886 o/d

Cheque number 606221 was a payment made to Royal Sports Limited. The cheque was issued and sent by post on 4 June. On its receipt, Royal Sports paid the cheque into their account with Barker Bank plc. As clearing banks, the head office of National Bank plc and Barker Bank plc exchange cheques with each other. Cheque 606221 would at that stage be passed by Barker Bank to National Bank. Which of the two banks would now owe money to the other bank in respect of this cheque?

Barker Bank plc / National Bank plc

9 (AAT CA J94)

David Cater has received a cheque for £1,000 from MEL Motor Factors Limited and has paid it into his account at the Mid-West Bank. When he asks if he can draw out some cash against the cheque, he is told by the cashier that he will have to wait four days from the date that the cheque was paid in.

Explain briefly why the bank might ask David to wait before he can draw out some or all of the £1,000.

10 (AAT CA D94)

The cheque shown below has been issued by Chang Fashions Limited. Give the name of:

(a) the drawer;

(b) the drawee;

(c) the payee.

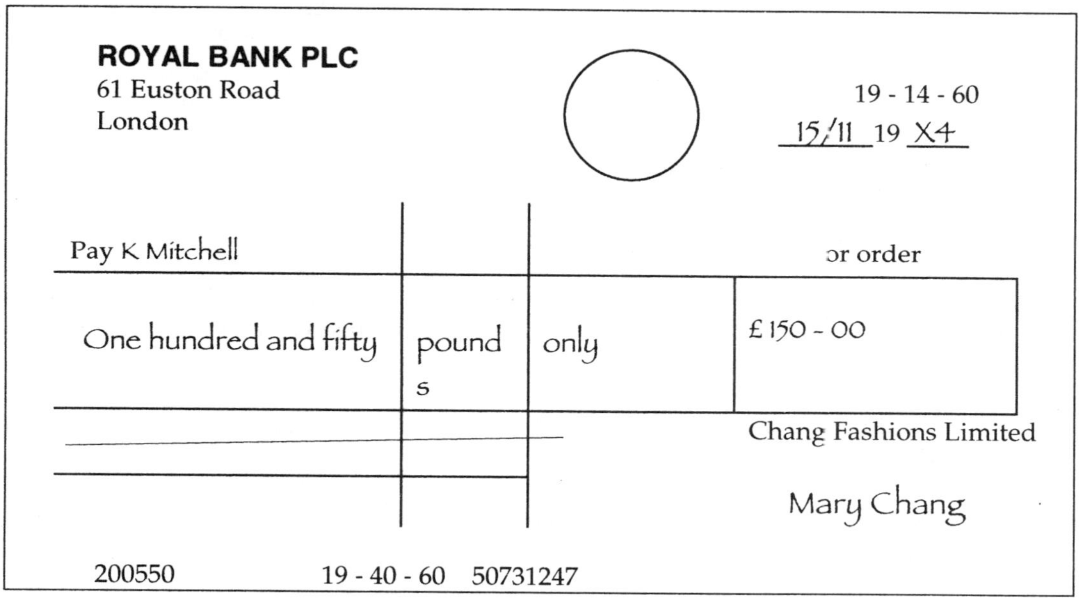

11 (AAT CA J93)

A cheque for £374 has been accepted by one of the cashiers in payment for a washing machine. As you record the cheque, you notice that it has been dated 1 June 19X2. Today's date is 1 June 19X3.

(a) Will payment of the cheque by the drawer's bank be affected by the incorrect date?

(b) Having noticed the error, is it acceptable for you to alter the cheque to the correct date?

12 (AAT CA J94)

The cheque shown below is received in the post from Autoparts Limited in part payment of their debt. The reverse of the cheque has been signed 'A Hallchurch'.

(a) Could the cheque be paid into MEL Motor Factors Limited's bank account?

(b) Briefly explain the reason for your answer.

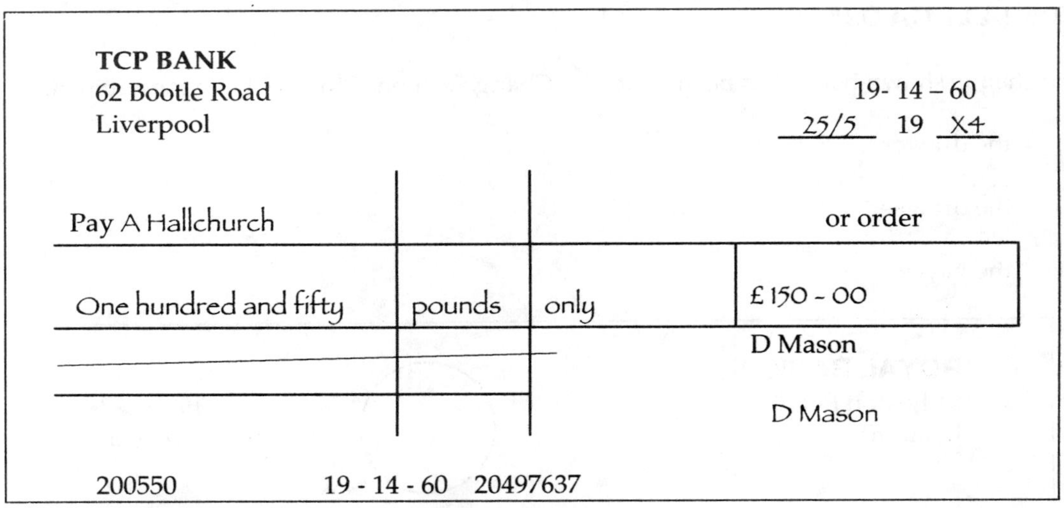

13 (AAT CA J92)

A cheque has been received from Roper Sports for £327. The drawer is D Barber, the payee G Rance and the drawee Midwest Bank plc. On examining the cheque, you notice that on the back of it is the signature of G Rance.

(a) Would National Bank plc normally allow the cheque to be paid into Allsport Limited's account?

(b) Would National Bank plc allow the cheque to be paid into Allsport Limited's account if the cheque has been crossed 'A/c payee only'?

14 (AAT CA D93)

Music World Limited receives a cheque in the post which has a special crossing.

(a) Explain briefly what is meant by a 'special crossing'.

(b) Explain briefly the effect of a special crossing.

15 (AAT CA D94)

The cheque shown below has been issued by Chang Fashions Limited. Briefly explain the effect of the crossing.

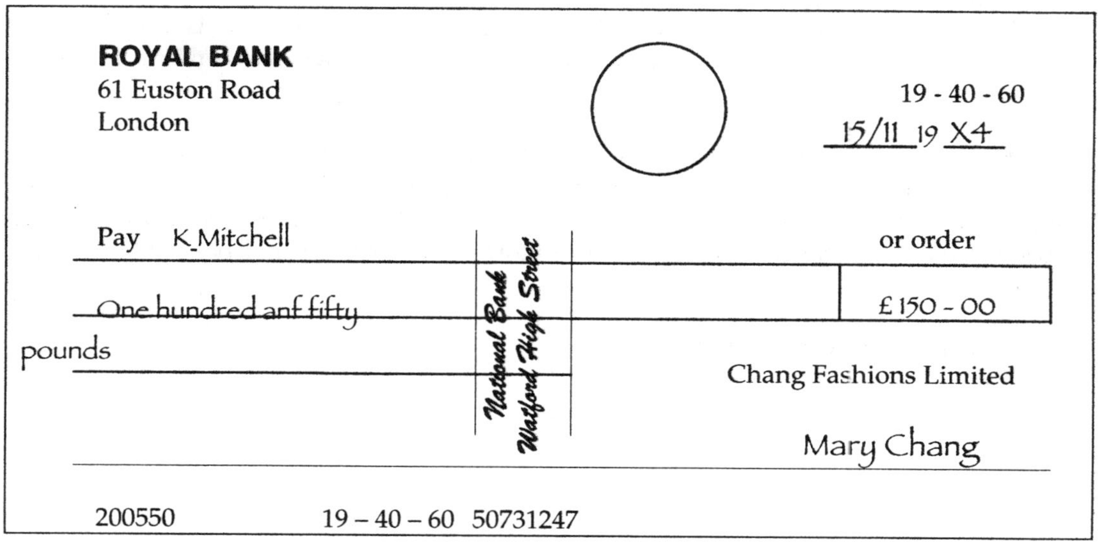
ROYAL BANK
61 Euston Road
London

19 - 40 - 60
15/11 19 X4

Pay K.Mitchell or order

One hundred anf fifty pounds

£ 150 - 00

National Bank
Watford High Street

Chang Fashions Limited

Mary Chang

200550 19 – 40 – 60 50731247

16 (AAT CA D93)

Music World Limited needs to make regular monthly payments to Firmcare Finance Limited. The amount of the payment varies from month to month. Which service provided by the banks would appear to be the most appropriate?

17 (AAT CA D94)

A cheque issued by a bank and drawn upon itself is known as a: ....

Briefly explain the advantage to a creditor in receiving such a cheque from a debtor in preference to the debtor's own cheque.

18 (AAT CA D93)

The company bank account tends to swing from overdraft to credit balances. Over the last six months:

Number of days overdrawn	42 days
Number of days in credit	140 days
Maximum overdraft	£22,000
Overdraft limit	£25,000
Maximum credit balance	£84,525
Average balance	£38,640 credit

Draft a memo from Tony Bryant (the Managing Director) to Jane Alder (the Accountant and Company Secretary) suggesting why it might be appropriate to have a bank deposit account as well as a current account and asking, if she is in agreement, for her authorisation to instruct the bank to make the necessary arrangements.

19 (AAT CA J93)

Curran Stores Limited are valued customers of Future Electrical Limited and have their offices at 14 Woolford Road, Lanchaster L14 8QS. Ben Travers is the managing director. He telephones with a query and you take the call. Apparently, a statement was sent out the previous day by Future Electrical showing a balance of £10,325. Curran Stores Limited's records show a balance of £7,325. One item on the statement that Ben Travers does not understand is a debit for £3,000 with the details 'unpaid cheque'. You promise to investigate and write to Ben Travers as he will be out of the office for the rest of the day.

The £3,000 debit turns out to be a cheque recently returned by Curran Stores Limited's bank marked 'Words and figures differ'. In issuing the cheque, the words had been written in error as three pounds. Although Curran Stores Limited's account had been debited, no further action had been taken with the cheque and Curran Stores had therefore not been informed of the situation.

Draft a suitable letter to be sent to Ben Travers.

Summary

Bank customer

- Someone with a current or similar account (length of time is not important)
- Someone who has agreed to open a current or similar account

Relationship between bank and customer

- **Debtor/creditor** (ie bank owes money to the customer or vice versa)
- Bank agrees to hold, receive and collect customer's money
- Bank agrees not to close the customer's account without reasonable notice
- Customer agrees to take care in writing cheques
- Customer can only ask for repayment in writing
- **Principal/agent** – When dealing with parties
- **Bailor/bailee** – Bank acts as bailee by looking after customer's property

Rights of the bank

- Charge for services
- Reclaim losses from customers
- Exercise a lien over customer's property
- Use the customer's money any way it wishes, provided it pays cheques written by customer
- Expect customer to use reasonable care when writing out cheques

Duties of the customer

- To use reasonable care when writing cheques
- To tell the bank of any known forgery of his or her signature

Duties of the bank

- To pay customer's cheques
- To obey any express mandate (eg standing order)
- To keep customer's details confidential
- To give reasonable notice of closure of account
- To provide regular bank statements
- To tell customer balance on account when asked
- To accept cash and cheques paid in by customer
- To repay customer's money when the customer asks
- To tell customer immediately of any possible forgery
- To exercise proper skill and care (fiduciary relationship).

Services offered by high-street banks

Deposit-taking

- Current accounts
- Deposit accounts

Money transfer

- Out of customer's account:
  - Cheques

  Standing orders

  Direct debits

  Cash from cash dispensers (ATMs)

  Debit cards

  BACS

- Into customer's account:
  - Cheques
  - Postal orders
  - Standing orders
  - Direct debits
  - Credit card sales
  - BACS
  - Bank giro credit

Advances

- Overdraft
- Credit cards
- Loans
- Mortgages
- Business loans

Other services

- Foreign currency
- Safe deposit boxes
- Nightsafes
- Investment advice
- Share dealing
- Advice on wills
- Insurance

Getting payment for the customer

- Customer pays in cheque
- Bank credits customer's bank account with value of cheques
- Collects money from third party's bank

Paying in cash and cheques

- Cash is bagged up before being taken to the bank
- Cashier checks items before accepting
- Cash is credited to customer's account at the end of the working day
- Cheques are sorted and processed through clearing system

Clearing system

- Many banks are now members
- Process takes three days

Day 1

- Cheques are sorted at branch
- Cheques are sent to bank's own clearing department

Day 2

- Cheques are sent to central clearing house
- Cheques are sent to other bank's clearing department

Day 3

- Cheques are sent to branch of person who wrote cheque

Cheques accepted by bank

- Bank must check:
  - date (out of date, post–dated, un–dated)
  - payee
  - words and figures
  - signature
  - crossings
  - endorsements.

Endorsements

- Form of signature:
  - titles
  - married women.
- Types:
  - blank/general
  - specific
  - restrictive.
- Required when:
  - cheques to joint payee paid into the sole account of one of the payees
  - when cheques are cashed over the counter
  - when R (receipt) is printed on the cheque
  - when cheques are negotiated (ie transferred).
- Not required when:
  - cheque paid into payee's account
  - cheques to an individual are paid into a joint account.

Cheques paid by the bank

- Bank must check:
  - sufficient funds exist in account
  - cheque correctly completed
  - customer not dead, bankrupt, mentally incapacitated
  - cheque not lost or stolen
  - drawer's signature not forged.

- Bank must pay cheque guaranteed by cheque guarantee card.
  - Cheque details to check:
    - date
    - payee
    - endorsements
    - crossings
    - alterations
    - drawer's signature
    - torn cheques
    - stopped cheques
    - Bank will return cheques it cannot pay.

Crossings

- Instruction to paying bank
  - Warning to collecting bank
  - Can be hand-written or printed
  - General crossings:
    - two parallel lines with or without words 'and Co', 'and Company' or 'not negotiable'
    - Special crossings
    - name of the bank (and sometimes branch name)
    - with or without parallel lines
    - cheque must be paid into bank/branch mentioned.
- Other instructions:
  - 'account payee only', 'account J Smith' or 'account payee'
  - instruction to collecting bank
  - cheque can only be paid into account of named payee
  - cannot be overridden by endorsement

Special forms of payment

- Bills of exchange:
  - forerunner of cheques
  - not used much nowadays
  - order to pay a certain amount on a particular date.
- Banker's draft:
  - like a cheque
  - but guaranteed by bank
  - useful for large payments.

Standing order

- Instruction to customer's bank to make regular payments
- Usually fixed amount
- Usually at fixed intervals

Direct debits

- Instruction to customer's bank to allow a third party to collect money from the customer's account
- Suitable for irregular amounts
- Suitable for irregular payment dates

Bank giro credits

- Method of transferring money into someone else's bank account
- Businesses often offer credit transfer slip as part of their bills
- Cleared through credit clearing system

BACS

- Method of electronic clearing
- Transactions recorded electronically instead of on paper
- Used by banks and companies

- Used to clear:
  - standing order payments
  - salary payments
  - bank giro credits.

CHAPS

- Method of electronic clearing
- Used for large sums only

CHAPTER 5

Maintaining a Cash Book and Petty Cash

Objectives

This chapter covers the following performance criteria.

When accounting for cash and bank transactions

- Entries in the cash book are accurately transferred to correct ledger accounts.
- Bank reconciliation statements are accurately prepared and are presented within specified timescales.
- Recorded transactions are supported by properly authorised primary documentation.
- Details for the relevant primary documentation are recorded in the cash book and analysed accurately.
- Totals and balances are correctly calculated.

When maintaining petty cash records

- Transactions are accurately recorded and analysed to the correct expenditure heads.
- Cash withdrawals from the main cash account are accurately recorded.
- Claims are properly authorised, are within prescribed limits and are supported by accurate evidence.
- Totals and balances are correctly calculated.
- The balance of cash in hand is reconciled with the petty cash records at appropriate intervals.
- Documentation is correctly filed.
- Cash handling, security and confidentiality procedures are followed.

Recording receipts and payments

Every business uses a **cash book** to record receipts and payments. Cash book is a slightly inaccurate name because it usually records receipts and payments through the business's bank account (ie the items which also appear on the bank statement).

Receipts can include cash which is paid into the bank account (particularly in a retail business) but payments would not include cash payments which would be made from petty cash.

The simplest cash book would be a book in which receipts are recorded on the left hand page and payments on the right hand page. The business will normally keep a separate cash book for each bank account held.

Entries in the cash book must only be made where they are supported by proper documentation.

All entries on the receipts side must agree to a paying-in slip. However, if the paying-in slip includes several cheques received the cash book may be written up from the cheques themselves, or from the remittance list.

All entries on the payments side must agree to cheques drawn which have been properly signed. (In practice, the entries may be made from the cheque stubs.)

Analysing receipts and payments

As the cash book is an important source of accounting information the nature of receipts and payments will normally be analysed.

Mini case study – cash book A

Joyce Brooks is the part-time cashier and bookkeeper for a small furniture manufacturing company. She maintains the cash book records for both receipts and payments.

Let us look first of all at the receipts side of the cash book.

Joyce prefers to write all cheques into the cash book, although she realises she could enter the totals from remittance lists, remittance advices or paying-in slips instead.

Some cash books also have a separate column which shows the total banked.

Let us look at the cash book for the week commencing 3 July 19X3.

(*Note*. This business does not have to be registered for VAT.)

Cash book receipts for the week commencing 3 July 19X3

Date	Narrative	Paying-in slip	Total			
3 July	A Brown	112	20.12			
5 July	S Smith & Co Limited	113	9.30			
	P Priest	113	60.80			
	James & Jeans	113	38.21			
	LS Moore	113	17.00			
6 July	L White Limited	114	5.16			
7 July	MN Furnishers Limited	115	112.58			
	RB Roberts	115	23.65			
	Light and Shade	115	86.95			
			373.77			

Joyce is now going to analyse the receipts by type. She will then use the totals by type later on when she writes up the accounting records.

MN Furnishing Limited is a business which rents a shop owned by the business. James & Jeans and A Brown are not credit customers. These are analysed as sales because this is the first time these sales have been recorded. The payments from debtors are for sales which have already been recorded.

This is an important point.

Let us look now at the cash book.

Cash book receipts for the week commencing 3 July 19X3

Date	Narrative	Paying-in slip	Total	Debtors	Rent	Sales
3 July	A Brown	112	20.12			20.12
5 July	S Smith & Co Limited	113	9.30	9.30		
	P Priest	113	60.80	60.80		
	James & Jeans	113	38.21			38.21
	LS Moore	113	17.00	17.00		
6 July	L White Limited	114	5.16	5.16		
7 July	MN Furnishers Limited	115	112.58		112.58	
	RB Roberts	115	23.65	23.65		
	Light and Shade	115	86.95	86.95		
			373.77	202.86	112.58	58.33

Note. The combined totals of the analysis columns (debtors, sales and rent) equal the overall total of receipts.

Let us look at the payments side of the cash book. Note that the business makes various payments other than those to creditors (suppliers who give the business credit).

The business also makes payments by direct debit (DD) and standing order (SO). Cheques are used in strict number order and cancelled cheques are noted. Joyce has included the interest charge made by the bank which has appeared on the bank statement.

Date	Narrative	Cheque no.	Total	Creditors	Insurance	Salaries	Electricity	Interest	Glue
3 July	PBR Solvents	558	95.61	95.61					
	Cancelled	559	–						
4 July	Norweb	DD	50.19				50.19		
	Joyce Brooks	560	46.00			46.00			
	Reg Watts	561	160.00			160.00			
	Woodstores Limited	562	86.95	86.95					
5 July	Greenbrook brokers	SO	10.50		10.50				
6 July	JW Sparks	563	102.13	102.13					
7 July	LV Stores	564	25.30						25.30
	Dowes Wood Supplies	565	115.83	115.83					
	Barclays Bank	–	23.50					23.50	
			716.01	400.52	10.50	206.00	50.19	23.50	25.30

The impact of value added tax

Some businesses which are registered for VAT make non-credit sales (ie customers are not given credit but pay immediately by cash or cheque). When writing-up these sales in the cash book this is the first recording of these sales. The business must analyse the VAT element of these sales.

Mini case study – cash book B

Peter Craddock is the cashier for a limited company which manufactures writing paper from recycled paper. There is a small shop at the front of the factory which makes sales to employees only for cash or cheques.

Let us look at the cash book for one week.

Cash book receipts for the week commencing 15 September 19X4

Date	Narrative	Paying-in slip	Total	Debtors	Cash/cheque sales	VAT
15 Sept		584	653.90	653.90		
16 Sept		585	864.60	864.60		
17 Sept		586	953.58	887.54	56.20	9.84
18 Sept		587	559.57	559.57		
19 Sept		588	234.23	48.00	158.49	27.74
			3,265.88	3,013.61	214.69	37.58

The bankings on 17 September and 19 September are a mixture of cash sales and payments from debtors. The totals of the analysis columns still equal the main total.

Let us look at the payments side of the cash book.

Cash book payments for the week commencing 15 September 19X4

Date	Cheque no.	Total	Creditors	Electricity	Salaries	Rent	Insurance	Interest	VAT
15 Sept	1151-1163	2,125.57	2,125.57						
	SO	168.15				168.15			
	DD	153.90		130.98					22.92
16 Sept	1164-1193	1,092.75	1,092.75						
	1194	103.18					103.18		
	1195	Cancelled							
17 Sept	1196-2012	742.60	742.60						
	2013	Cancelled							
18 Sept	2014-2015	131.89	131.89						
19 Sept	BACS	4,150.09			4,150.09				
	Interest	156.28						156.28	
		8,824.41	4,092.81	130.98	4,150.09	168.15	103.18	156.28	22.92

There is no VAT on salaries. Electricity is standard-rated for non-domestic users. Rent, interest and insurance are exempt.

The link with the other accounting records

The analysed cash book is an important source of accounting information. Each month details of cash receipts and payments by type are recorded in the accounting records.

The information to be posted (ie transferred) is normally summarised in the form of a journal entry. Many businesses use standardised pre-printed journal entry forms to reduce the likelihood of errors occurring.

Here is a typical journal entry form to post the totals from the cash book for one month.

Journal entry		No:	
Cash book Week ending 19 Sept 19X4 Prepared by TB Jones Authorised by			
Account	**Code**	**Debit**	**Credit**
Cash at bank (receipts)	0163	3,265.88	
Cash sales	0250		214.69
Debtors	0158		3,013.61
VAT	5390		37.58
Creditors	0175	4,092.81	
Interest	0263	156.28	
Wages and salaries	0290	4,150.09	
Rent	0299	168.15	
Insurance		103.18	
Electricity		130.98	
VAT		22.92	
Cash at bank (payments)	0163		8,824.41
Totals		12,090.29	12,090.29

Recording cash discounts

Accounting for discounts allowed and received

Businesses often offer discounts to customers. There are two main types of discount: trade discounts and cash (or settlement) discounts.

Trade discounts

Trade discounts are given to trade customers (ie wholsesalers and retailers) rather than the general public. They are given to customers who buy regularly or who buy large quantities. The effect of a trade discount is to reduce the selling price from the published list price. The calculation of the trade discount is shown on the invoice recording the transaction. The sale is recorded at the reduced selling price.

Cash (settlement) discounts

Cash (or settlement) discounts are given to customers for payment within a stated credit period. The customer may or may not take advantage of the discount. Therefore, the invoice shows the **full amount payable** and the sale is recorded at this amount.

If a customer takes advantage of a cash discount, the amount received will be **less** than the amount on the sales invoice. The difference is the **expense** and is described in the profit and loss account as **discount allowed**.

If a business takes advantage of cash discounts on items purchased, the discount is treated as **income** and is described in the profit and loss account as **discounts received**.

Cash or settlement discounts are recorded in a **memorandum column** in the cash book. The memorandum column does *not* form part of the double-entry.

Whether the business is offering or receiving these cash or settlement discounts, they both represent a discount in the total amount payable.

The business must therefore record these discounts. Trade discounts are not recorded in the cash book.

An extra column is included in the analysed cash book. This should be the final right-hand column for both receipts and payments.

Let us look at an entry in the receipts side of the cash book.

Date	Narrative	Paying-in slip	Total	Debtors	Discount
19 Feb	SJ Boddy	239	975.00	975.00	25.00

The original debtor was £1,000. The settlement discount was 2.5%. The total figure is the same as the debtors' figure not the debtors' figure plus the discount figure. This is because the total figure must be the actual amount received.

The discount column is described as a **memorandum column**. This is because it is a reminder to record the discount in the accounting records.

A discount taken by the business would be recorded in the same way in the payments side of the cash book.

Date	Narrative	Cheque No.	Total	Creditors	Discount
21 Feb	D Bates & Co Limited	834	545.43	545.43	16.87

Individual receipts and payments are also recorded against the relevant debtor or creditor.

The double-entry to record discounts is as follows:

		Dr	*Cr*
Discounts allowed:			
Dr	Discounts allowed	25.00	
Cr	Debtors		25.00
Discounts allowed			
Dr	Creditors	16.87	
Cr	Discount received		16.87

Another form of cash book

So far you have seen the analysed cash book which is a book of prime entry and is therefore not part of the double entry system.

Some businesses (particularly small businesses) use a cash book that is part of the double entry system. The cash book is effectively two cash books in one: one for cash receipts and payments and another for transactions that go through the bank account.

As well as columns for cash and bank it also has columns for VAT and discounts. The VAT and discount columns are **memorandum columns.** They are used when writing up the transactions in the ledgers.

Remember that this type of business will not have nominal ledger accounts for cash and bank because it uses the cash book instead. The cash book is written up and then the double entry is completed using the totals from the cash book.

Format of the cash book

See the example below.

Note how the balances on the cash and bank accounts are carried forward by balancing off the columns.

The **folio** column gives the ledger which the individual transactions are to be posted to as follows.

DL	Debtors' ledger
CL	Creditors' ledger
NL	Nominal ledger

If the transaction is a transfer between the cash and bank accounts the folio is C or CB. In this case the petty cash book is also maintained in the form of a ledger account.

You will learn more about the petty cash book later.

Cash and bank book

Date	Details	Folio	Disc all'd	VAT	Cash	Bank	Date	Details	Folio	Disc rec'd	VAT	Cash	Bank
19X4													
1 Apr	Balances b/f				123.56	560.88	2 Apr	Supplier A	CL	2.60			152.52
3 Apr	Cash sale	NL		5.25	35.25		2 Apr	Telephone	NL		13.65		91.65
3 Apr	Customer X	DL	2.72			159.32	2 Apr	Wages	NL			22.50	
3 Apr	Cash banked	C				50.00	3 Apr	Cash banked	C			50.00	
							4 Apr	Salary	NL				57.34
							5 Apr	Petty cash	PCB			20.00	
							5 Apr	Balance c/f				66.31	468.69
			2.72	5.25	158.81	770.20				2.60	13.65	158.81	770.20
5 Apr	Balance b/f				66.31	468.69							

Exercise

Here is the blank cash book for Jupiter Limited.

Date	Details	Folio	Disc all'd	VAT	Cash	Bank	Date	Details	Folio	Disc rec'd	VAT	Cash	Bank
19X9													
1 July	Balance b/f				23.66	509.77							

You are required to write up the following transactions in the cash book and carry forward the balances at the end of the week.

1 July	Cash sale of £7.05.	
2 July	Received a cheque for £45.90 from Hill and French Limited (no settlement discount allowed).	
2 July	Corrected a salary error with a cheque for £56.89.	
3 July	Paid £96.65 by cheque to Preston Brothers after deducting a settlement discount of £1.65.	
3 July	Cash sale of £35.25.	
3 July	Banked £30 of cash held.	
4 July	Received a cheque from Green and Holland for £245.89. They were allowed a settlement discount of £3.68.	
5 July	Received the bank statement which showed the following transactions not yet recorded in the cash book:	
	Bank charges and interest	£54.23
	Direct debit payment to English Telecomm	£94.00
	Credit transfer from Jones & Co (settlement discount of £1.56)	£123.90
5 July	Reimbursed the petty cash account with £34.89 of cash.	

Solution to exercise

Date	Details	Folio	Disc all'd	VAT	Cash	Bank	Date	Details	Folio	Disc rec'd	VAT	Cash	Bank
19X9													
1 July	Balance b/f				23.66	509.77	2 July	Salary error	NL				56.89
1 July	Cash sale	NL		1.05	7.05		3 July	Preston Brothers	CL	1.65			96.65
2 July	Hill & French	DL				45.90	3 July	Bank cash	C			30.00	
3 July	Cash sale	NL		5.25	35.25		5 July	Bank charges	NL				54.23
3 July	Bank cash	C				30.00	5 July	English Telec	NL		14.00		94.00
4 July	Green & Holland	DL	3.68			245.89	5 July	Petty cash	PCB			34.89	
5 July	Jones & Co	DL	1.56			123.90							
							5 July	Balance c/f				1.07	653.69
			5.24	6.30	65.96	955.46				1.65	14.00	65.96	955.46
5 July	Balance b/f				1.07	653.69							

Now list out the entries you will have to make in the nominal ledger and petty cash book to complete the double entry. Note that most of these will be *single entries*.

Entries in nominal ledger and petty cash book

		Dr	*Cr*
Nominal ledger			
Dr	Discounts allowed	5.24	
Cr	Debtors' ledger control		5.24
Cr	VAT		6.30
Cr	Sales		36.00
Cr	Debtors' ledger control		415.69
Dr	Creditors' ledger control	1.65	
Cr	Discounts received		1.65
Dr	VAT	14.00	
Dr	Wages and salaries	56.89	
Dr	Creditors' ledger control	96.65	
Dr	Bank charges	54.23	
Dr	Telephone	80.00	

		Dr	*Cr*
Petty cash book			
Dr	Petty cash	34.89	

You can check that this balances by including the other entries which are in the cash book:

Dr	Cash	42.30	
Dr	Bank	445.69	
Cr	Cash		64.89
Cr	Bank		301.77
		831.54	831.54

The debits and credits are equal.

Performing a bank reconciliation

At regular intervals (normally at least once a month) the cashier must check that the cash book is correct.

The best way to do this is to compare the cash book with the bank statements.

At any date the balance shown on the bank statement is unlikely to agree with the balance in the cash book for the following reasons.

- Cheques received by the business and paid into the bank which have not yet appeared on the bank statement (**deposits in transit**).
- Cheques written by the business but which have not yet appeared on the bank statement (**unpresented cheques**).
- Items charged or credited directly by the bank (charges, interest, etc).
- Errors in the cash book (eg transposition of numbers, addition errors).

This comparison is known as a **bank reconciliation**.

How to perform a bank reconciliation

- The first thing to do is to compare the cash book and bank statement and perform one-for-one matching of items to identify items which do not appear on both.
- The cash book may have to be corrected for errors or missing items.
- The revised cash book balance should then be compared with the bank statement balance using a simple proforma.

	£
Balance per bank statement	
Less: Unpresented cheques	
Add: Deposits in transit	
Balance per cash book	

Debits and credits in bank statements

- When we pay money into the bank, we debit our cash account but the bank credits our account.
- This is because a debit in our cash book represents the increase in our asset 'cash'. For the bank, the situation is different: they will debit *their* cash account and credit *our* account because they now owe us more money; we are a creditor. When our account is overdrawn, we owe the bank money and consequently our cash account will show a credit balance. For the bank the reverse is true.

Mini case study – bank reconciliation

The treasurer of the Bridge Club is performing the monthly bank reconciliation. He uses the bank statement and cash book to identify the deposits in transit and unpresented cheques.

First Bank Statement Page 23

Account No. XXXXXXX

Account Name Bridge Club

	No	*Debit* £	*Credit* £	*Balance* £
Balance b/f from Page 22				73
Cheque	58	12		
	59	10		
	61	9		
Deposit	112		23	
Cheque	64	17		
	62	21		
	63	18		
	67	7		
Deposit	113		41	
	115		53	
Balance c/f to page 24				96

Analysed cash book – payments

Date	Narrative	Cheque No.	Voucher No.	Total
X	X	58	X	12
X	X	59	X	10
X	X	60	X	*13
X	X	61	X	9
X	X	62	X	21
X	X	63	X	18
X	X	64	X	17
X	X	65	X	*19
X	X	66	X	*3
X	X	67	X	7
X	X	68	X	*15
				144

* Unpresented cheques

Analysed cash book – Receipts

Date	Narrative	Paying-in slip	Voucher No.	Total
X	Balance b/f			73
X	X	111	X	6Δ
X	X	112	X	23
X	X	113	X	41
X	X	114	X	17Δ
X	X	115	X	53
				213
	Less payments			(144)
	Balance c/f			69

Δ Deposits in transit

Bank reconciliation

		£
Balance per bank statement		96
Less:	Unpresented cheques *(13 + 19 + 3 + 15)	(50)
Add:	Deposits in transit Δ (6 + 17)	23
Balance per cash book		69

Dishonoured cheques and out of date cheques

Cheques may be 'Referred to drawer', or dishonoured by the bank. This may occur for a number of reasons, including insufficient funds in the drawer's account. Dishonoured cheques appear on the bank statement.

The cash book should be adjusted for any dishonoured cheques. If a customer's cheque is dishonoured, the cheque must be deducted from receipts or added to payments. If a cheque paid to a supplier is dishonoured, the cheque must be added to receipts or deducted from payments.

A cheque ceases to be valid after six months from the date of issue. Any unpresented cheques which are more than six months old should be written back into the cash book. These cheques will then cease to appear as part of the bank reconciliation.

Why does a business need petty cash

Most businesses need to keep small amounts of cash to make small payments.

These are usually for items such as stamps, cleaning materials, coffee, tea and newspapers. Wages and salaries should not be paid out of petty cash because of the requirements of the PAYE taxation system. You will see this in Unit 3. The cash will usually come from small amounts of cash received, eg cash sales to customers, staff sales for cash or from cheques from the business' bank account cashed over the counter at the bank.

Where petty cash is replenished from the main bank account, the withdrawal should be recorded in the cash book, as well as in the petty cash book.

Maintaining petty cash records

The format of the analysed petty cash book will be similar to the analysed cash book.

The petty cash book can be kept as a T-account (part of the double-entry system) or as a book of prime entry (not part of the double entry system).

The petty cash book is written up from numbered vouchers. Each voucher should be supported by a receipt and authorised. Some organisations may set limits for petty cash claims (for example, no claims over £20 allowed). Authorisation limits may operate in the same way that limits operate for cheque signatories. Receipts should be attached to the vouchers and the vouchers filed in numerical order.

As a minimum, the following information should appear on a petty cash voucher:

- date
- voucher number
- details of expense
- amount
- VAT amount (if applicable; if VAT is to be claimed, a VAT invoice must be attached)
- signature of person authorising payment.

Let us look at an extract from an analysed petty cash book. The sundry column is used for any other items.

Note how this petty cash book is in itself a ledger account with a debit and a credit side, balance brought forward and carried forward.

The analysis columns are memorandum columns used to complete the double-entry.

Receipts **Payments**

Date	*Narrative*	*Total*	*Date*	*Narrative*	*Voucher no*	*Total*	*Postage*	*Cleaning*	*Tea & coffee*	*Sundry*	*VAT*
1 Nov											
Bal b/f		35.50									
1 Nov	Cheque 394		1 Nov	ASDA	58	23.50			23.50		
		114.50									
			2 Nov	Post Office counters	59	29.50	29.50				
			2 Nov	Cleaning materials	60	14.76		12.56			2.20
			3 Nov	Postage	61	16.19	16.19				
			3 Nov	ASDA	62	10.35		8.81			1.54
			4 Nov	News-papers	63	18.90				18.90	
			5 Nov	ASDA	64	11.85				10.09	1.76
							45.69	21.37	23.50	28.99	5.50
			5 Nov	Bal c/f		24.95					
		150.00				150.00					
5 Nov	Bal b/f	24.95									
6 Nov	Cheque 411	125.05									

The journal entry to record the petty cash payments would be as follows.

Journal entry	**No:**	
Petty cash book		
Week ending 5 Nov 19X3		
Prepared by A J Smith		
Authorised by		
Account	**Debit**	**Credit**
Postage	45.69	
Cleaning	21.37	
Tea & coffee	23.50	
Sundry	28.99	
VAT	5.50	
Petty cash		125.05
	125.05	125.05

The journal entry to record the replenishment of the float on 6 November would be:

Dr	Petty cash	£125.05	
Cr	Bank		£125.05

The effect of value added tax

VAT on payments must be analysed separately if the business is able to reclaim that VAT.

However, the company cannot reclaim VAT on certain items, eg entertaining.

Security

Although only small amounts of cash are involved, petty cash is an area where theft or fraud can easily occur. The petty cash box must be kept under lock and key, preferably in a safe.

Cash should not be given to anyone other than in support of a voucher and a receipt. Cheques should not normally be cashed, neither should IOUs normally be allowed. As part of their security arrangements, many businesses only allow petty cash claims to be made at certain times of day.

Petty cash must be counted at regular intervals (daily, weekly or monthly, depending on the volume and frequency of transactions) and reconciled to the balance in the petty cash book. This reconciliation should normally be performed or checked by someone other than the person who keeps the petty cash book and makes payments.

The imprest system

Many businesses use the imprest system for petty cash. Using an imprest system makes petty cash easier to control and therefore reduces the possibility of error and fraud.

The business decides on a fixed amount of petty cash (the imprest) which is just large enough to cover normal petty cash requirements for a period (usually a week). This amount of petty cash is withdrawn from the bank.

Claims are paid out of petty cash in the usual way. A voucher is completed for each amount of petty cash paid out and the vouchers are kept in the petty cash box so that the amount of cash held decreases and is replaced by vouchers.

At any given time, the total contents of the box (ie petty cash plus amounts withdrawn represented by vouchers) must equal the amount of the imprest.

At the end of the period, a cheque is drawn for the total of the vouchers which restores the petty cash float to the amount of the imprest. The vouchers are removed from the petty cash box and filed.

Bookkeeping exercise

The tasks in this exercise are based on the transactions of Passiflora Products Limited, a small company which produces herbal remedies and cosmetics and supplies them to shops and beauty parlours.

The accounting system is manual.

Data

Cheques received

	Paying-in slip/customer	*Amount*	*Discount allowed*
		£	£
1/5/X6	Paying-in slip 609		
	Natural Beauty	11,797.05	176.95
	Grapeseed	417.30	6.26
	New Age Remedies	6,379.65	95.69
	The Aromatherapy Shop	9,130.65	136.96
3/5/X6	Paying-in slip 610		
	Comfrey Group	5,689.20	85.34
	Natural Elegance	2,056.89	30.85
8/5/X6	Paying-in slip 611		
	The Herbalist	8,663.45	129.95
12/5/X6	Paying-in slip 612		
	Edwards Pharmacy	106.42	
	Healthworks	17,213.94	258.21
19/5/X6	Paying-in slip 613		
	The Beauty Box	11,195.85	167.94
	Crystals	54.19	
25/5/X6	Paying-in slip 614		
	The Village Chemist	7,662.55	114.94
29/5/X6	Paying-in slip 615		
	Brewer Brothers	2,504.61	37.57
30/5/X6	Paying-in slip 616		
	Lapis Lazuli	112.58	
31/5/X6	Paying-in slip 617		
	Lorelei	5,618.40	84.27
	Spain & Co, Chemists	197.93	

Cheque payments

Narrative	*Date*	*Cheque No.*	£
Imperial Oils	1/5/X6	3385	8,839.33
Curtis Herb Farms	2/5/X6	3386	828.95
Brandon Glassworks Limited		3387	17,383.25
Paper Bag Company Limited		3388	7,182.50
Drewstead Supplies	8/5/X6	3389	1,167.22
Coopers Laboratories		3390	883.19
Phillips & Sons	9/5/X6	3391	2,721.56
The Plantcare Company		3392	386.78
Sullivan Limited		3393	1,858.16
The Natural Oil Company		3394	6,337.49
Provencal Herbalists	15/5/X6	3395	271.96
Thyme and Sage Products		3396	11,947.17
Houndsbane and Hellebore	16/5/X6	3397	4,666.25
Provencal Herbalists		3398	56.16
Drewstead Supplies	17/5/X6	3399	3,416.64
Finch's Hardware		3400	173.30
Winter & White Limited		3401	5,002.21
Grants Gardens	22/5/X6	3402	4,783.88
Imperial Oils		3403	8,667.39
Curtis Herb Farms		3404	1,942.91
Jones Plumbers		3405	133.78
Ross Stationers		3406	122.93
Ellis & Edwards	24/5/X6	3407	422.10
Thyme & Sage Products	29/5/X6	3408	9,397.47
The Garlic Grower		3409	5,169.63
Finch's Hardware		3410	2,840.05
Harpers Printers		3411	302.51

Other payments

Salaries totalling £37,601.88 were paid by BACS on 25 May 19X6.

Quarterly rent payments are made by standing order. Rent of £3,273.72 was due on 25 May 19X6.

During May 19X6 the following payments were made by direct debit:

English Telecomm	£189.32 (including VAT @ 17.5%)
English Electricity	£273.45 (including VAT @ 17.5%)

Bank reconciliation at 30 April 19X6

		£
Balance per bank statement		34,232.15
Less:	Unpresented cheques (see attached list)	(52,094.65)
Add:	Deposits in transit (see attached list)	60,227.17
Balance per cash book		42,364.67
Balance per cash book brought forward		5,953.19
Receipts		118,457.84
Payments		(82,046.36)
Balance per cash book carried forward		42,364.67

Unpresented cheques:	
3377	10,172.89
3378	5,283.49
3379	6,352.25
3380	4,337.66
3381	5,937.04
3382	7,228.38
3383	3,844.22
3384	8,938.72
	52,094.65

Deposits in transit:	
606	20,337.95
607	1,716.61
608	38,172.61
	60,227.17

Summary of bank statement at 31 May 19X6

	Withdrawals	*Deposits*	*Balance*
	£	£	£
Balance at 1/5/X6			34,232.15
Counter credit 606		20,337.95	
3378	5,283.49		
3382	7,228.38		42,058.23
Counter credit 607		1,716.61	
3377	10,172.89		
3384	8,938.72		24,663.23
Counter credit 608		38,172.61	
3386	828.95		
3391	2,721.56		
3396	11,947.17		47,338.16
Counter credit 609		27,724.65	
3403	8,667.39		
3387	17,383.25		
3389	1,167.22		
3393	1,858.16		
3399	3,416.64		42,570.15
Counter credit 610		7,746.09	
3400	173.30		
3405	133.78		
3408	9,397.47		40,611.69
Counter credit 611		8,663.45	
3380	4,337.66		
3385	8,839.33		
3390	883.19		35,214.96
Counter credit 612		17,320.36	
3407	422.10		
3411	302.51		
3379	6,352.25		
3381	5,937.04		39,521.42
Counter credit 613		11,250.04	
3383	3,844.22		
Salaries BACS	37,601.88		
Greythorpe Estate SO	3,273.72		
3397	4,666.25		
3402	4,783.88		
3404	1,942.91		(5,341.40)
Carried forward			(5,341.40)

	Withdrawals	*Deposits*	*Balance*
	£	£	£
Brought forward			(5,341.40)
Counter credit 614		7,662.55	
3410	2,840.05		
English Telecomm DD	189.32		
English Electricity DD	273.45		
Balance at 31/5/X6			(981.67)

Task 1

Write up the cash receipts book.

Task 2

Write up the cash payments book.

Task 3

Total both sides of the cash book.

Task 4

Prepare a bank reconciliation as at 31 May 19X6.

(For solutions, turn to the end of this chapter.)

Task 1

Cash book receipts

Date	*Narrative*	*Paying in slip*	*Total*	*Debtors*	*Other*	*VAT*	*Discount allowed*

Task 2

Cash book payments

Date	*Narrative*	*Cheque No*	*Total*	*Creditors*	*Salaries*	*Other*	*VAT*

Task 3

Cash book payments

Date	*Narrative*	*Cheque No*	*Total*	*Creditors*	*Salaries*	*Other*	*VAT*

Task 4

BANK RECONCILIATION

Date

Prepared by

	£
Balance per bank statement	
Less: Unpresented cheques (see attached list)	
Plus: Deposits in transit (see attached list)	
Other items (please describe)	
Balance per cash book	
Balance per cash book brought forward	
Receipts	
Payments	
Balance per cash book carried forward	

UNPRESENTED CHEQUES

Date	Number	£

DEPOSITS IN TRANSIT

Date	Paying-in-slip No.	£

Questions

1 (AAT CA D92)

A cheque for £172 from a customer had been banked two weeks ago, but had been returned by the bank to Hairdressing Supplies Limited marked 'R/D' (refer to drawer).

(a) What does 'Refer to drawer' usually signify?

(b) What entries will be made in the general ledger accounts of Hairdressing Supplies Limited in respect of this returned cheque?

2 (AAT CA D92)

The cheque received from Euro Hair Style Limited was net of cash discount. If the cash discount had not been entered in the cash book, would this have resulted in an imbalance between the totals of the closing debit and credit balances in your general ledger?

3 (AAT CA J92)

The following bank statement is received from the company's bankers, National Bank plc.

National Bank plc

Allsports Limited – Statement of account

Account No. 80439561 Statement date: 15 June 19X2

Date	*Details*	*Debits*	*Credits*	*Balance*
5 June	Balance forward			10,822 o/d
8 June	606218	23		
8 June	Sundry credit		46	10,799 o/d
9 June	606219	387		
9 June	Direct debit	86		
9 June	Standing order	131		11,403 o/d
10 June	Bank giro credit		249	
10 June	606221	1,181		
10 June	606224	346		12,681 o/d
15 June	Dividend		81	12,600 o/d
16 June	Bank charges	286		12,886 o/d

How will cheque number 606221 appear in Allsports Limited's cash book? As a debit entry or as a credit entry?

4 (AAT CA D93)

Would bank charges of £67 shown in the cash book appear on the bank statement as a debit entry or a credit entry?

5 (AAT CA D94)

Would bank interest received of £411 shown in the cash book appear on the bank statement as a debit entry or a credit entry?

6 (AAT CA J94)

Once presented to the bank, would a cheque issued to Lombard Products Limited appear as a debit entry or a credit entry in the company's account at the Royal Bank Limited?

7 (AAT CA J94)

Would a direct debit paid by the Royal Bank Limited out of the company's account appear in the company's cash book as a debit entry or a credit entry?

8 and 9

Please read the following which relates to questions 8 and 9.

The following bank statement was received from a company's bankers on 2 June 19X3

Midwest Bank plc

Future Electrical Limited – Statement of account

Account No. 60413658 Statement date: 1 June 19X3

Date	*Details*	*Debit*	*Credit*	*Balance*
1 June	Balance forward			1,791
1 June	Dividend		104	1,895
1 June	Counter credit		7,084	8,979
1 June	GR insurance DD	89		8,890
1 June	000415	300		8,590

The following transactions took place on 1 June 19X3

Cash book

				£
Opening balance at start of day				1,491 (debit)
Receipts		*Discount*	*Net receipt*	
		£	£	
Electromart		84	4,126	
Denman Stores		60	2,958	
				7,084
				8,575
Payments	*Cheque No.*	*Discount*	*Net payment*	
		£	£	
Hammond & Co	000416	75	3,683	
				3,683
Closing balance at end of day				4,892 (debit)

8 (AAT CA J93)

In updating the cash book balance of £4,892:

(a) Which item or items should now be debited to the cash book?

£104 / £7,084 / £89 / £300

(b) Which item or items should now be credited to the cash book?

£104 / £7,084 / £89 / £300

9 (AAT CA J93)

In preparing a bank reconciliation statement:

(a) Which item, if any, should be added to the updated cash book balance or, alternatively, should be deducted from the bank statement balance?

None / £7,084 / £3,683 / £3,758

(b) Which item, if any, should be deducted from the updated cash book balance or, alternatively, should be added to the bank statement balance?

None / £7,084 / £3,683 / £3,758

10 (AAT CA J94)

The following transactions all occurred on 1 June 19X4 and have yet to be entered into the ledger system. The bank statement was received on 2 June but again contains transactions relating to 1 June.

Cheques issued

	£
Lombard Products Limited (in full repayment of a debt for £2,958)	2,817
Cash purchases (inclusive of VAT of £203)	1,363

Cheques received

	£
Motormania (in full repayment of a debt for £1,550)	1,472

Bank statement received

Royal Bank Limited

MEL Motor Factors Limited

Statement of account – Account No. 40319442

Date	*Details*	*Debit*	*Credit*	*Balance*
		£	£	£
1 June	Balance forward			4,120
1 June	Bank interest		122	4,242
1 June	Bank charges	210		4,032

The following balance is available to you at the start of the day on 1 June 19X4

Bank (debit balance) £4,120

What would have been the balance of the company's account at the Royal Bank Limited if all the items shown in the cash book at the end of the day on 1 June had also passed through the account at the bank on the same date?

11 (AAT CA D94)

The closing balance on a company's cash book was £184 (credit) at 2 December 19X4.

If, at the end of the day on 2 December 19X4, all the entries in the cash book match the entries which have passed through the bank statement apart from:

(a) unpresented cheques for £30,291; or

(b) receipts not yet banked for £26,435,

what would be the balance shown on the bank statement as at 2 December 19X4?

12 (AAT CA D94)

The following letter has been received.

Star Line Insurance Limited

23 Vicarage Road, Watford HE9 0BU (Tel: 01923 76824)

Mr Rahul Divan
Company Accountant
Chang Fashions Limited
142 Regent Court
London WE4 1NN

30 November 19X4

Dear Mr Divan

Motor policy no. ST9992342 on vehicle E156 ESY

I wrote to you on 10 November concerning the renewal of the above policy and requesting a cheque for £526.

Since I have not received a reply, the policy has now been cancelled and the vehicle is therefore no longer covered with this company.

Yours sincerely

R Massey

Robert Massey
Policies Manager

On checking, the following is found:

(a) A cheque for £526 payable to Star Line Insurance Limited was issued on 17 November.

(b) The cheque referred to in (a) above was debited to Chang Fashion Limited's bank account on 24 November.

Draft an appropriate letter to Robert Massey pointing out the facts concerning the cheque and requesting confirmation that the vehicle is covered under the Star Line policy. The letter is to be signed by Rahul Divan, the accountant and company secretary.

13 (AAT CA J94)

MEL Motor Factors Limited is about to purchase a new delivery van costing £7,821.

(a) Would it normally be appropriate to make a purchase of this sort out of the petty cash?

(b) Explain briefly the reason for your answer.

14 (AAT CA J92)

Give two ways in which the company might attempt to maintain security over the petty cash.

15

Why does the chief accountant normally insist that the amount paid is shown in both words and numbers on the petty cash voucher?

16 (AAT CA D92)

Name four items of data appearing on a petty cash voucher other than the 'Amount payable'.

17 (AAT CA J92)

Allsports Limited maintains an imprest amount for the petty cash of £250. During the current period, the sum of £180 is paid out. At the end of the period, what amount should be drawn out of the bank?

18 (AAT CA J93)

In a petty cash system, what in money terms is the relationship between the imprest amount, the cash in hand and the value of the vouchers held by the petty cashier?

19 (AAT CA D94)

The company operates its petty cash using the imprest system. The imprest amount is £250. At the end of a particular period, the five analysis columns were totalled to give the following amounts.

Column 1	£26.19
Column 2	£45.27
Column 3	£6.94
Column 4	£12.81
Column 5	£14.38

How much cash would be required to restore the amount for the following period?

20 (AAT CA D92)

> **HAIRDRESSING SUPPLIES Limited**
>
> **MEMORANDUM**
>
> To: Chris — Date: 29 March 1992
>
> From: Phyllis Cranborne
>
> Subject:
>
> Marjorie Thistlethwaite mentioned to me yesterday that she wanted me to take responsibility for petty cash commencing on 1 June.
>
> Could you please let me have a brief summary of how the petty cash imprest system works?
>
> Thanks.
>
> Phyllis

Draft a suitable reply.

Solutions to Bookkeeping exercise

Cash book receipts

Date	*Narrative*	*Paying-in slip*	*Total*	*Debtors*	*Other*	*VAT*	*Discount allowed*
1/5/X6	Cheques	609	27,724.65	27,724.65			415.86
3/5/X6	Cheques	610	7,746.09	7,746.09			116.19
8/5/X6	Cheques	611	8,663.45	8,663.45			129.95
12/5/X6	Cheques	612	17,320.36	17,320.36			258.21
19/5/X6	Cheques	613	11,250.04	11,250.04			167.94
25/5/X6	Cheques	614	7,662.55	7,662.55			114.94
29/5/X6	Cheques	615	2,504.61	2,504.61			37.57
30/5/X6	Cheques	616	112.58	112.58			
31/5/X6	Cheques	617	5,816.33	5,816.33			84.27
			88,800.66	88,800.66			1,324.93

Cash book payments

Date	*Narrative*	*Cheque No.*	*Total*	*Creditors*	*Salaries*	*Other*	*VAT*
1/5/X6	Imperial Oils	3385	8,839.33	8,839.33			
2/5/X6	Curtis Herb Farms	3386	828.95	828.95			
	Brandon Glassworks Limited	3387	17,383.25	17,383.25			
	Paper Bag Company Limited	3388	7,182.50	7,182.50			
8/5/X6	Drewstead Supplies	3389	1,167.22	1,167.22			
	Coopers Laboratories	3390	883.19	883.19			
9/5/X6	Phillips & Sons	3391	2,721.56	2,721.56			
	The Plantcare Company	3392	386.78	386.78			
	Sullivan Limited	3393	1,858.16	1,858.16			
	The Natural Oil Company	3394	6,337.49	6,337.49			
15/5/X6	Provencal Herbalists	3395	271.96	271.96			
	Thyme and Sage Products	3396	11,947.17	11,947.17			
16/5/X6	Houndsbane & Hellebore	3397	4,666.25	4,666.25			
	Provencal Herbalists	3398	56.16	56.16			
17/5/X6	Drewstead Supplies	3399	3,416.64	3,416.64			
	Finch's Hardware	3400	173.30	173.30			
	Winter & White Limited	3401	5,002.21	5,002.21			
22/5/X6	Grants Gardens	3402	4,783.88	4,783.88			
	Imperial Oils	3403	8,667.39	8,667.39			
	Curtis Herb Farms	3404	1,942.91	1,942.91			
	Jones Plumbers	3405	133.78	133.78			
	c/f		88,650.08	88,650.08			

Date	*Narrative*	*Cheque No.*	*Total*	*Creditors*	*Salaries*	*Other*	*VAT*
	b/f		88,650.08	88,650.08			
24/5/X6	Ross Stationers	3406	122.93	122.93			
25/5/X6	Ellis & Edwards	3407	422.10	422.10			
	Salaries	BACS	37,601.88		37,601.88		
29/5/X6	Rent	SO	3,273.72			3,273.72	
	Thyme & Sage Products	3408	9,397.47	9,397.47			
	The Garlic Grower	3409	5,169.63	5,169.63			
	Finch's Hardware	3410	2,840.05	2,840.05			
	Harpers Printers	3411	302.51	302.51			
	English Telecomm	DD	189.32			161.12	28.20
	English Electricity	DD	273.45			232.72	40.73
			148,243.14	106,904.77	37,601.88	3,667.56	68.93

BANK RECONCILIATION

Date 3/6/X6

Prepared by A N Accountant

		£
Balance per bank statement		(981.67)
Less:	Unpresented cheques (see attached list)	(24,529.66)
Plus:	Deposits-in-transit (see attached list)	8,433.52
Other items	(please describe)	
Balance per cash book		(17,077.81)
Balance per cash book brought forward		42,364.67
Receipts		88,800.66
Payments		(148,243.14)
Balance per cash book carried forward		(17,077.81)

UNPRESENTED CHEQUES

Date	Number	£
2/5/X6	3388	7,182.50
9/5/X6	3392	386.78
9/5/X6	3394	6,337.49
15/5/X6	3395	271.96
16/5/X6	3398	56.16
17/5/X6	3401	5,002.21
22/5/X6	3406	122.93
29/5/X6	3409	5,169.63
		24,529.66

DEPOSITS IN TRANSIT

Date	Paying-in slip no	£
29/5/X6	615	2,504.61
30/5/X6	616	112.58
31/5/X6	617	5,816.33
		8,433.52

Summary

Cash book

- Records receipts and payments into and out of business' bank account
- Keep a separate cash book for each bank account
- Analyse receipts and payments by type

VAT

- Cash sales must have VAT analysed as this is the first time the sale has been recorded
- Cash from debtors does not need to have VAT analysed. (VAT on sale has already been accounted for when sale first recorded.)

Cash discounts

- Actual amount received or paid recorded in total and analysis columns
- Discount recorded in separate column as a reminder to record these discounts

Link with other accounting records

- Cash book is a major source of accounting information

Bank reconciliation

- A method of ensuring that the cash book has been written up correctly
- The bank statements are compared with the cash book

Petty cash

- Used to make small cash payments
- Cash is received from cashing cheques from business' bank account, cash sales or staff sales

Authorisation

- All payments are recorded on numbered vouchers as well as in petty cash book
- Receipts are attached to vouchers as proof
- Vouchers are authorised before money is paid out

VAT

- VAT on payments must be analysed separately if business can reclaim the VAT paid
- VAT must be analysed because these are not payments to credit suppliers therefore the purchases have not been recorded before

Imprest system

- Reduces risk of theft or fraud
- Based on realistic requirements, petty cashier is given the same amount of cash each week
- Each time cash is paid out, a voucher is completed
- At any time during the week, the cash held and the vouchers equal the original amount of cash
- At the end of the week, petty cashier is reimbursed for value of vouchers

CHAPTER 6

Legal Relationship of Buyer and Seller

Objectives

The purpose of this chapter is to provide you with a basic understanding of the principles of contract law.

Nature of a contract

When a business agrees to buy goods or services from a supplier or to sell goods to a customer, then the business is entering into a **contract**.

A contract is a legally binding agreement. The law of contract is the branch of the civil law which determines whether or not a particular agreement is **legally binding**, that is, enforceable by a court of law.

The essential characteristics of a contract

There are seven fundamental requirements if a contract is to be valid:

- **offer and acceptance**, that is, an agreement;
- the intention to **create legal relations**, that is, the parties must be willing to accept the authority of the law, and to be bound by their contracts;
- **consideration**, in that both parties must do, or promise to do, something as their side of the contract;
- written formalities must be observed in some situations;
- the parties must have the capacity, or ability, to contract and accept the authority of the law;
- the parties must genuinely consent to the terms of the contract; and
- the contract itself must be both legal and possible.

If one or more of these fundamental characteristics is absent, the contract may be described as **void, voidable or unenforceable.**

A **void** contract is one under which:

- no rights may be enforced by either party; but
- the parties return any money or goods handed over.

A **voidable** contract is one where:

- one of the parties may affirm or reject (avoid) the contract at his option;
- a party may wish to avoid the contract if, for example, one party lied to the other to get him to enter the contract;
- the contract is valid until the point when it is avoided; and
- anything which happens before it is avoided is deemed to happen while the contract is still valid (so the subsequent action is valid in its own right).

Example

Voidable

Original contract

A ◄────► B

avoids contract with B on 29 January | sells goods on 10 January

↓

C

Result: C keeps goods (at the time he bought from B there was no doubt as to B's ability to sell)

Compare with

Void

Original contract

A ◄────► B

declares contract with B void on 20 January | sells goods on 10 January

↓

C

Result: A recovers goods from C (contract is void and therefore third party gets no right to goods)

Rule: when a contract is voidable, if a sale to a third party takes place before the contract is avoided, the third party may keep the goods; when a contract is void, the original owner will recover them.

An **unenforceable** contract is one which is valid, but owing to the lack of some required formality or sufficient legal evidence:

- it cannot be sued upon;
- it will not be enforced by the court.

For example, a hire purchase contract which is not in writing is unenforceable.

The offer

Agreement

The first essential of a contract is that there must be an agreement between the parties.

Agreement is usually expressed in the terms of offer and acceptance. It must be shown that an offer was made by one party (the offeror) and accepted by the other party (the offeree) and that legal relations were intended. Therefore:

OFFER + ACCEPTANCE = AGREEMENT

The offer

An offer is an expression of willingness to contract on certain terms, made with the intention that it shall become binding as soon as it is accepted by the person to whom it is addressed.

An offer may be made to a specific person, to a group of people, or to the world at large.

Example of offer to world at large:

- collecting coupons to exchange for gifts.

Examples of conditions:

- collecting coupons;
- while stocks last.

The offer may be conditional, but the offer must be certain. It may be express or implied.

Implied offer: boarding a bus is an implied offer to buy a ticket.

It must be communicated to the offeree: a person who returns property without knowing that a reward has been offered would not be entitled to the reward.

Invitation to treat

An offer must be distinguished from an invitation to another party to make an offer himself (referred to as an invitation to treat).

In the case of an offer, the agreement is complete when the offeree agrees unconditionally to the terms of the offer. However, with an invitation to treat it is the person to whom the invitation is directed who may make the offer, which the party issuing the invitation (now the offeree) is free to accept if he wishes to do so.

No agreement (and hence no contract) arises until acceptance is made by the party originating the invitation.

Examples of invitations to treat include:

- notices in shop windows;
- prospectuses for the issue of company shares;
- mail order 'bargain offers'; and
- the display of goods in supermarkets.

Lapse of the offer

Once an offer lapses, it cannot be accepted.

An offer may lapse in two main situations.

- On the death of the offeror or the offeree before acceptance.
- If it is not accepted within:
  - the time stipulated in the offer for acceptance; or
  - a reasonable time (determined on the facts in each case) if no time for acceptance has been prescribed.

Revocation of offer

An offer may be revoked (or withdrawn) by the offeror at any time before it has been accepted.

Notice of the revocation must reach the offeree before he has accepted, or the revocation is ineffective. This has caused problems when offer, acceptance and revocation are sent by post.

Example

1 October	–	VT posted a letter in Cardiff to B in New York, offering to sell B tinplate.
8 October	–	VT wrote to B revoking the offer.
11 October	–	B received VT's offer and at once telegraphed acceptance.
15 October	–	B confirmed acceptance by letter.
20 October	–	B received letter of revocation (dated 8 October) from VT.

By this time, VT had entered another contract to sell the tinplate elsewhere.

Held: Revocation of an offer is not effective unless notice reaches the offeree before he has accepted the offer.

Mere posting (or other means of notifying) to the offeree is not enough; revocation must actually be communicated to (ie reach the attention of) the offeree before he accepts.

VT is therefore liable for breach of contract with B.

If the offeror says the offer is to be left open for a certain time, the offer can be revoked before the expiry of that time unless:

- the offeree has already accepted it; or
- the offeree provided consideration for the offeror's promise to keep the offer open.

Rejection of offer

The offeree may notify the offeror that he does not wish to accept the offer. This may be express or implied.

If the offeree makes a counter-offer, then this destroys the first offer.

- Express rejection (eg 'No, I do not accept your offer')
- Implied rejection (eg the making of a counter-offer or proposal of different terms)

However, a mere inquiry by the offeree for further information is not in itself a rejection of the offer.

The acceptance

Acceptance is a final expression of assent to the terms of an offer. Offer and acceptance constitute agreement.

In order to be effective, the acceptance must be:

- made while the offer is still in force, ie before it has been revoked or before it has lapsed;
- absolute and unqualified: if the terms of the offer are altered, then there has been a counter-offer;
- communicated to the offeror in cases where notification of acceptance is specifically or tacitly required.

Generally, silence does not constitute acceptance.

Illustration

F wrote to his nephew, offering to buy the latter's horse, and said 'If I hear no more, I shall consider the horse to be mine for £30'. Bindley, an auctioneer, who was selling a number of the nephew's horses, was instructed not to sell that particular one but inadvertently did so. He was then sued by F. It was held that F had no claim against either B or the nephew as the original offer to buy had not been accepted. It is impossible to interpret silence as consent in such a situation.

Acceptance must also be made in whatever form (if any) has been prescribed by the offeror.

Acceptance by post

Where the person making the offer indicates that acceptance is to be made through the post, acceptance is effective as soon as the letter is posted, even if it never reaches the offeror.

Acceptance by telephone, telex or fax

Where a means other than the post is used for acceptance, the general rule is that the contract is made when and where the acceptance is received by the offeror. For example, if an offeree in Manchester sends a fax of his acceptance to the offeror in London, the contract is made when the fax is received in London.

Intention to create legal relations

Introduction

Even if an accepted offer creates an agreement, it does not automatically make the agreement a contract. If one of the parties wishes the help of the law in enforcing the terms of the agreement against the other party, he must show, amongst other things, that there had been an intention by both parties that the agreement was to create legal relations.

Social or domestic agreements

There is a presumption in social or domestic agreements that legal relations are not intended.

Agreements between spouses living together are usually assumed to be of a domestic nature only.

Commercial agreements

In commercial agreements there is a presumption that legal relations are intended, although this can be changed by an 'honourable pledge' clause which expressly states that the agreement is not to be legally binding: if this is the case, the agreement will not be legally enforceable.

Formality

The requirement of formality

The general rule of English law is that contracts can be made quite informally, even verbally in numerous situations, and the form in which a contract is made does not matter and will have no effect upon the validity of the contract.

There are, however, certain exceptions, especially:

- contracts which must be made by deed;
- contracts which must be in writing; and
- contracts which must be evidenced in writing.

Where the required formality is not observed, the contract is generally unenforceable or void.

Contracts made by deed

A contract under deed is a written document which is signed and often sealed. Such contracts are described as 'specialty contracts', all others being simple contracts.

The types of contract which must be made by deed are as follows.

- Contracts where one of the parties provides no consideration (for example a contract to establish a covenant to a charity for a number of years whereby the charity claims the amount paid plus the related income tax). Such contracts are often referred to as 'deeds of gift'.
- Contracts for the transfer of a British registered ship or aeroplane.
- Documentation for the legal conveyance of land or leases of land (for more than three years); therefore for house purchases or sales, the completion documents must be made by deed.

Contracts which must be in writing

The following simple contracts are required to be wholly in writing otherwise they are invalid and of no legal effect.

- Contracts for the future sale of interests in land:
  - such contracts must be signed; and
  - all terms which the parties have expressly agreed must be included in the document (or be identifiable by reference to some other document).
- Contracts of marine insurance.
- Regulated agreements under the Consumer Credit Act 1974, for example hire purchase contracts.
- Transfers of company shares.
- Bills of exchange, whereby one party (A) instructs another party (B) to pay money to a third party (C) to settle a debt due from A to C (eg cheques).

Contracts which must be evidenced in writing

Some contracts need not necessarily be in writing (although they often are) but in order for a court to recognise and, if necessary, enforce such contracts, there must be some kind of written evidence of their existence.

Such evidence could be something as basic as a letter acknowledging the existence of the contract, although the evidence must contain a number of components.

The two main types of such contracts are as follows.

- Contracts of guarantee, whereby one party (A) accepts liability to pay the debt of another party (B) to a third party (C), **should B not pay**.
- Money-lending agreements.

Capacity

Minors (persons under 18) cannot enter into any contract that they wish. They may enter into the following:

- contracts for 'necessaries' (eg clothes, hire of a car, a haircut);
- contracts which benefit the minor (eg contracts for training, education and apprenticeship).

Certain contracts are **voidable** when entered into by a minor:

- contracts for a lease;
- contracts for the acquisition of shares; and
- contracts of partnership.

These contracts bind the minor unless and until he takes active steps to avoid them either during his minority or within a reasonable time thereafter.

Any contract entered into by a minor other than the above is **unenforceable** by the third party against the minor, but is enforceable by the minor against the third party.

Contracts entered into by persons suffering from mental disorder are voidable by them if the other party to the contract was aware of their disability at the time the contract was executed.

Mistake and misrepresentation

If a contract is to be valid, the parties to the contract must have genuinely consented to its terms. The genuineness of the consent will be affected if mistake or misrepresentation has occurred.

Mistake

There are three possible types of mistake.

- **Common mistake** – each party makes the same mistake.
- **Mutual mistake** – both parties make a mistake but a different mistake; they are at cross-purposes.
- **Unilateral mistake** – only one of the parties is mistaken and the other knows, or must be taken to know, of his mistake.

Common mistake

A common mistake has no effect whatsoever unless it is such as to eliminate the very subject matter of the agreement; for example, one of the parties to a contract contracts to buy something which no longer exists or which already belongs to the purchaser.

In these cases the contract will be *void*.

Mutual mistake

Mutual (non-identical bilateral) mistake occurs where one party refers to a particular item, while the other party thinks that another item is being considered. Effectively, the parties are talking at cross purposes. In this case, there is no consensus from the start (unlike cases of common mistake in which the parties at least have the same item in mind). It applies even where a third party was responsible for the mistake.

A feature of cases involving mutual mistake is that, wherever possible, the courts will try to find 'the sense of the promise' and may, on occasion, enforce the contract on the terms understood by one of the parties.

However, if this 'sense of promise' cannot be detected, the contract will be void on the grounds of uncertainty.

Unilateral mistake

Unilateral mistake arises where one party is mistaken as to some material fact concerning the contract and *the other party knows, or ought to know* (given the situation), that the mistake exists.

Knowledge by the other party of the mistake's existence is essential, otherwise the first party is liable under the contract.

Misrepresentation

A representation is a statement made by one party to the other before or at the time of contracting with regard to some existing fact or to some past event which is one of the causes that induce the contract.

A misrepresentation, therefore, is a false statement of fact made by one party to induce the other to enter the contract.

Because it must fulfil the definition above, misrepresentation excludes a number of matters.

- As it must be a statement of *fact*, it cannot be a statement of future conduct or intent.
- A false statement of opinion cannot constitute a misrepresentation, unless it can be shown that the person making the statement had no such opinions.
- Since a statement must be involved, silence cannot generally be deemed to be misrepresentation.
- Trade puffs do not amount to representation (eg phrases such as 'whiter than white').

If misrepresentation is proved, the remedies are:

- rescission of the contract – the contract is set aside as if it had never been made and property and monies are restored to the original owner;
- refusal by the injured party to perform his part of the contract; or
- an action in damages by the injured party for any loss suffered by him.

Criminal penalties

In addition to the civil law remedies referred to above, the *Trade Descriptions Act 1968* prescribes certain criminal penalties for which a person may become liable if he falsely or misleadingly describes goods which he is selling.

Questions

1 (AAT CA J94)

John Burns, one of MEL Motor Factors Limited's sales staff, recently sent a quotation to Sally Dawson at Autosports Limited offering to sell 100 Hirama car radios at £70 each plus VAT. In reply, Sally writes to say that Autosports would like to accept the offer provided that the radios can be delivered by the end of June.

(a) At this stage, does a contract exist between the two companies? Yes/no.

(b) Briefly explain the reason for your answer.

2 (AAT CA D92)

Due to a printer's error, one of the items in Hairdressing Supplies' equipment catalogue was under-priced. Subsequently a letter was received from a customer ordering one of these items.

(a) Are Hairdressing Supplies obliged to supply the goods at this price? Yes/no.

(b) Explain briefly why.

3 (AAT CA D93)

Music World Limited has received an enquiry from ABC Music to purchase 100 assorted CDs. A quotation is sent out offering to supply these at £7 per disc. Two days later Tony Bryant realises that a mistake has been made. He immediately writes to ABC Music informing it that unfortunately the quoted price was incorrect and that the discs cannot therefore be supplied as offered. The following day Anne Todd from ABC Music telephones to say that although she has received Tony's letter she now wants to accept the original offer and she insists that the discs should be supplied at £7 each.

(a) Does a valid contract exist between Music World Limited and ABC Music? Yes/no.

(b) Explain briefly the reason for your answer.

4 (AAT CA J93)

Chris Payne has been given £50 and wants to buy himself a Walkman. He is told that Future Electrical Limited is out of stock of the model he wants but it can supply one within 48 hours for £49.50. Chris agrees and signs an order form.

(a) Does a valid contract appear to exist between Chris and Future Electrical Limited? Yes/no.

(b) Explain briefly the reason for your answer.

(c) Could Future Electrical Limited insist that Chris makes the purchase under the agreed terms if the £50 given to him had been for a recent 17th birthday present? Yes/no.

(d) Explain briefly the reason for your answer.

5 (AAT CA J94)

MEL Motor Factors Limited has placed an advertisement in a motoring magazine for a new line of car fire extinguishers. The price stated in the advert is £19 for each extinguisher but an error has been made by the printer, in that the price should have been £79. One of the sales staff receives a telephone call from Peter Burridge of Autospares who wants to place an order for 100 extinguishers. He insists that these should be supplied at £19 each since that was the offer in the advert.

(a) Does MEL Motor Factors Limited have to supply the extinguishers at £19 each? Yes/no

(b) Explain briefly the reason for your answer.

Summary

Nature of contract

- Legally binding
- Based on agreement of parties
- Can be enforced by courts
- Part of civil law

Essential characteristics

- Agreement (offer and acceptance)
- Intention to create legal relations
- Consideration
- Written formalities (certain contracts only)
- Capacity
- Genuine consent
- Legality and possibility

Void contract

- No rights for either party
- Parties return any goods or money handed over

Voidable contract

- One of the parties may reject the contract if he wishes
- One party may wish to avoid the contract in certain circumstances
- Valid until avoided
- Anything which happens before the contract is avoided is valid

Unenforceable

- Valid in theory
- Cannot be sued upon or enforced by the court
- Formality or evidence missing

Offer

- Expression of willingness to contract on certain terms
- Intention that it will become binding if accepted by the other party
- Made to a specific person or the world at large
- May be conditional, but must be certain
- May be express or implied
- Must be communicated to the other party

Invitation to treat

- Invitation to another party to make an offer

Acceptance

- Offer must still be in force
- Must be absolute and unqualified
- Must be communicated to the offeror where notification is specifically or tacitly required

Intention to create legal relations

- Both parties must intend to create legal relations
- Social or domestic arrangements – presumption that legal relations are not intended
- Commercial agreements (presumption that legal relations are intended)

Formality

- General rule – contracts can be informal (sometimes even verbal)
- Exceptions – contracts which must be made by deed, in writing, evidenced in writing
- Deed: written document – signed and often sealed
- In writing: wholly in writing
- Evidenced in writing (eg referred to in a letter)

Capacity

- Contracts enforceable against minors:
- for necessaries
- for their benefit

Genuine consent

- Affected by mistake or misrepresentation

CHAPTER 7

Trading on Credit Terms

Objectives

This chapter covers the following performance criteria.

When recording and accounting for credit transactions

- Invoices and credit notes are correctly authorised and coded and despatched to customers.
- The calculations on invoices and credit notes, including discounts and VAT, are correct.
- Invoices and credit notes are correctly entered as primary accounting records in a form acceptable to the organisation.

Credit control

Many businesses buy and sell goods or services on credit, rather than for cash. This allows them to delay payment to their suppliers until they have been paid by their customers. When a business agrees to supply another business or individual with goods or services, the two parties are entering into a contract. The contract can be **written** or **oral**, but it becomes legally binding when the two parties agree. The exact moment of agreement will depend upon the nature of the contract itself. Because of the legal nature of the agreement, the business must carefully decide whether or not it wishes to supply a particular customer.

New customers

New customers would probably be expected to supply **trade references** (ie they give the names of other businesses they have dealt with who vouch for the customer's creditworthiness). The business may also check the new customer's creditworthiness through an agency, such as Dun and Bradstreet, or by asking for references from the customer's bank. The business should not enter into the contract until it is satisfied that the new customer is creditworthy. A **credit limit** should then be set for that customer.

Credit limit – The maximum unpaid amount which a customer may have outstanding at any time.

Established customers

Before the business accepts an individual order from an existing customer it must ensure that:

- the new order will not exceed the credit limit; and
- the customer does not appear to have any problems in paying amounts already outstanding.

Credit limits should be reviewed regularly and adjusted if necessary.

Occasionally a customer may be considered to be too risky to supply more goods or services to. In this case, the customer is put on a **stop list**. This means that no more goods or services are to be supplied until existing debts have been paid.

Purchase orders from all customers must be carefully reviewed to ensure that:

- prices quoted;
- delivery terms;
- payment terms; and
- discount claimed

are approved by the business.

Confirming sales orders

To avoid misunderstandings, a supplier will normally confirm a customer's order by completing a **sales order**, even if the customer has already sent a written **purchase order**.

Sales order – Document confirming:

- quantity/type of good or service
- date of supply
- location of supply
- price and terms

The sales order might be a four-part document.

Part one	–	sent to customer to confirm order
Part two	–	kept by sales order department
Part three	–	sent to purchasing department to prompt ordering/manufacture of goods
Part four	–	sent to despatch department to authorise despatch of goods

Sales orders must be authorised by someone outside the sales order function (eg credit control) before goods or services can be provided.

City Wood Suppliers
192 Old Kent Road, London SE9

Tel: 0171 248 7009 – Fax: 0171 248 7890

To:	**Delivery:**	**Delivery date:**
Alpha Limited Mountjoy St London W12	26 New Road Milton Keynes MK25 2BA	10 November 19X3

Date: 25 September 19X3

We confirm the following order to be delivered as above.
Please note our credit terms are strictly 30 days net.

Code	*Quantity*	*Description*	*Unit Price (exc VAT)*	*Discount*
CB0351	10	Chipboard sheeting 6′ × 4′	£23.00	NIL

Authorised: Date:

Invoicing the customer

Supplying goods

When a business supplies goods to a customer, the despatch department raises a **delivery note**.

Delivery note – Document accompanying goods despatched to a customer.

The delivery note would normally have four parts.

Part one – kept by customer after receiving goods

Part two – kept by despatch department

Part three – sent to stores department to update records

Part four – sent to sales invoicing department to invoice customer

Delivery notes should have **preprinted sequential** numbers and should be used in order. Spoiled delivery notes should be cancelled and kept. The delivery note should be signed by the customer to acknowledge receipt of the goods. A delivery note may also be called a **despatch note**.

Supplying services

When a business supplies a service to a customer, a record must be kept of the work done. This could be a three-part **advice note.**

Part one	–	given to customer to inform him of hours worked, part used, etc
Part two	–	kept by service department to record payroll details, etc
Part three	–	sent to sales invoicing department to invoice customer

Preparing sales invoices

Invoice – Document showing quantity of goods, services supplied and amount payable by customer.

Sales invoices must be prepared from the details shown on delivery notes or advice notes. Delivery notes do not normally show details of prices, discounts or VAT. (This is because the customer might mistake the delivery note for a sales invoice.)

Sales invoices should have **preprinted sequential numbers** and should be used in order. Spoiled sales invoices should be cancelled and kept.

Controls over invoicing

Checks should be made to ensure that:

- all deliveries have been invoiced (ie each delivery note has a related sales invoice);
- only genuine deliveries have been invoiced (ie each sales invoice relates to a particular delivery note); and
- invoicing has been carried out accurately (ie quantities/types of goods/services have been transferred correctly from the delivery note to the invoice).

This might be achieved in different ways by different businesses.

Examples

- In a fabric wholesaling business (which sells only complete rolls of fabric):
  - the despatch department calculates the number of rolls of fabric by type despatched that week (from its copy of the delivery notes);
  - the sales invoicing department calculates the number of rolls of fabric by type invoiced that week (from its copies of sales invoices);
  - the two totals are compared and any discrepancies are investigated (eg different overall total/misclassification between types) and corrected.

  (This is an example of using **control totals.**)

- In a fancy goods wholesaling business:
  - all sales invoices issued during the week are checked to delivery notes individually by the sales invoicing supervisor.

  (This is an example of **one-for-one checking**.)

Sales invoices might have three parts.

Part one	–	sent to customer to ask for payment
Part two	–	kept by sales invoicing department
Part three	–	sent to debtors' ledger clerk to record in sales records

Pricing goods and services

Unit prices for goods or services are kept in **master files** which must be updated regularly.

Prices will normally be quoted exclusive of value added tax (VAT), as this is the true selling price to the business.

The effect of value added tax

If the business is registered for VAT, VAT must be charged on taxable supplies.

Most goods and services are standard-rated (ie 17.5% rate of VAT must be charged).

The invoice must include certain details by law.

Illustration

INVOICE 68553

A J BROOM & Co Ltd

59 Parkway,
Manchester M2 6EG

Tel: 0161 560 3392 **Fax: 0161 560 5322**

VAT registration no: 625 9911 58
Tax point: 23 August 19X3

Customer order **28596**

Despatch **68553**

J Hardy Construction
Poplar Works
Poplar Street
OLDHAM OL4 6QB

Code	*Supply*	*Description*	*Quantity*	*VAT rate*	*Unit price* £	*Amount exc of VAT* £
950 BB3	Sale	Cotswold	3	17.5%	300.00	900.00
159 504	Sale	Bricks	5	17.5%	195.50	977.50
874 KL5	Sale	Roof Tiles – Red Brick Tiles	1	17.5%	56.65	56.65
Total amount payable excluding VAT						1,934.15
VAT at 17.5%						338.48
Total amount payable						**2,272.63**

A proper VAT invoice must show:

- an identifying number;
- the date of the supply;
- the name, address and registration number of the supplier;
- the name and address of the person to whom the goods or services are supplied;
- the type of supply, eg sale, sale or return;
- for each item or service supplied:
  - a description;
  - quantity supplied;
  - rate of VAT;
  - amount payable, excluding VAT, in sterling;
- total amount payable, excluding VAT, in sterling;
- rate of any cash discount offered;
- amount of VAT charged at each rate, with the rate to which it relates;
- total amount of VAT chargeable.

On a proper VAT invoice, the date is called the **tax point**. This can be either the date of supply of goods or services (the basic tax point); or the date the invoice is made out (actual tax point). The invoice must be made out within 14 days of the supply.

This tax point is very important when accounting for VAT to Customs and Excise.

VAT and discounts

If a bulk or trade discount is offered, this is deducted before VAT is calculated as follows.

Sales invoice no: 148

To: Smith & Issacs
Sloane Street
LONDON
SW3

Creative Clothing

3 The Mall
Wanstead
LONDON
E11 3AY

VAT Reg No 487 3921 12
Tax point 14 February 19X0

Quantity	*Description*	*Amount exclusive of VAT*	*VAT rate*	*VAT net*
		£		£
250	Ear muffs (adults)	2,125.00	17.5%	
Discount	2%	(42.50)		364.44
		2,082.50		
VAT		364.44		
Total		2,446.94		

Terms: 3% 30 days, otherwise net

If a cash or settlement discount is offered, the VAT is calculated on the lowest value which the customer may pay. For example, the VAT-exclusive invoice value is £100. A 3% discount is offered for payment within 30 days, ie £97 would be payable.

VAT is calculated on the £97, ie £16.98. The amount invoiced is £100 plus £16.98 VAT. The customer therefore pays £116.98 (full price) or £113.98 (£97 discounted price plus £16.98 VAT).

The discount recorded in the cash book on receipt of the £113.98 is therefore £3.

The customer cannot discount the VAT again, as the supplier has already discounted the VAT.

Sales invoice no: 149

To: Smith & Issacs
Sloane Street
LONDON
SW3

Creative Clothing

3 The Mall
Wanstead
LONDON
E11 3AY

VAT Reg No 487 3921 12
Tax point 14 February 19X0

Quantity	*Description*	*Amount exclusive of VAT*	*VAT rate*	*VAT net*
		£	17.5%	£
				16.98
2	Fairisle sweaters (adults)	100.00		
Cash discount	£3.00			
Discounted price	£97.00			
		100.00		
VAT		16.98		
Total		116.98		

Terms: 3% 30 days, otherwise net

Other terms found on invoices

You may also find other terms and conditions shown on invoices or other documents. Here are some of the more common:

E & OE – Errors and omissions excepted. The seller is claiming the right to correct any genuine errors on the invoice (eg prices) at a later date.

Carriage paid – The invoice value includes delivery of the goods to the customer's premises.

Ex works – Prices quoted do not include delivery to the customer's premises. The customer must organise and pay for the delivery of the goods.

Cash on delivery – The customer is expected to pay for the goods when they are delivered.

Authorising invoices

Invoices should not be sent out to customers until they have been checked by an independent person.

Invoices must be coded to allow them to be analysed within the accounting records. This coding must be carefully checked.

The coding will cover two aspects:

- allocation to the customer's individual record of the amount payable;
- analysis of sales by type/product.

Segregation of duties

If only one person is responsible for the recording and processing of a complete transaction, the risk of errors is greatly increased. There is also a risk that the records may be fraudulently altered or assets (such as cash or goods) may be misappropriated without this being discovered.

Separation of responsibilities reduces the risk of intentional manipulation or errors. This separation of responsibilities is known as **segregation of duties** and is a very important form of **internal control.**

We have seen several examples of segregation of duties within this chapter, including:

(a) sales orders authorised by someone outside the sales order department (separation of recording and authorisation);

(b) goods despatched by someone other than the person who raised the sales order (separation of recording and physical custody over assets);

(c) invoices raised by someone other than the person who prepared the delivery note;

(d) invoices checked and authorised by someone other than the person who prepared the invoice.

You will come across other examples as you work through the Study Pack.

Questions

1 (AAT CA J92)

List six items of data which you would expect an invoice to contain.

2 (AAT CA J93)

A customer orders 10 Sansui radios priced at £25 each. The customer is given a 20% trade discount and a 10% cash discount for prompt payment. Calculate the VAT charged on the sale.

3 (AAT CA D94)

Explain briefly why Chang Fashions Limited might add 'E & OE' to invoices issued to customers.

4 (AAT CA D93)

Music World Limited has received a quotation for £2,160 ex works. Explain briefly the meaning of the term ex works.

5 (AAT CA J94)

You have received a telephone call from Jim Ellis (the owner of Motormania). Motormania currently receives an 8% trade discount on all purchases. Jim Ellis requests that this should be increased to 10%. You tell him that this will have to be referred to the Managing Director (Andrew Bolton) and that you will respond to his request in writing within 7 days. You are subsequently unable to contact Andrew Bolton and decide therefore to leave a memorandum with his secretary explaining the situation. Motormania's current balance is £25,220 and their annual turnover with your company is £230,910.

Draft your memorandum to Andrew Bolton.

Summary

Need for credit control

- Business enters into legally binding contracts
- Risk of non-payment:
  - new customers:
    - trade references
    - Dun and Bradstreet
    - bank references
    - set credit limit.
- Established customers:
  - review orders against credit limit
  - review payment history
  - review credit limits regularly
  - consider putting on stop list.

Sales order

- Confirms order with customer
- Prompts business to buy/manufacture necessary goods

Delivery note

- Advice note used externally to advise customer of goods delivered and internally to update stock records and initiate invoicing

Sales invoice

- Request for payment from a customer
- Sequentially numbered
- Use in order; keep spoilt copies
- Check periodically that all deliveries and only proper deliveries are invoiced

Bulk or trade discounts

- Discounts offered to certain customers – deducted from selling price when sales invoice is prepared

VAT

- Certain details must be shown on invoice
- Discounts (trade or settlement) are deducted before calculating VAT

Authorisation and coding

- Invoices must be authorised before being sent to customer
- Coding required to allocate:
  - amount payable to individual customer's account.

Despatch department

- Sends goods to customer by company's own transport
- Driver asks customer to sign delivery note
- Driver splits four-part delivery note:

Part one	–	customer
Part two	–	despatch department
Part three	–	stores department
Part four	–	sales invoicing department.

Sales invoicing clerk

- Receives copy of delivery note
- Prepares sales invoice (within 14 days)
- Passes sales invoice (three-part document) and delivery note to sales department supervisor

Sales department supervisor

- Checks invoice;
- Distributes parts as follows:

  Part one – customer

  Part two – sales invoicing clerk (with copy of delivery note)

  Part three – debtors' ledger clerk in accounts department

  – sale to its particular product group within accounting records.

CHAPTER 8

Maintaining the Sales Day Book

Objectives

This chapter covers the following performance criteria.

- Invoices and credit notes are correctly entered as primary accounting records in a form acceptable to the organisation.
- Suppliers' invoices and credit notes are correctly checked against ordering documentation and evidence that goods/services have been received.
- Calculations on suppliers' invoices and credit notes are correct.
- Documents are correctly entered as primary accounting records in a form acceptable to the organisation.
- The analysis and totalling of the primary records are completed accurately.

Recording sales invoices

All sales invoices despatched to customers should immediately be recorded in the sales day book or a similar record. This is effectively a diary of all the credit sales transactions of the business in date order.

Analysing sales invoices

Sales invoices should be coded to show:

- product group/type for analysis of sales;
- customer account number.

The sales day book is then used to analyse invoices to produce information needed by the accounting system.

There are several different systems of coding outlined below.

Sequence codes

Allocate a number, or a letter, to items in a simple list.

For example:

Code	*Name*
01	ADAMS, John
02	AITKEN, James
03	ALCOCK, Fred
04	BROWN, Joe

Block codes

These allocate bands of numbers to particular categories.

For example, consider a tobacco manufacturer who produces several types of cigarettes, cigars and pipe tobaccos. He could assign a code to each particular brand as follows

Product type	*Block code*
Cigarette	01 – 19
Cigar	20 – 29
Pipe tobacco	30 – 39

Significant digit codes

These are a particular type of group classification code where individual digits and letters are used to represent features of the coded item. The example given is one used to describe different kinds of vehicle tyres.

Code	*Item*
TT67015B	Tube Tyre 670 × 15 Blackwall
LT67015W	Tube Less Tyre 670 × 15 Whitewall

Faceted codes

Faceted codes are another type of group classification code by which the digits of the code are divided into facets of several digits and each facet represents some attribute of the item being coded. These codes are similar to significant digit codes but are purely numerical.

Example: faceted code for types of carpet

Facet 1 = type of weave (1 digit)	1	=	cord
	2	=	twist
	3	=	short tufted, etc.
Facet 2 = material (1 digit)	1	=	all wool
	2	=	80% wool, 20% nylon
	3	=	50% wool, 50% nylon, etc.

Facet 3 = pattern (2 digits)	01	=	self colour (plain)
	02	=	self colour (embossed)
	03	=	figleaf, etc.
Facet 4 = colour (2 digits)	01	=	off white
	02	=	jaundice yellow
	03	=	scarlet fever, etc.

A typical code would be 220302 representing a twist carpet in 80% wool, 20% nylon, pattern figleaf and colour jaundice yellow.

Note that a two-digit facet allows up to 99 different codings, but if there were only 20 possibilities for this facet, it would result in a large amount of wastage.

Decimal codes (or hierarchical codes)

These are yet another form of a group classification code. The most obvious example of a decimal code is the Universal Decimal Code (UDC) devised by Dewey and widely used for the classification of books in libraries. UDC divides all human knowledge into more and more detailed categories as shown.

Code	*Item*
3	Social science
37	Education
372	Elementary
372.2	Kindergarten
372.21	Methods
372.215	Songs and games

Sales day book example

Joyce Potts is the sales ledger clerk for a toy manufacturer and wholesaler.

Each day she receives a batch of invoices from the sales invoicing department which she writes up in the sales day book.

Let us look at this week's entries.

Invoices have been entered in order and the total sales value recorded in the total column.

The sales then need to be analysed into:

- net value by product (the true sales value to the business) and
- VAT element (all supplies are standard–rated).

Sales day book

Date	*Invoice No*	*Customer name*	*Code*	*Total*	*Group 01*	*Group 02*	*Group 03*	*Group 04*	*VAT*
				£	£	£	£	£	£
23 July 19X8	1228	Jennings Toys	J02	148.23	56.85	69.30			22.08
	1229	Playstop	P03	281.15		83.11		156.17	41.87
24 July 19X8	1230	Playstop	P03	135.07			114.95		20.12
	1231	Cancelled							
	1232	C&C Products	C12	97.80	36.80	31.53		14.90	14.57
25 July 19X8	1233	AJ Halpern	H11	80.84		68.80			12.04
	1234	Jennings Toys	J02	64.31	54.73				9.58
26 July 19X8	1235	Toystore	T08	290.68	210.85			36.54	43.29
27 July 19X8	1236	H&J Limited	H13	248.50	185.26		26.23		37.01
	1237	Pullmans	P12	269.05		98.30	130.68		40.07
	1238	Toystore	T08	89.30	63.20		12.80		13.30
				1,704.93	607.69	351.04	284.66	207.61	253.93

The four product groups represent:

01	Board games
02	Soft toys
03	Outdoor games
04	Baby toys

The link with the accounting records

Each week or month information is transferred from the **sales day book** to the accounting records.

The information which is to be **posted** (ie transferred) is summarised using a **journal entry.**

This is likely to be a pre–printed standard form for routine transactions like sales.

This is the journal entry to be prepared by Joyce.

Account		*Code*	*Debit*	*Credit*
			£	£
Sales –	Product group 01	2101		607.69
–	Product group 02	2102		351.04
–	Product group 03	2103		284.66
–	Product group 04	2104		207.61
VAT control account		3506		253.93
Debtors' ledger control account			1,704.93	
Totals			1,704.93	1,704.93

Issuing credit notes

A business must keep strict control over credit notes issued.

Credit note – Document issued by a supplier to a customer cancelling part or all of a sales invoice.

A business normally issues a credit note:

- when a customer has returned **faulty** or **damaged** goods;
- when a customer has returned **perfect** goods by agreement with the supplier;
- to make a refund for short deliveries;
- to settle a dispute with a customer;
- to refund for goods sold on a sale or return basis.

Customers must have written approval, in all cases, before returning goods.

Returned goods must be inspected, counted and recorded on receipt. They would normally be recorded on a **returns inwards note** (similar to a **goods received note**).

Returns inwards note – Document recording returned goods received by supplier.

The return inwards note would normally have three parts:

Part one	–	kept by goods inwards department
Part two	–	sent to stores to update records
Part three	–	sent to sales invoicing department to raise credit note

Authorising credit notes

All credit notes must be authorised by a supervisor prior to being issued.

Credit notes would normally have three parts:

Part one	–	sent to customer
Part two	–	kept by sales invoicing (matched with returns inwards note)
Part three	–	sent to debtors' ledger department to update records

Some credit notes may be issued **without a returns inwards note**. For example, an error may have been made in pricing on an invoice but the customer is satisfied with the goods and does not need to return them.

These credit notes must be issued only after **written authorisation** has been received and must be reviewed and approved before being sent to the customer or recorded.

Preparing credit notes

A credit note is effectively an invoice in reverse.

Effect of value added tax

If a business is registered for VAT, the credit note must show:

- an identifying number;
- date of issue;
- supplier's name, address and registration number;
- customer's name and address;
- reason for credit, eg returned goods;

- for each item:
  - (i) description of the goods or services to which the credit relates;
  - (ii) quantity and amount credited;
- total amount credited excluding VAT;
- rate and amount of VAT credited;
- number and date of original tax invoice, if possible.

It is not acceptable for a business registered for VAT to issue credit notes to recover bad debts. VAT is charged on the original supply of goods or services, not on the payment from the customer.

The proper procedure is to account for the VAT on the original supply as normal. Then, if the debt is still not paid after six months, the business can reclaim the VAT by a different procedure.

Recording credit notes

Credit notes should be issued in **sequential** number order and recorded in that same order. Spoilt copies should be cancelled and kept.

The debtors' ledger clerk will record the credit notes in the **sales returns day book.**

This is effectively the reverse of the sales day book. It is *analysed* in the same way as the sales day book.

The sales returns day book is then used to update the **debtors' ledger** and the **debtors' ledger control account** in the same way as the sales day book.

Each month each transaction is posted to the individual supplier's account in the debtors' ledger and the total of returns is posted to the debtors' ledger control account.

Deposits

A business may ask customers to pay a deposit when ordering goods, for example, because special work is to be carried out to the customer's own requirements.

The deposit is posted to the sales day book when it is received. When the customer is invoiced, the total shown on the invoice is net of the deposit.

If the business is registered for VAT, the VAT is effectively apportioned between the deposit and the remainder of the invoice total. When the deposit is posted to the day book, the VAT element must be shown separately.

Computerised accounting systems

So far we have only considered manual accounting systems. In practice, many organisations maintain some or all of their accounting records on computers.

Computer systems were developed to replace manual systems because they are more efficient at storing, retrieving and processing information. They basically work in the same way.

A computerised accounting system contains the same records as a manual accounting system. For example, sales invoices are entered in a sales day book and information from the sales day book is posted to the nominal ledger. As you work through the Study Pack, you will be introduced to other accounting records. These also have exactly the same purpose in a computerised system as they would have in a manual system.

There are two main methods of processing transactions using a computer: batch processing and real time processing.

Batch processing

In batch processing, large numbers of similar transactions (eg sales invoices) are grouped together and processed at the same time.

Advantages of batch processing

- Error detection is easier compared with real-time processing. Systems normally use control or batch totals. The amounts on the documents are totalled manually and this total is input to the computer. The computer also totals the documents and will not accept the batch if the totals do not agree.
- It is relatively inexpensive as no special hardware/software is needed (all computer systems should be able to adopt this).
- It contributes large-scale economies due to bulk processing.
- It is flexible in that, if necessary, part of the data could be processed now, the remainder later.
- It is easy to schedule processing at set times (therefore easier to organise work for competing users).
- It is easier to control input and processing than on-line methods (see below).

On-line, real-time processing (OLRT)

On-line means that transactions can be input as they occur. Real-time means that processing takes place and the results are obtained immediately.

Transactions are processed as they arise (as opposed to being batched).

Advantages of real time processing

- There is no delay in information processing, so that output can be received back as soon as processing is complete.
- With the transactions being processed as they arise, data is more up to date.
- Due to data being up to date and the system being on-line, any enquiries made of the system should give as responses an accurate picture.
- Systems can be programmed to initiate transactions. For example, processing a transaction may:
  - create a condition such as reordering stock which has now hit a minimum stock level;
  - signal (another) transaction (eg a purchase invoice leads to the production of cheques for suppliers).

Files

Not all data is manually input to the computer every time it is required. It is stored in files.

A file is an organised collection of individual *records* which share a common structure. For example:

- a pricing master file (contains unit prices for each product or service sold by a business);
- a personnel file contains details (such as address, start date, gross pay, tax code and bank details) for each member of staff.

Hierarchy of information

- A **file** is a collection of related *records* (eg a collection of employees will have their personnel records stored on a file).
- A **record** is a collection of related facts about an entity (eg a personnel record for John Smith will consist of various facts about him). It is a component of a *file*, containing a number of *fields*.
- A **field** is a section of a record (eg 'John Smith' is the field containing employee name. '07394' is the field containing employee number). Each field contains a single item of information.
- A **character** is a unit which is a letter, number or symbol making up a field (eg '6', '9', or '£').

Questions

1 (AAT CA J93)

The cheque numbers used in a cheque book are an example of a sequential code or a hierarchical code?

2 (AAT CA J94)

Cathy Payne is keen to have a computerised accounting system for the company. She is particularly interested in obtaining a microcomputer, which would include a keyboard, a central processing unit, a VDU and a hard disk, together with a printer.

(a) Which of the items of hardware given above would be regarded as a backing storage device?

(b) Give one reason why it would be necessary to have a backing storage device.

3 (AAT CA D94)

Batch processing is a system whereby transactions are processed as and when they arise in order to keep the ledgers totally up to date.

True / False

4 (AAT CA J93)

In using a computer to process accounting data, there are two main systems which can be adopted.

(a) What is the processing system system where documents or transactions for a period are grouped and processed together is known as?

(b) Give one advantage of the system in (a).

(c) What is the processing system where documents or transactions are processed as they occur is known as?

(d) Give one advantage of the system in (c).

5 (AAT CA D93)

In a computerised accounting system will the following be a file, record or field:

(a) The purchase ledger will be a ....

(b) The amount owed to a particular supplier will be a ....

(c) The account details of a particular supplier will be a ....

6 (AAT CA J93)

Give two different circumstances which would necessitate a credit note being issued.

7 (AAT CA D92)

The credit balance of £92 (including VAT @ 17.5%) on the debtor's account of Euro Hair Style Ltd on 1 March arose because of an overcharge on a sales invoice which was subsequently corrected. However, Euro Hair Style has paid the original amount shown on the invoice.

(a) What document would have been sent to Euro Hair Style when the overcharge was corrected?

(b) Show the entries in the general ledger accounts, including amounts, made when this document was issued.

Summary

Sales day book

- Records sales invoices in number/date order
- Diary of credit transactions
- Analyse sales by product type excluding VAT
- Analyse VAT separately
- Totals posted to accounting records using journal entry

Credit note

- Note issued by a supplier cancelling part or all of a previous sale
- Issued: (i) to refund for goods returned and (ii) to settle a dispute
- Must be authorised
- If business registered for VAT, must include specific information
- Cannot be issued to cancel a debt which will not now be paid because customer is insolvent or in receivership
- Recorded in sales returns day book
- clerk should not have access

Computerised accounting systems

- More efficient at storing, retrieving and processing information
- Batch processing where large number of similar transactions are processed together

On line real time (OLRT) transactions input and processed as they occur

CHAPTER 9

Maintaining the Debtors' Ledger

Objectives

This chapter covers the following performance criteria.

- Entries in the primary records are correctly transferred to the correct ledger accounts.
- Adjustments involving debtors' accounts are properly authorised and documented, and are correctly transferred to the correct ledger accounts.
- The control account in the general ledger is reconciled with the total of balances in the sales (debtors) ledger.

Customers' individual accounts

So that the business knows how much is owed by each credit customer (debtor), the business maintains a book called the debtors' ledger (or sales ledger). The debtors' ledger consists of records of amounts owed by each debtor. Each customer has his or her own page (or account) in the ledger.

The account will look something like this.

Customer name: AJ Halpern **Customer code:** H11

Date	*Transaction*	£	*Date*	*Transaction*	£
25/7/X8	Inv. 1233	80.84			

Sales invoices are recorded on the left-hand side (debit side). Individual transactions are transferred from the sales day book. Note that the amount recorded for each sales invoice is the total including VAT as this is what is owed by the customer. As each invoice is paid, the remittance advice is used to match the cash paid to the related invoice. Cash received is recorded on the right-hand side (credit side).

The easiest way to match cash is to mark off items as matched.

Customer name: A J Halpern

Date	*Transaction*	£	*Date*	*Transaction*	£
25/7/X8	Inv. 1233	✓80.84	25/9/X8	Cash 2653	✓80.84
30/8/X8	Inv. 1254	112.13			
02/9/X8	Inv. 1257	254.68			

Example

Here is an account from the debtors' ledger of Frosty Limited, a glass manufacturer which specialises in glassware for the catering trade.

Account name: **Account number:**

Date	*Transaction*	£	*Date*	*Transaction*	£

You have taken over writing up the sales ledger because the debtors' ledger clerk has been ill for several months.

You have gathered together the following information about sales and cash receipts. The customer is a new customer whose name is Arthur Pickering. The account code will be SP05.

Sales invoices

		£
02/5/X1	325	585.60
03/6/X1	468	238.90
15/6/X1	503	113.43
16/7/X1	510	48.70
17/7/X1	604	441.12

Cash received

		£	
06/6/X1	p.23	585.60	(Invoice 325)
20/7/X1	p.28	268.23	(Invoice 468, part Invoice 503)
25/7/X1	p.29	132.80	(part Invoice 503, Invoice 510)

Solution

Account name: Arthur Pickering **Account number:** SP05

Date	Transaction	£	Date	Transaction	£
02/5/X1	Inv. 325	✓585.60	06/6/X1	Cash p.23	✓585.60
03/6/X1	Inv. 468	✓238.90	20/7/X1	Cash p.28	✓268.23
15/6/X1	Inv. 503	✓113.43	25/7/X1	Cash p.29	✓132.80
16/6/X1	Inv. 510	✓ 48.70			
17/7/X1	Inv. 604	441.12		Bal c/f	441.12
		1,427.75			1,427.75
	Bal b/f	441.12			

Example

You are the sales ledger clerk of Francis plc a firm that provides interpreter services to news agencies. It is your job to maintain the debtors ledger. You have been handed a batch of invoices that Mrs Thomas has previously recorded in the sales day book and she has provided the journal entry for the batch. There are ten invoices.

The journal entry gives the following information.

		Code	Debit £	Credit £
Debtors control account		015	8,225	
Sales a/c:	Russian	051		5,500
	Polish	052		100
	Spanish	053		400
	German	054		600
	French	055		400
	VAT	016		1,225
Batch total			8,225	8,225

The entries in the sales day book are given below.

Required

From the information given, produce the individual sales ledger accounts

Date	*Inv. no.*	*Customer*	*Code*	*Total*	*Ru*	*Po*	*Sp*	*Ge*	*Fr*	*VAT*
15.8.X1	167	Worldwide News	W5	2,937.50	2,500					437.50
	168	Local News	L1	235.00			200			35.00
	169	The Press Today	P2	352.50				300		52.50
	170	Home Call	H1	235.00			200			35.00
	171	States Press	S5	117.50		100				17.50
	172	Tomorrow	T1	117.50					100	17.50
	173	Worldwide News	W5	3,525.00	3,000					525.00
	174	The Press Today	P2	352.50				300		52.50
	175	States Press	S5	117.50					100	17.50
	176	Home Call	H1	235.00					200	35.00
				8,225.00	5,500	100	400	600	400	1,225.00

Solution

Account no. W5

Worldwide News

Date	Transaction	Amount	Date	Transaction	Amount
		£			£
15.8.X1	Inv. 167	2,937.5		Balance c/f	6,462.5
15.8.X1	Inv. 173	3,525.0			
		6,462.5			6,462.5

Account no. L1

Local News

Date	Transaction	Amount	Date	Transaction	Amount
		£			£
15.8.X1	Inv. 168	235.0		Balance c/f	235.0
		235.0			235.0

Account no. P2

The Press Today

Date	Transaction	Amount	Date	Transaction	Amount
		£			£
15.8.X1	Inv. 169	352.5		Balance c/f	705.0
15.8.X1	Inv. 174	352.5			
		705.0			705.0

Account no. H1

Home Call

Date	Transaction	Amount	Date	Transaction	Amount
		£			£
15.8.X1	Inv. 170	235.0		Balance c/f	470.0
15.8.X1	Inv. 176	235.0			470.0
		470.0			

Account no. S5

States Press

Date	Transaction	Amount	Date	Transaction	Amount
		£			£
15.8.X1	Inv. 171	117.5	Balance c/f		235.0
15.8.X1	Inv. 175	117.5			
		235.0			235.0

Account no. T1

Tomorrow

Date	Transaction	Amount	Date	Transaction	Amount
		£			£
15.8.X1	Inv. 172	117.5	Balance c/f		117.5
		117.5			117.5

Accounting for cash or settlement discounts

If the business has offered a customer a cash or settlement discount, the customer may pay less than the original amount invoiced. When writing up cash received the discount given must also be recorded.

Account name: AJ Wilde **Account number:** SW53

Date	Transaction	£	Date	Transaction	£
19/11/X0	Inv. 4220	✓237.80			
27/11/X0	Inv. 4390	359.65	30/11/X0	Bal c/f	597.45
		597.45			597.45
01/12/X0	Bal b/f	597.45	20/12/X0	Cash 354	✓233.04
				Disc 354	✓4.76
			31/12/X0	Bal c/f	359.65
		597.45			597.45
01/1/X1	Bal b/f	359.65			

If the discount was not written into the ledger account, the total still outstanding would be £364.41 (£359.65 plus £4.76) which would be incorrect.

The information on discounts allowed comes from the discounts memorandum column in the analysed cash book.

Other unusual items in the debtors' ledger

Occasionally other adjustments may be needed in the customer's individual account in the debtors' ledger.

Adjustments may be needed for:

- bad debts;
- contras;
- errors
- dishonoured cheques.

Bad debts

Bad debt – A debt which is highly unlikely to be received; it is therefore not prudent for the business to consider this debt as an asset.

A business may decide that a debt is bad for a number of reasons:

- customer is in liquidation – no cash will be received;
- customer is having difficulty paying although not officially in liquidation;
- customer disputes the debt and refuses to pay either part or all of it.

The business must make an adjustment to write off the bad debt from the customer's account in the debtors' ledger.

Notice that the bad debt becomes an expense in the profit and loss account. Writing off bad debts decreases the profits made by a business. (Note that the bad debt is *not* deducted from sales.)

Doubtful debts

A doubtful debt is a debt which may still be recovered, even though this is doubtful. In this situation, management usually want the debt to stay in the books, as a reminder to chase it up. A provision is created against the debt. This provision is deducted from the figure for debtors in the balance sheet when the accounts are eventually prepared.

A provision may be specific (against particular debts) or general. A general provision may be made if a business knows from experience that a certain proportion of its debts will not be recovered.

Doubtful debts, like bad debts, result in an expense to the business. In practice, the expense is the movement in the provision during a period.

Bad debts and VAT

VAT may be reclaimed on bad debts over six months old. The debt must have been removed from the books. It is necessary to make a formal claim to Customs and Excise and the business must produce a VAT invoice in respect of the sale.

Contras

Contra – When another business or individual is both a customer and supplier (ie both a debtor and a creditor), a contra entry can be made (with the permission of the other party) to cancel the asset against the liability.

This means that a contra entry will be made in the individual customer's accounts in both the debtors' and creditors' ledgers.

The double–entry is:

Dr	**Creditor's ledger account**	
	Cr	**Debtors ledger account**

with the difference.

Example

Celia sells goods to Godfrey but also purchases some supplies from him. At the end of the period, Godfrey owes Celia £40 but Celia also owes Godfrey £50. The balances on the accounts in the debtors' ledger and creditors' ledger in Celia's books will be:

Debtors' ledger

Godfrey

	£		£
Balance b/f	40		

Creditors' ledger

Godfrey

	£		£
		Balance b/f	50

The maximum amount which can be offset is £40 and after passing the contra entries the accounts will show:

Debtors' ledger

Godfrey

	£		£
Balance b/f	40	Contra with creditors ledger	40
	—		—

Creditors' ledger

Godfrey

	£		£
Contra with debtors ledger	40	Balance b/f	50
Balance c/f	10		
	50		50
		Balance b/f	10

Celia still owes Godfrey £10. Debtors and creditors have both been reduced by £40.

Errors

Errors may sometimes be discovered and need to be dealt with, such as:

- discounts not written off;
- discounts written off in error;
- transactions written up in the wrong customer's account.

Dishonoured cheques

Cheques received from customers may be 'referred to drawer', or dishonoured by the bank. This may occur for a number of reasons, including insufficient funds in the drawer's account. Both the cash book and the debtors' ledger must be adjusted to reflect this.

The double–entry is:

Dr Debtors ledger account
Cr Cash at bank

Authorisation

Adjustments should only be made after authorisation from someone outside the debtors' ledger function, eg financial controller. All adjustments must be documented.

Debtors' ledger control account

Within the nominal ledger the total amount outstanding from debtors is shown in the debtors' ledger control account (sometimes called the sales ledger control account).

The totals of credit sales (from the sales day book) and cash received and discounts (from the analysed cash book) are posted to this account (via a journal entry).

This account therefore shows the total debtors outstanding. It does *not* give detail about individual customers' balances. (This is available in the debtors' ledger.)

However, as both records are compiled from the same sources, the total balances on the customers' individual accounts must equal the outstanding balance on the control account at any time.

The double-entry system operates as follows.

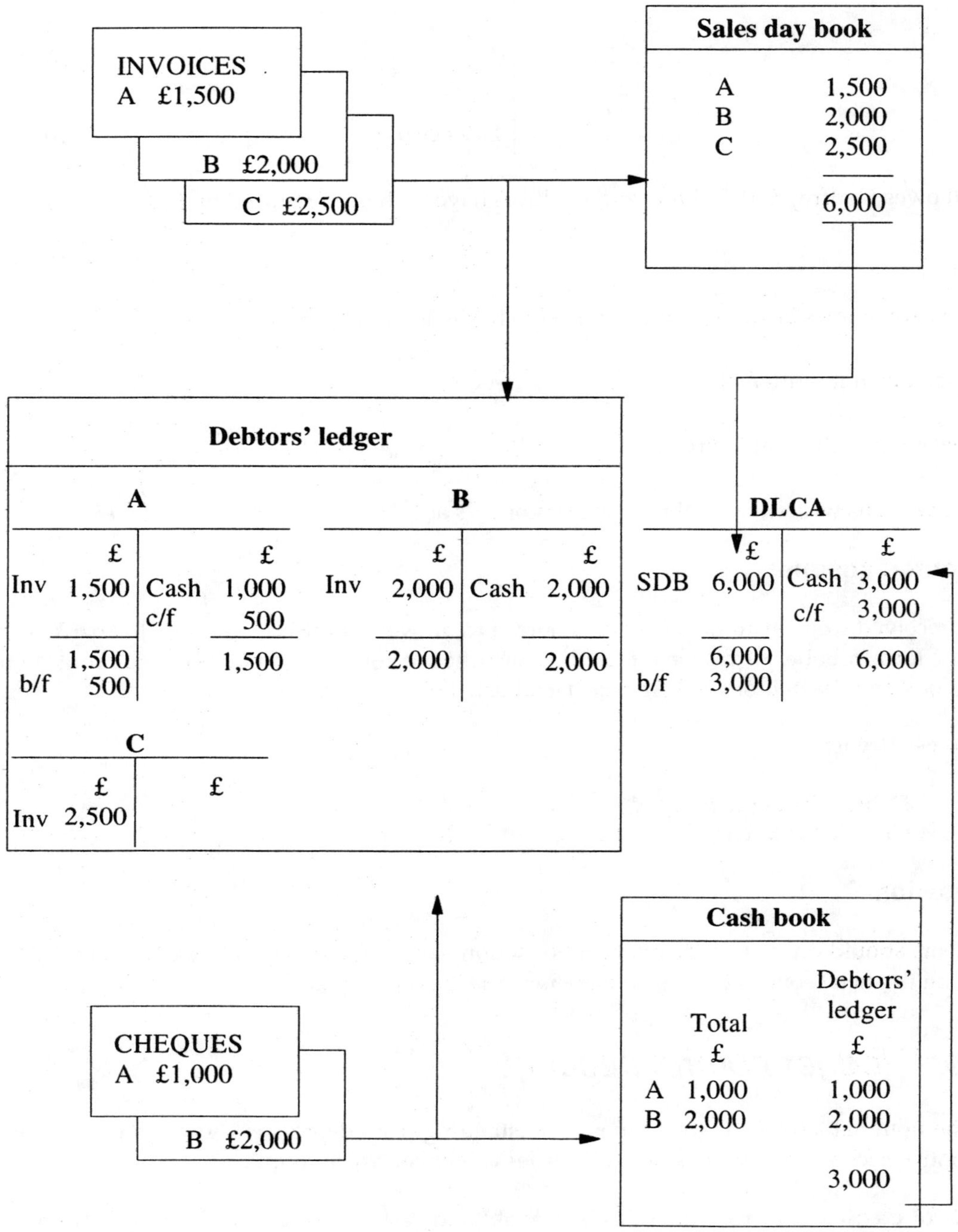

Key: DLCA = debtors' ledger control account

Notice that the remaining balance on the control account (£3,000) is equal to the sum of the remaining balances on the individual debtors' accounts (A £500 + C £2,500).

A debtors' ledger control account normally appears like this.

Debtors' ledger control account

	£		£
Balance b/f	X	Returns per returns day book	X
Sales per sales day book	X	* Cash from debtors	X
		* Discounts allowed	X
		Bad debts written off	X
		Contra with creditors ledger control account	X
		Balance c/f	X
	X		X
Balance b/f	X		

* Per cash book

Advantages of maintaining control accounts

The advantages of using control accounts are as follows.

- They provide a quick total of debtors, creditors, etc. so that trial balances can be conveniently drawn up without having to total up all the subsidiary balances each time.
- They provide a check on the postings to the individual accounts when the control account balance is reconciled to the total of the subsidiary balances. Errors can therefore be corrected quickly.
- Preparers of accounts can be confident of the period-end debtors and creditors figures, so that balance sheets can be drawn up more quickly.
- They may help to prevent fraud.

Mini case study

James has been trading for two months. He has four credit customers. James is not registered for VAT. Here is the day book for the first two months:

Sales day book (SDB)

Date	*Customer*	*Invoice*	£
02.2.Y4	Peter Brown	01	50.20
05.2.Y4	Ian Smith	02	80.91
07.2.Y4	Sid Parsons	03	73.86
23.2.Y4	Eva Lane	04	42.30
	Total		247.27
09.3.Y4	Ian Smith	05	23.96
15.3.Y4	Sid Parsons	06	34.72
20.3.Y4	Peter Brown	07	12.60
24.3.Y4	Sid Parsons	08	93.25
31.3.Y4	Total		164.53

Here is the receipts side of the analysed cash book for March 19Y4 (no cash was received from debtors in February).

Analysed cash book (ACB)

Date	*Narrative*	*Total*	*Sales*	*Debtors*	*Rent*
01.3.Y4	Peter Brown	50.20		50.20	
03.3.Y4	Clare Jones	63.80	63.80		
04.3.Y4	Molly Dell	110.00			110.00
12.3.Y4	Sid Parsons	50.00		50.00	
13.3.Y4	Emily Boyd	89.33	89.33		
20.3.Y4	Frank Field	92.68	92.68		
25.3.Y4	Eva Lane	42.30		42.30	
31.3.Y4	Total	498.31	245.81	142.50	110.00

The debtors' ledger will then appear as follows.

Debtors' ledger

Peter Brown

		£			£
02.2.Y4	01	50.20	28.2.Y4	c/f	50.20
		50.20			50.20
01.3.Y4	b/f	50.20	01.3.Y4	Cash	50.20
20.3.Y4	07	12.60	31.3.Y4	c/f	12.60
		62.80			62.80
01.4.Y4	b/f	12.60			

Eva Lane

		£			£
23.2.Y4	04	42.30	28.2.Y4	c/f	42.30
		42.30			42.30
01.3.Y4	b/f	42.30	25.3.Y4	Cash	42.30

Sid Parsons

		£			£
07.2.Y4	03	73.86	28.2.Y4	c/f	73.86
		73.86			73.86
01.3.Y4	b/f	73.86	12.3.Y4	Cash	50.00
15.3.Y4	06	34.72	31.3.Y4	c/f	151.83
24.3.Y4	08	93.25			
		201.83			201.83
01.4.Y4	b/f	151.83			

Ian Smith

		£			£
05.2.Y4	02	80.91	28.2.Y4	c/f	80.91
		80.91			80.91
01.3.Y4	b/f	80.91	31.3.Y4	c/f	104.87
09.3.Y4	05	23.96			
		104.87			104.87
01.4.Y4	b/f	104.87			

Nominal ledger (extract)

Debtors' ledger control account

		£			£
28.2.Y4	SDB	247.27	28.2.Y4	c/f	247.27
		247.27			247.27
01.3.Y4	b/f	247.27	31.3.Y4	ACB	142.50
31.3.Y4	SDB	164.53	31.3.Y4	c/f	269.30
		411.80			411.80
01.4.Y4	b/f	269.30			

Let us compare balances at 31 March 19Y4.

Debtors' ledger

	£
Peter Brown	12.60
Eva Lane	–
Sid Parsons	151.83
Ian Smith	104.87
	269.30
Debtors' ledger control account	269.30

Debtors' ledger reconciliation

Comparing the control account balance with the total of the debtors' ledger personal accounts, is a form of internal control. The reconciliation should be performed on a regular basis by the sales ledger clerk and reviewed and approved by an independent person.

Adjustments to the debtors' ledger control account

Any corrections or adjustments made to the debtors' ledger control account must be documented as a journal entry (including a narrative).

For instance, the total sales for the month were posted from the sales day book as £4,657.98 instead of £4,677.98. The business only has one product group.

The journal entry to correct this error will be as follows.

JOURNAL ENTRY	**No: 97**		
Prepared by: A Grimm			
Authorised by: L R Ridinghood			
Date: 23.7.X3			
Narrative: To correct error in posting to debtors' ledger control account			
Account	*Code*	*Debit*	*Credit*
Debtors' ledger control	x11	20	
Sales	m56		20
TOTALS		20	20

Adjustments in the debtors' ledger

Adjustments in the debtors' ledger do not need to be documented on a journal entry. Journal entries are only required for adjustments to the nominal ledger.

These adjustments should be recorded somewhere, for instance, in a separate notebook.

Control account reconciliations (a summary)

(1) The balances on the individual debtors' ledger accounts are extracted, listed and totalled.

(2) The debtors' ledger control account is balanced.

(3) If the two figures differ, then the reasons for the difference must be investigated.

Reasons may include the following:

- An error in the casting of the day book. (The *total* is posted to the control account whereas the individual invoices are posted to the individual accounts and, therefore, if the total is incorrect, a difference will arise.)
- A transposition error which could be made in posting either:

  (i) to the control account; or

  (ii) to the individual accounts.
- A contra which has been made between the individual accounts in the debtors and creditors ledgers but has not been recorded in the control account or vice versa.
- A bad debt which has been written off in the individual account but not in the control account or vice versa.
- A casting error in the cash book column relating to the control account. (The *total* is posted).
- A balance omitted from the list of individual accounts.
- A credit balance on an individual account in the debtors' ledger which has automatically and wrongly been assumed to be a debit balance.

(4) Differences which are errors in the control account should be corrected in the control account.

(5) Differences which are errors in the individual accounts should be corrected by adjusting the list of balances.

Questions

1 (AAT CA D93)

What double entry would you make in the general ledger in respect of the following.

(a) A set off of £20 is to be made between Tompkinson & Co's accounts in the sales ledger and in the purchase ledger.

(b) The account of D L Mason who owes £1,214 is to be written off as a bad debt.

2 (AAT CA D93)

Explain briefly why a business would be anxious to minimise the amount of bad debts written off.

3 (AAT CA D92)

One of the company's customers has been declared bankrupt with little probability of paying his debt to the company of £147. The outstanding amount is to be written off as a bad debt.

(a) In which record of original entry would the write-off first be entered?

(b) Which general ledger account would be debited and which credited in this respect?

4 (AAT CA J92)

Is it possible under certain circumstances to reclaim the VAT component of a bad debt written off?

5 (AAT CA D92)

Give two reasons for maintaining the debtors' ledger control account.

6 (AAT CA D93)

Would the following errors cause a difference to occur between the balance of the debtors' control account and the total of the balances in the sales ledger?

(a) The total column of the sales day book was overcast by £100.

(b) In error H Lambert's account in the sales ledger was debited with £175 instead of M Lambert's account.

(c) An invoice for £76 was recorded in the sales day book as £67.

Summary

Debtors' ledger

- Separate from nominal ledger
- Contains individual accounts for each customer
- Shows how much each customer owes the business
- Compiled from detailed information from books of prime entry

Debtors' ledger control account

- One of the accounts in the nominal ledger
- Shows total debtors' balance outstanding
- Compiled from totals from books of prime entry

CHAPTER 10

Using Information to Control Debtors

Objectives

This chapter covers the following performance criteria.

- When required, statements of account are sent to debtors promptly.
- The organisation's policies, procedures and timescales are observed.?
- Discrepancies, unusual features or queries are identified and either resolved or referred to the appropriate person.
- Communications with debtors regarding accounts are handled promptly, courteously and effectively.

Preparing an aged analysis of debtors

Each month a listing of debtors is produced from the debtors' ledger. This shows how much each individual customer owes the business.

By producing a more detailed listing which shows the age of the invoices making up the balance, credit control (ie chasing debtors for payment) is much easier.

Aged debtors' listing – Debtors' ledger listing which shows the age of invoices making up each customer's balance.

The aged debtors' listing can be prepared in various formats. Here is one example.

NEMO Limited

Aged debtors' listing as at 31 August 19X3

Code		*Total*	*Current*	*30+*	*60+*
01	William Allan Limited	1,123.90	901.30	222.60	
02	James Allcroft	68.50		68.50	
03	Allied Products	0.20			0.20
04	Beard & Bell	586.37	418.67	113.90	53.80
05	Chambers Video	256.80	238.96		17.84
06	Cowper & Co	394.55		394.55	
09	Double Vision	101.73	78.93	22.80	
10	Glendale Kitchens	992.15	879.59	112.56	
11	Globe Travel	115.13	20.02	95.11	
14	High Class Limited	97.93	74.20	23.73	
28	Pacific Sales	5.53		5.53	
29	Percival & Williams	297.84	297.84		
33	Quill Products	756.89	50.02	706.87	
34	Scott Brothers	835.19	529.94	236.50	68.75
35	Turner & Bates	86.90	86.90		
37	United Services	63.80	43.60	20.20	
38	Walter & Ward	1,210.35	399.15	654.30	156.90
39	Staff Sales	53.96			53.96
	Totals	10,597.72	6,419.12	3,677.15	501.45

Preparing statements

The debtors' ledger clerk prepares monthly statements to send to debtors:

- to remind them that certain invoices are due for payment;
- to reconfirm amounts outstanding where credit notes have been issued.

Statement – Document issued (monthly) by supplier to customer showing unpaid sales invoices.

Statements can be prepared in a number of different ways. Some also have remittance advices attached to them.

From: NEMO Limited
23 Park Road, Oldham OL1 1VR

To: Scott Brothers (34)
Festival Way, Oldham OL2 3BD

Date: 31 August 19X3

STATEMENT

Date	*Transaction*	*Debit*	*Credit*	*Balance*
12 May 19X3	Inv. 2569	92.35		92.35
13 June 19X3	CN 2659		23.60	68.75
09 July 19X3	Inv. 2701	102.69		171.44
18 July 19X3	Inv. 2753	133.81		305.25
02 August 19X3	Inv. 2889	56.50		361.75
10 August 19X3	Inv. 2901	230.20		591.95
28 August 19X3	Inv. 3114	243.24		835.19
	Balance due			835.19

May we remind you our credit terms are 30 days

Where the business has made an error, the customer will usually query the statement. Any queries should be handled by a different person to the one who prepared the original statement.

This is a useful type of **internal control** over debtors.

Chasing payment

If a debt has not been paid, the **credit controller** should contact the customer's **creditors' ledger clerk** by telephone and by letter and should politely ask for payment.

It may be that the customer is dissatisfied with the goods or service received.

If the credit controller becomes aware of any such circumstances he must tell the relevant departments immediately.

If the customer still refuses to pay after an unreasonable length of time and after the business has put right any complaints, the business may have to resort to the courts.

Example

You are the credit controller for GoGo Limited, a wholesaler of discount children's clothing. You have been reviewing the aged debtors' listing. The following customer is causing you concern!

	Total	*Current*	*30+*	*60+*
Candy Limited	556.78	0	0	556.78

You must write a letter to this customer to ask for payment. Invent any details you need (names, dates, etc).

Solution

GoGo Limited

225 Western Road
Anytown
Anyshire AN1 2RN

Creditors' Ledger Clerk
Candy Limited
53 High Street
Anytown
Anyshire AN1 6BN

23 August 19X4

Dear Sir

Outstanding balance

According to our records your company has an outstanding balance of £556.78.

Our normal credit terms are 30 days. As this debt is now over 60 days old we would be very grateful if you could send us your payment immediately.

If you have any queries please do not hesitate to contact me.

Yours faithfully

AN Smith
Credit Controller

Questions

1 (AAT CA J94)

The account of Discount Motors appears in the ledger as follows.

			£				£
April	12	Sales	1,241	May	15	Bank	1,241
April	18	Sales	2,182	May	30	Bank	2,182
May	5	Sales	1,849				
May	10	Sales	1,654				
June	14	Sales	2,237				

(a) Complete the following age analysis at 15 June 1994 for Discount Motors.

Discount Motors – Age analysis at 15 June 19X4

Balance	*Up to 1 month*	*1 to 2 months*	*Over 2 months*
£	£	£	£
....	....	....	....

(b) Which of MEL Motor Factors Limited's departments would have the task of ensuring that payments are received promptly from credit customers?

.... department.

2 (AAT CA J92)

The account of Castle Sports Limited appears as follows.

			£				£
April	1	Balance b/d	842	April	2	Bank	402
	29	Sales	460				
May	2	Sales	175				
June	3	Sales	327				

Complete the following age analysis for this customer as at 17 June 1992.

Age analysis at 17 June 19X2

Balance	*Up to 1 month*	*Up to 2 months*	*Over 2 months*
£	£	£	£
....	....	....	....

3 (AAT CA J93)

The following is an extract from an age analysis report prepared on 1 June.

Name	*Balance*	*Up to 1 month*	*Up to 3 months*	*Over 3 months*
	£	£	£	£
West & Co	4,860	3,400	1,460	0
Star Limited	2,719	0	0	2,719
Norwood Limited	3,116	1,200	1,900	16
Just Electric	1,391	1,320	0	71

(a) With which one of the four accounts might you be most concerned?

(b) Explain briefly the reason for your answer.

4 (AAT CA J93)

Joan Brookes (the accountant) has been reviewing the accounts in the sales ledger and notes that no monies have been received from Moss Electrical for some months. She feels that if the owner has not been in touch within the next month, and this seems highly unlikely, then the debt should be written off. Such matters have to be sanctioned by Bob Wallis, the managing director. The file for Moss Electrical shows the following.

Moss Electrical

Today's date	1 June 19X3
Balance	£1,642
Last payment received	November 19X2
Last correspondence	Recorded delivery sent February 19X3 – returned 'premises unoccupied'
Solicitor's report	Unable to trace owner – James Moss

Joan Brookes asks you to draft a suitable memorandum to Bob Wallis informing him of the facts and seeking his authorisation.

Summary

Aged analysis of debtors

- Prepared from debtors' ledger
- Shows age of debts
- Useful for credit controller

Statements

- Produced regularly (monthly)
- Reminder to customers
- May reveal errors in debtors' ledger

Credit control

- By telephone
- By letter
- Through courts

CHAPTER 11

Receiving Purchase Invoices

Objectives

This chapter covers the following performance criteria.

- Suppliers' invoices and credit notes are correctly checked against ordering documentation and evidence that goods/services have been received.
- Suppliers' invoices and credit notes are correctly coded.
- Calculations on suppliers' invoices and credit notes are correct.

Ordering goods and services

Departments needing goods and services from outside suppliers make an internal request using a **purchase requisition.**

Purchase requisition – Document for internal use only to make requests for goods and services.

The departments send their purchase requisitions to the buying (or purchasing) department. The buying department then locates a supplier and confirms the order using a **purchase order.**

Purchase orders – Document sent to supplier confirming an order for goods or services.

These must be authorised by the relevant department head or supervisor before being sent to the supplier. Each department head has an **authorisation limit**. Orders above that value must be authorised by a director, eg managing director.

Only approved suppliers (shown on an official list) should be used. An **advice note** may be received from a supplier as confirmation that the goods have been despatched.

Suppliers must be instructed not to accept orders which are made without a proper purchase order.

Purchase orders should be sequentially numbered and carefully controlled. A four-part document might be used as follows:

Part one	–	sent to supplier
Part two	–	kept by buying department
Part three	–	to goods inwards department to check off goods received – unauthorised goods are returned immediately to the supplier
Part four	–	to creditors' ledger department to verify purchase invoices received.

Checking the accuracy of purchase invoices

Purchase invoices should be carefully checked when they are received. They should be:

- compared to purchase orders;
- compared to goods received notes/delivery notes;
- checked for accuracy of pricing, VAT and discounts;
- checked for clerical accuracy.

Note that VAT is calculated on the invoice amount *net* of any cash discount allowed, regardless of whether the discount is taken.

Goods received note – Document recording goods received prepared for internal use.

Staff in the buying department should not have access to blank goods received notes.

Goods received notes should be sequentially numbered and carefully controlled.

A three-part document would be used as follows:

Part one	–	kept by goods inwards department
Part two	–	sent to stores to update records
Part three	–	sent to creditors' ledger department to be matched to purchase invoice.

Coding and authorising purchase invoices

All purchase invoices should be date stamped on receipt, given a sequential number, coded, checked and recorded in a **purchase invoice register** or similar.

They should then be sent to the relevant department head for authorisation.

The creditors' ledger clerk must wait until they have been authorised before entering them in the **purchase day book**.

Authorising service invoices

For services received there may be no record kept by the business, although the supplier might supply an advice note for certain services.

Services purchase invoices should be authorised by some responsible person, eg department head.

Summary of procedures

Creditors' ledger clerk

- Matches purchase order, goods received note (and delivery note) and purchase invoice.
- Chases up any discrepancy/ problems.
- Stamps invoice.
- Records it in purchase invoice register.
- Sends invoice for coding/ authorisation.
- Notifies buying department of short delivery.

Buying department

- Photocopies original purchase order, writes additional amount to be received on photocopy.
- Distributes to warehouse and creditors' ledger clerk.

Example

Consider the following operations within Gathermore Limited's purchasing department. Gathermore deals with the manufacture of off-the-shelf, ready-to-hang curtains.

(1) Mrs Thomas in the cutting department has sent Suzie to tell Raymond in the purchasing section that they have run out of Greyshwins Rose Pink Cotton Satin.

(2) Raymond rings up Greyshwins in York and asks them to deliver 200 metres of Rose Pink Cotton Satin as soon as possible.

(3) When the cloth arrives, it is taken directly to the cutting department.

(4) The invoice arrives two days after the delivery and is paid by the purchasing manager the same day.

(5) Two weeks later Mrs Thomas is surprised that the cutting department has again run out of cloth before it has finished the production schedule's work load. She is convinced that they did not receive all of the cloth that had been ordered and paid for.

Required

Describe some control procedures that could be introduced into this inefficient system and indicate which problem they might avoid or benefit.

Solution

She completes the following information.

Internal control	**Problem area/benefit**
Requisition and ordering	
Written internal purchase requisition **signed** by Mrs Thomas.	Avoids errors by word of mouth. If there are later queries or problems concerning the requisition, written signed documentation is available. Ensures that requisitions are made only for official company business and not private items.
A purchase order should be made out from the requisition in the purchasing department (segregation of duties).	Helps avoid the ordering of private goods.
The order should have **four parts**.	Provides written evidence for: (1) comparison with purchase requisition in case of query; (2) sending to supplier to let him know in writing which goods are required and for future reference in case of query;
The order should be **matched** and filed accordingly.	(3) comparing with the delivery when the goods are received to ensure that the goods were as ordered; (4) comparing with the invoice before payment to ensure that only properly ordered and authorised goods are paid for.
Delivery of goods	
Cloth should be received into a goods inwards section, where it can be physically **checked**, recorded and monitored before distribution throughout the factory.	Enables immediate detection of problems/queries (quality, etc) to raise with supplier and inform purchasing department.
Delivery note should be compared and **matched** with the original purchase order.	Avoids goods being accepted that were not officially ordered. Matching highlights outstanding orders which may be causing production problems.

Internal control	**Problem area/benefit**
	Ensures that shortfall problems can be traced later and highlighted now to inform the supplier.
Goods received note should be prepared by a goods-in official detailing exactly what was received.	
GRN should be matched to delivery note.	Identifies shortfall errors made upon delivery where goods are not physically in accordance with the supplier's records of despatch. Need to inform supplier highlighted.
Multi-part GRN for subsequent **matching** and information.	Avoids paying an invoice without proof of delivery of goods invoiced. Provides written evidence for: (1) update stores records; (2) match with delivery notes; (3) comparison with invoice in creditors' section.
Invoice and payment	
Authorisation of invoice prior to payment.	Avoids paying for goods that have not been received.
Authorisation should include: (1) checking that invoice agrees to order and GRN. (2) Only then should the invoice be passed to a more senior individual for payment (segregation of duties).	Segregation of duties helps avoid fraud.

The effect of value added tax

Value added tax on standard-rated supplies may be reclaimed by the business on its allowable expenditure **only**.

Example

You are the creditors' ledger clerk for Princess Manufacturing Limited. You have received the following invoice from the business' landlord.

Required

(a) Check the invoice for clerical accuracy.

(b) Describe the procedures for dealing with this invoice.

Park Lane Properties Ltd

28 Higher Lane
Prestwich
Manchester M14 8PD

Tel: 0161 894 5677
Fax: 0161 894 8233

Tax point: 23 July 19X5

INVOICE **No. 75317** **VAT Reg No: 456 8993 78**

Princess Manufacturing Limited
456 Barlow Moor Road
Chorlton-cum-Hardy
Manchester M21 8TR

Date

Letting of property	£
Rent for the quarter ended 31 July 19X5	
4 months @ £330 per month	1,320
VAT @ 0%	0
Total payable	1,320

Solution

Errors

- The charge is for a quarter's rent (three months) but the invoice is for four months.
- Rent is an exempt supply not a zero-rated supply.

Action

You must:

- date stamp invoice;
- give it next number;
- code invoice;
- record in purchase invoice register;
- note problems in register;
- write to landlord and ask him to send a credit note.

Questions

1 (AAT CA J92)

You are asked to check some invoices received before they are entered into the appropriate book of original entry. List two checks which should be carried out as a matter of routine to ensure that the company does not pay too much.

2 (AAT CA J94)

What would be the appropriate document to be used in each of the following cases?

(a) MEL Motor Factors Limited sends out a document to a credit customer on a monthly basis summarising the transactions that have taken place and showing the amount owed by the customer.

(b) MEL Motor Factors Limited sends out a document to a credit customer in order to correct an error where the customer has been overcharged on an invoice.

(c) MEL Motor Factors Limited wishes to buy certain goods from a supplier and sends a document requesting that those goods should be supplied.

3 (AAT CA D94)

The company receives an invoice from a supplier offering a 5% cash discount which amounts to £120. What would be the total of the invoice inclusive of VAT?

4 (AAT CA D92)

When passing a purchase invoice for payment, what two aspects need to be checked, other than calculations?

Summary

Checking accuracy of purchase invoices

- Compare to purchase order
- Compare to goods received notes/ delivery notes
- Checked for accuracy of pricing, VAT and discounts
- Checked for clerical accuracy

Coding of purchase invoices

- Date stamped
- Numbered sequentially
- Authorised
- Coded

VAT

- Reclaim VAT only if:
  - business registered for VAT;
  - supplier registered for VAT;
  - expenditure not disallowed;
  - business holds proper VAT invoice.

CHAPTER 12

Maintaining the Purchase Day Book

Objectives

This chapter covers the following performance criteria.

- Documents are correctly entered as primary accounting records in a form acceptable to the organisation.
- Suppliers' invoices and credit notes are correctly checked against ordering documentation and evidence that goods/services have been received.
- Calculations on suppliers' invoices and credit notes are correct.

Recording purchase invoices

Once purchase invoices have been approved, they should be recorded in the purchase day book or a similar record.

This is effectively a diary of all the credit purchase transactions of the business.

The purchase day book is a book of prime entry.

As the purchase invoices are transferred from the purchase invoice register to the purchase day book, the purchase register should be marked. Any purchase invoices not transferred should then be followed up at least once a month.

Analysing purchase invoices

The purchases should be analysed according to type and VAT where it is recoverable.

There is an extract from a typical purchase day book on the next page.

Purchase day book

Date	*Invoice no.*	*Code*	*Supplier*	*Total*	*01*	*02*	*03*	*04*	*VAT*
1 Feb 19X5	3569	265	Norweb	148.29	126.20				22.09
	3570	053	Calderwood & Co	98.60		98.60			
2 Feb	3580	259	Mellor & Cross	661.09	221.43	562.63			98.46
3 Feb	3586	360	Thompson Bros Limited	260.18			18.90		38.75
	3581	023	Cooplin Associates	18.90			231.55		
4 Feb	3582	056	Heywood Suppliers	272.07				38.61	40.52
5 Feb	3583	395	William Leggett	45.37					6.76
	3584	271	Melville Products	366.49	311.91				54.58
	3585	301	Quick-Bake	99.68	84.83				14.85
	3589	311	Rogers & Roebuck	135.25				115.11	20.14
				2,105.92	744.37	661.23	250.45	153.72	296.15

The link with the accounting records

Each week or month information is transferred from the **purchase day book** to the accounting records.

The information which is to be **posted** (ie transferred) is summarised using a **journal entry**.

This is likely to be a pre-printed standard form for routine transactions like purchases.

Here is a blank journal entry form.

Journal entry		No:	
Purchase day book			
Week ending			
Prepared by			
Authorised by			
Account	Code	Debit	Credit
Creditors' ledger control account	05666		
Purchase Group 01	02501		
Group 02	02502		
Group 03	02503		
Group 04	02504		
Group 05	02505		
VAT control account			
Totals			

Making returns

Returns may be made for various reasons, eg:

- faulty goods;
- excess goods delivered by supplier;
- unauthorised goods delivered;
- unsold goods purchased on a **sale or return** basis.

All goods must be recorded on a **returns outwards note**.

Recording returns

The return should not be recorded until the business receives a **credit note** from the supplier. This confirms that there is no longer a liability for these goods. A credit note from a supplier is sometimes known as a **debit note**.

The credit note should be checked for accuracy against the **returns outwards note**. The calculations and extensions on the credit note should also be checked.

Returns outwards note – Document recording returned goods sent back to supplier.

Debit note – Document sent to or received from a supplier showing the amount to which the business should be entitled in respect of returned goods.

The return outwards note might have four parts:

Part one – to be sent to supplier

Part two – to be kept by despatch department

Part three – sent to stores department to update records

Part four – sent to creditors' ledger department

Credit notes are recorded in the **purchase returns day book**. This is effectively the reverse of the purchase day book. (Purchase returns day book is a book of prime entry.)

At the end of each month each transaction is posted to the supplier's individual account in the creditors' ledger.

The total is posted to the creditors' ledger control account.

Questions

1 (AAT CA D94)

The sales and purchases day books are primary records used for listing data taken from source documents. Double-entry is carried out by transferring relevant totals from the day books into the general ledger.

True / False

2 (AAT CA D93)

What would be the appropriate document to be used in each of the following cases?

(a) Music World Limited sends a document to a customer showing the amount to be adjusted in the customer's account in respect of returned goods.

(b) Music World Limited sends a document to a supplier showing the amount to which Music World should be entitled in respect of returned goods.

(c) Music World Limited issues a document to a customer detailing goods supplied and indicating the amount that should be paid in respect of those goods.

3 (AAT CA J92)

In which of the primary records (books of original entry) would the following be entered?

(a) Invoices issued

(b) Invoices received

(c) Credit notes issued

(d) Credit notes received

(e) Bad debts written off

4 (AAT CA J92)

In which ledger would the account of Royal Sports Limited (a customer) appear?

5 (AAT CA J92)

In which ledger would the account of Sportsworld Limited (a supplier) appear?

6 (AAT CA J92)

Using a table to record your answers, what debit and credit entries would you make to correct the following errors?

(a) An invoice relating to a sale for £275 to B Lowe was entered in D Lowe's account.

(b) A credit note for £67 received from C Dent was entered in the relevant book of original entry as £76.

(c) Repairs to the computer costing £82 were debited to the equipment account.

7 (AAT CA J93)

What double entry would you make in the general ledger if you had to correct the following errors?

(a) An invoice received from Smith's Electrics Limited had been entered in the relevant day book but the VAT element of £14 had been omitted.

(b) The £98 total of the discounts allowed column in the cash book had been debited to discounts received.

(c) A credit note issued to a customer for £23 plus £4 VAT had been posted to the general ledger as a credit note received.

8 (AAT CA D94)

You have been asked to help resolve a problem concerning one of Chang Fashion Limited's suppliers.

The following details have been provided:

12 October 1994, purchase order P00234 sent to Ace Imports Limited.

Order for two boxes of jeans.

Delivery 26 October. One box contains cotton trousers instead of jeans (trousers not ordered).

Telephone call made by Mary Chang (the managing director) to Mr Brian Moody at Ace Imports Limited on 27 October. Brian Moody promises to deliver a replacement box and take away the trousers within 14 days.

Invoice dated 16 November received from Ace Imports Limited on 18 November. Invoice is for two boxes of jeans at £764.92 each and refers to order P00234.

To date no further action from Ace Imports Limited.

Required

Draft a letter to Brian Moody at Ace Imports Limited, 165 Dell Trading Estate, Southampton SO10 4EP. The letter is to be signed by Rahul Divan (the company secretary) and should include the following.

(a) Details of the original error

(b) The arrangements made to correct the error.

(c) A request for the exchange of products to take place immediately.

(d) A request for early notification and the issue of a credit note if (c) is not possible.

Summary

Purchase day book

- Records purchase invoices
- Diary of credit transaction
- Analyses purchases by product type **excluding** VAT where it is recoverable
- Analyses VAT separately where it is recoverable
- Totals posted to accounting records using journal entry

Returns

- Faulty goods
- Excess goods
- Unauthorised goods
- Recorded on returns outwards note

Purchase returns day book

- Records credit notes received from suppliers
- Analysed like purchase day book

CHAPTER 13

Maintaining the Creditors' Ledger

Objectives

This chapter covers the following performance criteria.

- Entries in the primary records are correctly transferred to the correct ledger accounts.
- Adjustments involving creditors' accounts are properly authorised and documented, and are correctly transferred to the correct ledger accounts.
- The control account in the general ledger is reconciled with the total of balances in the purchases (creditors') ledger.

Suppliers' individual accounts

So that a business knows how much it owes to each credit supplier, it maintains a book called the creditors' ledger (or purchase ledger). The creditors' ledger consists of records of amounts owed to each supplier (or creditor). Each supplier has his or her own page or card (or account) in the ledger.

The account will effectively be the reverse of the accounts in the debtors' ledger.

Account name: Robert Jones **Code:** J53

Date	*Transaction*	£	*Date*	*Transaction*	£
			01.8.X3	Invoice 0992	✓ 236.93
			03.8.X3	Invoice 0996	✓ 92.58
31.8.X3	Balance b/f	399.04	10.8.X3	Invoice 1032	69.53
		399.04			399.04
03.9.X3	Cash 293	✓ 329.51	01.9.X3	Balance b/f	399.04
30.9.X3	Balance c/f	69.53			
		399.04			399.04

Purchase invoices are recorded on the right-hand side (credit side). Individual transactions are transferred from the **purchase day book**.

Note that the amount recorded for each purchase invoice is the **total including VAT**, as this is what is **owed** to each supplier.

The source for the cash payments is the analysed cash book. Again, items are matched as they are paid.

Example

Here is an account from the creditors' ledger of Frosty Limited.

Account name: **Code:**

Date	*Transaction*	£	*Date*	*Transaction*	£

Required

Write up the account for Jones Brothers, account number PJ06. This is a new customer.

Frosty Limited has only been trading for a short time and is not yet registered for VAT.

Purchase invoices

02.5.X1	9268	£638.26
06.6.X1	9369	£594.27
15.6.X1	9402	£368.24
19.6.X1	9568	£268.54

Cash payments

01.6.X1	9268	£619.11 (3% discount taken)
28.6.X1	9369	£582.38 (2% discount taken)

Solution

Account name: Jones Brothers **Account number:** PJ06

Date	*Transaction*		£	*Date*	*Transaction*		£
31.5.X1	Balance c/f		638.26	02.5.X1	Invoice 9268	✓	638.26
			638.26				638.26
01.6.X1	Cash 9268	✓	619.11	01.6.X1	Balance b/f		638.26
28.6.X1	Discount	✓	19.15	06.6.X1	Invoice 9369	✓	594.27
30.6.X1	Cash 9369	✓	582.38	15.6.X1	Invoice 9402		368.24
	Discount	✓	11.89	19.6.X1	Invoice 9568		268.54
	Balance c/f		636.78				
			1,869.31				1,869.31
				30.6.X1	Balance b/f		636.78

Note. The discounts taken have been written off. The information on discounts taken would normally come from the **memorandum** column of the analysed cash book.

Other unusual items in the creditors' ledger

Adjustments may be needed in the individual suppliers' accounts in the creditors' ledger for:

- contras
- errors.

Example

You are the creditors' ledger clerk for Davies and Chapman Limited, a wholesaler of dairy products.

You are new to your current job. You have been reviewing the following accounts of Foster Brothers, a fairly small supplier.

Account name: Foster Brothers **Account number:** F97

Date	*Transaction*	£	*Date*	*Transaction*	£
05.5.X1	Cash overpaid	2.96	09.9.X1	Invoice 536	✓ 53.98
30.9.X1	Balance c/f	51.02			
		53.98			53.98
13.12.X1	Cash	✓ 53.98	01.10.X1	Balance b/f	51.02
31.12.X1	Balance c/f	110.00	12.12.X1	Invoice 628	112.96
		163.98			163.98
15.2.X2	Cash	62.50	01.1.X2	Balance b/f	110.00
28.2.X2	Balance c/f	195.30	03.2.X2	Invoice 698	73.90
			03.2.X2	Invoice 698	73.90
		257.80			257.80
			01.3.X2	Balance b/f	195.30

(1) Invoice 698 has been posted twice in error.

(2) The cash payment of 15.2.X2 relates to another supplier.

(3) Foster Brothers is also a customer. The balance on its account in the debtors' ledger is £56.90.

Required

Write up the account for these items.

Solution

Account name: Foster Brothers **Account number:** F97

Date	*Transaction*	£	*Date*	*Transaction*	£
05.5.X1	Cash overpaid	2.96	09.9.X1	Invoice 536	✓ 53.98
30.9.X1	Balance c/f	51.02			
		53.98			53.98
13.12.X1	Cash	✓ 53.98	01.10.X1	Balance b/f	51.02
31.12.X1	Balance c/f	110.00	12.12.X1	Invoice 628	112.96
		163.98			163.98
15.2.X2	Cash	✓ 62.50	01.1.X2	Balance b/f	110.00
28.2.X2	Balance c/f	195.30	03.2.X2	Invoice 698	✓ 73.90
			03.2.X2	Invoice 698	73.90
		257.80			257.80
01.3.X2	Error –		01.3.X2	Balance b/f	195.30
	invoice 698	✓ 73.90	01.3.X2	Cash error	✓ 62.50
	posted twice	<u>C</u> 56.90			
01.3.X2	Contra	127.00			
	Balance c/f				
		257.80			257.80

Creditors' ledger control account

Within the nominal ledger the total amount payable to suppliers (creditors) is shown in the **creditors' ledger control account.** It is also known as the **purchase ledger control account**.

The total of **credit purchases** (from the purchase day book) and **cash payments** and **discounts** (from the analysed cash book) are posted to this account via a journal entry.

This account shows the total amount payable to creditors. It does *not* give details about individual amounts owed to suppliers. (These are in the creditors' ledger.)

However, the total outstanding on the **control account** must equal the total of the balances on the customers' individual accounts in the **creditors' ledger.**

A creditors' ledger control account normally appears like this.

Creditors' ledger control account

	£		£
Payments to suppliers per analysed cash book		Balance b/f	X
		Purchases per purchase day book	X
Cash	X		
Discount received	X		
Returns – per day book	X		
Contra with debtors' ledger control a/c	X		
Balance c/f	X		
	X		X
		Balance b/f	X

Creditors' ledger reconciliation

At each month end the creditors' ledger clerk must **reconcile** the **creditors' ledger control account** and the **creditors' ledger,** just as the debtors' ledger clerk performed the debtors' ledger reconciliation.

Remember that as well as investigating and discovering the differences, the **control account** and the individual accounts in the **creditors' ledger** must also be amended for any errors.

Adjustments to the creditors' ledger control account

Any corrections or adjustments made to the creditors' ledger control account must be documented as a journal entry (including a narrative).

For instance, the total purchases for the month were posted from the purchase day book as £2,547.98 instead of £2,457.98. The business only purchases one product.

The journal entry to correct this error will be as follows.

Journal entry		**No:** 253	
Prepared by: P Charming			
Authorised by: U Sister			
Date: 29.8.X5			
Narrative: To correct error in posting to creditors' ledger control account			
Account	**Code**	**Debit**	**Credit**
Creditors' ledger control	c56	90	
Purchases	w34		90
TOTALS		90	90

Adjustments in the creditors' ledger

Adjustments in the creditors' ledger do not need to be documented on a journal entry. Journal entries are only required for adjustments to the nominal ledger.

These adjustments should be recorded somewhere, for instance in a separate notebook.

Illustration

Gemma is the purchases section leader. It is her job to identify problems and errors in the creditors' ledger and deal with them accordingly. She has decided to prepare a creditors' ledger control account to determine whether there are any errors or discrepancies she can easily correct.

The following information is available.

Creditors' ledger: accounts with balances outstanding

Thomas Limited

Date	*Transaction*	£	*Date*	*Transaction*	£
05.1.X1	Cash paid pg 6	2,350	01.1.X1	Invoice 115	2,000
17.1.X1	Returns/CRN 5	520	26.1.X1	Invoice 121	2,350
Balance c/f		1,480			
					4,350
		4,350			

Horace Shades

Date	*Transaction*	£	*Date*	*Transaction*	£
15.1.X1	Discount received	80	06.1.X1	Invoice 116	6,000
Balance c/f		14,270		Invoice 117	2,350
				Invoice 116	6,000
		14,350			14,350

Zipped & Buttoned Limited

Date	*Transaction*	£	*Date*	*Transaction*	£
15.1.X1	Cash paid	4,600	06.1.X1	Invoice 119	2,350
Balance c/f		2,450	12.1.X1	Invoice 120	4,700
		7,050			7,050

Northumbrian Water

Date	*Transaction*	£	*Date*	*Transaction*	£
Balance c/f		1,000	06.1.X1	Invoice 118	1,000
		1,000			1,000

Extract from purchase day book

Date	*Inv. No.*	*Description*	*Value*	*Purchases*	*Heat & light*	*Rent & rates*	*VAT*
01.1.X1	115	Thomas Limited	2,350	2,000			350
06.1.X1	116	Horace Shades	6,000	6,000			1,050
06.1.X1	117	Horace Shades	2,350	2,000		1,000	350
06.1.X1	118	Northumbrian	1,000				
06.1.X1	119	Water	2,350	2,000			350
12.1.X1	120	Zipped & Buttoned	4,700	4,000			700
		Zipped & Buttoned					
			18,750	16,000		1,000	2,800

Extract from cash book (payments)

Date	*Cheque No.*	*Supplier*	*Bank*	*Discount received 'memo'*
05.1.X1	CQ No. 1110	Thomas Limited	2,350	
15.1.X1	CQ No. 1111	Zipped & Buttoned	4,600	80
			6,950	80

Extract from cheque stubs

Cheque stub 1110 £2,350

Cheque stub 1111 £4,620

Extract from returns day book

Date	*CRN No.*	*Supplier*	*Reason*	*Amount*	*Goods*	*VAT*
17.1.X1	5	Horace Shades	Faulty goods	611	520	91

Required

Identify the problems and draft correcting journal adjustments, assuming there was nothing owed to suppliers at the start of January.

Approach

First compare carefully the creditors' ledger accounts with the purchase day book – tick off each item or note the errors.

1 Zipped & Buttoned Limited

		£		£
Payments			Balance b/f	–
	Cash (point 2)	6,950	Purchases from purchase day book (point 1)	19,800
	Discounts received	80		
Returns (from day book)		611		
Balance c/f		12,159		
		19,800		19,800

Point 1 – Cross casts of purchase day book show an error on invoice 116. The total column should read £7,050 instead of £6,000 as given.

The revised total for the purchase day book should be £19,800 instead of originally totalling £18,750.

Point 2 – Checking cash book payments with the cheque stubs reveals that cheque 1111 to Zipped & Buttoned was incorrectly recorded as £4,600 instead of £4,620. A bank reconciliation should have detected this error. However, both the creditors' ledger control account and the cash book are incorrect. Therefore a journal adjustment is required.

Dr	Creditors' ledger control account	£20	
Cr	Cash		£20

2 Listing of creditors' balances extracted from the original ledger cards

	£
Thomas Limited	1,480
Horace Shades	14,270
Zipped & Buttoned	2,450
Northumbrian Water	1,000
	19,200
Balance per creditors' control account	12,159
Balance of extracted creditors	19,200
Total difference	7,041

3 Creditors' ledger control account

	£
Balance per creditors' control account	12,159
Less: Cash omitted in the cash book (point 2 above)	(20)
	12,139
Add: Thomas invoice 121 omitted from the purchase day book	2,350
Corrected total per creditors' ledger	14,489

4 Correction of individual ledger accounts

Thomas Limited

Invoice 115 should be included gross in the creditors' ledger, not net

Cr				£350

Credit note 5 in returns day book was from Horace Shades for £611.

Its value and its creditors' ledger account are wrong.

Dr	Horace Shades Limited		£611	
	Cr	Thomas Limited		£520

Horace Shades

Discount received was from Zipped & Buttoned, **not** Horace Shades. Therefore:

Dr	Zipped & Buttoned		£80	
	Cr	Horace Shades		£80

Invoice 116 has been included twice in error.

Dr	Horace Shades		£6,000	

It is also given net instead of gross:

	Cr	Horace Shades (the VAT element)		£1,050

(*Note.* The creditors' ledger is not part of the double-entry system; it is the creditors' control account which is. Corrections in the creditors' ledger may be one-sided, but the list of balances must always reconcile to the creditors' control account in total.)

5 Revised creditors' ledger account

Thomas Limited

Date	*Transaction*	£	*Date*	*Transaction*	£
05.1.X1	Cash paid	2,350	01.1.X1	Invoice 115	2,350
Balance c/f		2,350	26.1.X1	Invoice 121	2,350
		4,700			4,700

Horace Shades

Date	*Transaction*	£	*Date*	*Transaction*	£
17.1.X1	Returns CR 5	611	06.1.X1	Invoice 116	7,050
Balance c/f		8,789	06.1.X1	Invoice 117	2,350
		9,400			9,400

Zipped & Buttoned Limited

Date	*ransaction*	£	*Date*	*Transaction*	£
15.1.X1	Cash paid	4,620	06.1.X1	Invoice 119	2,350
15.1.X1	Discount received	80	12.1.X1	Invoice 120	4,700
Balance c/f		2,350			7,050
		7,050			

Northumbrian Water

Date	*Transaction*	£	*Date*	*Transaction*	£
Balance c/f		1,000	16.1.X1	Invoice 118	1,000
		1,000			1,000

Note. These accounts would normally be corrected by adjustments. These accounts have been rewritten to make the solution clearer.

6 New extraction of balances

	£
Thomas Limited	2,350
Horace Shades	8,789
Zipped & Buttoned	2,350
Northumbrian Water	1,000
	14,489

This reconciles with the corrected creditors' ledger control account (see 3).

Questions

1 (AAT CA J94)

Which account in the general ledger would you debit and which account in the general ledger would you credit in respect of the following:

(a) A set-off is to be made between Peter Allen's' account in the sales ledger, which has a balance of £200, and his account in the purchase ledger, which has a balance of £450.

(b) The correction of an error where it has been found that an invoice for £36, received from Allied Brokers Limited for insurance, has been entered in the various columns of the purchase day book as £63. (*Note.* There is no VAT charged on insurance.)

(c) The correction of an error where it has been discovered that the purchase of £10 of stationery has been debited to the purchases account.

2 (AAT CA D92)

State the document appropriate to each of the following stages for purchasing and paying for goods.

(a) Notification to purchasing manager of need to order.

(b) Request to supplier to supply goods.

(c) Postal notification by supplier that goods have been despatched.

(d) Form accompanying goods sent by supplier.

(e) Physical receipt of goods by purchaser.

(f) Notification by purchaser to supplier of amount paid.

3 (AAT CA J94)

Give one reason for maintaining a creditors' ledger control account.

4 (AAT CA D92)

Would each of the following cause a difference between the totals of the general ledger debit and credit account balances at 31 March?

Yes / No

(a) A purchase invoice for £36 from P Swift was credited to P Short's account in the creditors' ledger.

(b) A purchase invoice for £96 not entered in the purchases day book.

(c) An undercast of £20 in the total column of the purchases day book.

(d) A purchase invoice from Short & Long for £42 for goods for resale, entered as £24 in the purchases day book.

5 (AAT CA D92)

Show the transfer journal entry for correcting item 4(d) above in the general ledger, including an appropriate narrative.

Summary

Creditors' ledger

- Separate from nominal ledger
- Contains individual accounts for each customer
- Shows how much the business owes each supplier
- Compiled from **detailed information** from books of prime entry

Creditors' ledger control account

- One of the accounts in the nominal ledger
- Shows **total** creditors payable
- Compiled from totals from books of prime entry.

CHAPTER 14

Using Information About Creditors

Objectives

This chapter covers the following performance criteria.

- The organisation's policies, regulations, procedures and timescales are correctly observed.
- Discrepancies, unusual features and queries are identified and either resolved or referred to the appropriate person.
- Communications with creditors regarding accounts are handled promptly, courteously and effectively.

Supplier statement reconciliation

Statements are normally received monthly. If they are not normally received, then they should be requested.

The statements can be used to check the balances payable according to the individual suppliers' accounts in the creditors' ledger.

The comparison of the statement and the supplier's account is a type of reconciliation.

The reconciliation has a set format:

		£
Balance per supplier statement		X
Less:	Goods in transit (1)	(X)
	Cash in transit (2)	(X)
Other items		X
Balance per creditors' ledger		X

(1) Goods in transit must be deducted because they have been recorded as sales by the supplier, but not by the business as they have not yet been received.

(2) Cash in transit (ie a cheque in the post) must be deducted because the business has recorded it in the creditors' ledger and nominal ledger, but it does not appear on the supplier's statement.

Mini case study

Here is an extract from the accounting records of Scott Brothers.

This is its account for Nemo Limited (a regular supplier) in the creditors' ledger.

Account name: Nemo Limited

Date	*Transaction*	£	*Date*	*Transaction*	£
13 Jun	Cn 19556	✓23.60	12 May	Invoice 19556	✓92.35
30 Jun	Balance c/f	68.75			
		92.35			92.35
			01 Jul	Balance b/f	68.75
31 Jul	Balance b/f	305.52	09 Jul	Invoice 20021	102.96
			18 Jul	Invoice 20523	✓133.81
		305.52			305.52
30 Aug	Cash p 911	✓305.52	01 Aug	Balance b/f	305.52
31 Aug	Balance c/f	286.70	02 Aug	Invoice 20738	56.50
			10 Aug	Invoice 21101	✓230.20
		592.22			592.22
			01 Sep	Balance brought forward	286.70

(*Note.* The invoices have a different reference (purchase invoice register number) in the books of Scott Brothers.)

NEMO Limited
23 Park Road
Oldham
OL1 1VR

To: Scott Brothers
34 Festival Way
Oldham
OL2 3BD

Date: 31 August 19X3

STATEMENT

Date	*Transaction*	*Total*	*Current*	*30+*	*60+*
12 May 19X3	Invoice 2569	92.35			92.35
13 Jun 19X3	CN 2659	(23.60)		102.69	(23.60)
09 Jul 19X3	Invoice 2701	102.69	56.50	133.81	
18 Jul 19X3	Invoice 2753	133.81	230.20		
02 Aug 19X3	Invoice 2889	56.50	243.24		
10 Aug 19X3	Invoice 2901	230.20			
28 Aug 19X3	Invoice 3114	243.24			
	TOTALS	835.19	529.94	236.50	68.75

May we remind you our credit terms are 30 days

Creditors' ledger reconciliation

		£
Balance per supplier statement		835.19
Less:	Goods in transit (Invoice 3114)	(243.24)
	Cash in transit (Cash p 911)	(305.52)
Other items – transposition error (Invoice 20021)		0.27
Balance per creditors' ledger		286.70

The transposition error occurred in the purchase day book.

The individual account of Nemo Limited in the creditors' ledger and the creditors' ledger control account in the nominal ledger must be corrected for the transposition error.

The other items (cash in transit; goods in transit) are timing differences which will correct themselves in the next month. No adjustment is required.

Corrected account

Account name: Nemo Limited

Date	*Transaction*	£	*Date*	*Transaction*	£
13 Jun	Cn 19556	✓23.60	12 May	Invoice 19556	✓92.35
30 Jun	Balance c/f	68.75			
		92.35			92.35
			01 Jul	Balance b/f	68.75
			09 Jul	Invoice 20021	✓102.96
31 Jul	Balance b/f	305.52	18 Jul	Invoice 20523	✓133.81
		305.52			305.52
30 Aug	Cash p 911	✓305.52	01 Aug	Balance b/f	305.52
31 Aug	Balance c/f	286.70	02 Aug	Invoice 20738	✓56.50
			10 Aug	Invoice 2101	✓230.20
		592.22			592.22
01 Sep	Transposition error (Invoice 20021)	✓0.27	01 Sep	Balance b/f	286.70

Communicating with creditors

Differences may arise between the supplier's statement and the individual supplier account as a result of errors made by the supplier. These might include:

- failure to deduct settlement discounts despite prompt payment;
- disputed invoices in the total balance;
- transposition or other clerical errors.

The business should make contact with the supplier by telephone or by letter. Communication should be prompt and courteous. Failure to resolve problems quickly may damage the relationship of the business with the supplier.

Example

You are the creditors' ledger clerk at Hay and Partners. Whilst performing a supplier's statement reconciliation for Netherfield Limited, you notice that it has deducted payments in respect of invoice numbers 0942 and 0945, but has not deducted the 5% settlement discounts of £100 and £157 respectively. From the statements it appears that payment was received within the time limit for the discounts.

Draft a letter to Netherfield Limited requesting that the discount be honoured.

Solution

Hay and Partners
8 Main Road
London EC1 4AA

Debtors' Ledger Clerk
Netherfield Limited
Unit 8
Leaside Industrial Estate
Everthorpe ET16 3FG

25 November 19X5

Dear Sir

Settlement discounts allowed

I refer to your invoices 0942 and 0945 for which payment was made, in accordance with your terms of trade, after deduction of a 5% settlement discount. I note from the supplier's statement dated 31 October 19X5 that you have not deducted this discount from our account, although the payments were made within the time stipulated and appear on the statement.

I would be grateful if you would amend our account to reflect the discount allowed as soon as possible.

Yours faithfully

Questions

1 (AAT CA D92)

Which of the following errors and omissions would be discovered by checking against suppliers' statements of account at the month end?

(a) A purchase invoice for £36 from P Swift was credited to P Short's account in the creditors' ledger.

(b) A purchase invoice for £96 not entered in the purchases day book.

(c) An undercast of £20 in the total column of the purchases day book.

(d) A purchases invoice from Short & Long for £42 for goods for resale, entered as £24 in the purchases day book.

2 (AAT CA D93)

A statement for Music World Limited has been received from International Records Limited showing a balance outstanding at yesterday's date (30 November) of £8,490. According to the purchases ledger the balance should be £7,160. The difference is due to the following items, neither of which appears on the statement.

(a) A cheque for £1,200 made payable to International Records Limited. Issued and sent off by Music World on 17 November (cheque no. 000549). The cheque should have arrived by now, particularly as it was sent by first class post.

(b) £130 of returned CDs despatched to International Records Limited on 15 November. A credit note was received by Music World on 19 November.

Draft a letter to be signed by Tony Bryant. This will be faxed to Cathy Price at International Records (142 Durham Road, Newcastle NN12 1BE). The letter should point out the difference in the balances and the reasons for it, and should ask for suitable action to be taken.

Summary

Supplier statement reconciliation

- Form of internal control
- Compares supplier's statement with creditor's individual account in creditors' ledger
- Timing differences will reverse next month – no adjustment required
- Errors may have to be corrected in both creditors' ledger and creditors' ledger control account (dependent upon type of error)

CHAPTER 15

Answers to Chapter Questions

Financial Accounting

1

(a) Revenue

(b) Capital

2

(a) Capital

(b) Capital

(c) Capital

3

(a) Asset

(b) Revenue

(c) Expense

(d) Liability

4

Bertie Dooks – Ledger accounts

Cash account

	£		£
Capital account	5,000	Rent	150
Sales	35	Purchases	140
Debtors	1	Repairs	25
		Advertising	2
		Creditors	175
		Cleaning	5
		Drawings	5
		Balance c/f	4,534
	5,036		5,036
Balance b/f	4,534		

Creditors' account

	£		£
Cash	175	Purchases	275
Balance c/f	100		
			275
	275		
			275
		Balance b/f	100

Debtors' account

	£		£
		Cash	1
Sales	3	Balance c/f	2
	3		3
Balance b/f	2		

Capital account

	£		£
Balance c/f	5,000	Cash	5,000
	——		——
	5,000		5,000
	——		——
		Balance b/f	5,000

Sales account

	£		£
Balance c/f	38	Cash	35
		Schoolmaster	3
	—		—
	38		38
	—		—
		Balance b/f	38

Purchases account

	£		£
Cash	140	Balance c/f	415
J Fox	275		
	——		——
	415		415
	——		——
Balance b/f	415		

Rent account

	£		£
Cash	150	Balance c/f	150
	——		——
	150		150
	——		——
Balance b/f	150		

Repairs account

	£		£
Cash	25	Balance c/f	25
	—		—
	25		25
	—		—
Balance b/f	25		

Advertising account

	£		£
Cash	2	Balance c/f	2
	—		—
	2		2
	—		—
Balance b/f	2		

Cleaning account

	£		£
Cash	5	Balance c/f	5
	—		—
	5		5
	—		—
Balance b/f	5		

Drawings account

	£		£
Cash	5	Balance c/f	5
	—		—
	5		5
	—		—
Balance b/f	5		

5

(a)	Debit	Asset
(b)	Credit	Liability
(c)	Credit	Liability
(d)	Credit	Capital (liability to owners)
(e)	Debit	Asset

Chapter 1

1

(a) Bank balance on 22 July 19T5 was £1,812.36

(b) Branch address is 10, Yorkshire Street, Headingley, Leeds.

2

To be retained by receiving bank

For the credit of TRADING COMPANY LIMITED

Cheques etc for collection to be included in total credit of £ ________ paid in __________ 19

	£	brought forward	£	brought forward	£
Carried forward		carried forward	£	Total cheques etc	£

Date 29/8/X4

Cashier's stamp and initials

56 – 28 – 48

FINANCIAL BANK PLC

EXETER HIGH STREET

Credit Trading Company Limited

Fee	No Chqs

Paid in by AN Other

Address/Ref No. ______

£50 Notes		
£20 Notes	60.	00
£10 Notes	20.	00
£5 Notes	15.	00
£1 Coins	28.	00
50p	7.	50
20p	3.	40
Silver	4.	10
Bronze	.	59
Total Cash	138.	59
Cheques, POs etc		
TOTAL £	138.	59

3

120

4

FINANCIAL BANK PLC
SHEPHERD'S BUSH GREEN BRANCH
352 SHEPHERD'S BUSH GREEN W12 6TH

fb

01 - 89 - 34

26 June 19 *X3*

Pay *S. Greenwood & Co Limited* or order

Twenty eight pounds 34 only

£ 28 - 34

MISS S SMITH

S. E. Smith

000267   01 – 89 – 34   47586909

5

8 × 1p	=	8p
5 × 2p	=	10p
1 ×10p	=	10p
		28p

6

Money can be defined as anything which is generally acceptable as a method of settling a debt.

Chapter 2

1

(a) No

(b) Any two from the following:

- (i) The cheque has not been signed.
- (ii) The cheque is out of date.
- (iii) The words and figures on the cheque are not the same.

2

Any three from:

(a) The cheque guarantee card should not have expired.

(b) The signature on the cheque should match with the one on the card.

(c) The amount of the cheque should not exceed the guarantee amount of the card.

(d) The drawer's name and any other details on the card should match with those on the cheque.

3

False

4

(a) The card is not on a list of stolen cards.

(b) The signature on the card agrees with the one given by the customer.

(c) The card is not out of date.

(Or alternative acceptable answers.)

5

(a) Yes

(b) The credit card company can be contacted by phone to authorise use of the card for the purchase.

6

The amount of cash that should be in the cash register at the end of the day can be calculated from the opening float and the value of the cash sales which will have been recorded. This sum can then be checked against the actual amount of cash held.

7

Night safe

8

(a) Yes

(b) Under the Sale of Goods Act, the jeans must be of satisfactory quality. In this case, it would appear that they were not and the customer is therefore entitled to a refund. The sign has no effect since it is not possible to avoid the conditions of the Sale of Goods Act in this way (Unfair Contract Terms Act 1977).

9

(a) No

(b) Contracts of sale are between the buyer and the seller, not the buyer and the manufacturer.

(c)

(c)	Debit sales returns	£200
	Debit VAT	£35
	Credit cash	£235

10

True

11

False

12

False

13

The trade discount.

The trade discount reduces the price of the goods without any conditions. A cash discount does not reduce the price as such but is a settlement discount. Music World will only receive a 10% reduction if they make payment within a stipulated period.

14

Draft letter

HAIRDRESSING SUPPLIES Limited
(Head Office)

Station Road, Dorking, Surrey GU10 1ZZ

The Accountant
Allied Hairdressers Limited
99 Castle Street
Chichester
Sussex

1 April

Dear Sirs

Cash discount

Thank you for your cheque for £195 in respect of our invoice dated 1 March.

We note, however, that you have deducted cash discount of 2.5% before payment, which was made at least two weeks after the date up to which discount was allowed.

You will be aware that our terms of payment are that 2.5% cash discount may be deducted if payment is made within 10 days of the date of receipt of the invoice, otherwise payment must be made in full by the end of the month following the date of the invoice.

We do not intend to press for payment of the balance in this instance, but would ask you to note our terms of payment in respect of future transactions.

Yours faithfully

Marjorie Thistlethwaite

Marjorie Thistlethwaite
Company Accountant

Chapter 3

1

Different aspects of the work or job are carried out by different people so that the work of each person is subject to an independent check in the course of another person's duty.

2

	Discount	*Take discount?*
(a)	£5.99	No
(b)	£6.88	Yes
(c)	£3.36	Yes
(d)	£7.83	No
(e)	£1.42	No

3

£21

Note. The answer is calculated as follows.

	£
Output VAT on sales (£846 × 17.5/117.5)	126
Less: Input VAT on purchases (80 × £7.50 × 17.5%)	(105)
	21

4

A zero-rated supply

5

£1,645,000

Note. The answer is calculated as follows.

	£
VAT on sales (£1,821,250 × 17.5/117.5)	271,250
Less: Balance on VAT account	(26,250)
VAT on purchases	245,000
Purchases = £245,000 × 117.5/17.5	£1,645,000

6

VAT registration number of the supplier. This is totally different from the invoice number and it is vital that it is included on a VAT invoice.

7

Draft letter

HAIRDRESSING SUPPLIES Limited

(Head Office)

Station Road, Dorking, Surrey GU10 1ZZ

Mr F Petersley
Sales Manager
Hairdressing Supplies Limited (Sales division)
Park Road
Guildford
Surrey GU1 1AA

31 March

Dear Fred

Sales commission scheme

Thank you for your letter dated 27 March.

As you probably know, the size of our turnover dictates that we register for VAT. This, in turn, makes it incumbent upon us to charge VAT on all taxable supplies invoiced to customers. The VAT is ultimately paid to Customs and Excise, less the VAT we have ourselves been charged on our purchases.

Thus, although VAT is charged to customers, it is not part of our sales turnover and is therefore not included as such when computing gross profit, upon which the sales bonus is calculated.

I trust that the above explanation clarifies the position for you. Please do not hesitate to contact me again should you have any further queries.

Yours sincerely

Marjorie Thistlethwaite

Marjorie Thistlethwaite
Company Accountant

Chapter 4

1

(a)	Customer – Bailor	Bank – Bailee
(b)	Customer – Debtor	Bank – Creditor
(c)	Customer – Principal	Bank – Agent
(d)	Customer – Mortgagor	Bank – Mortgagee

2

The funds held are owed by the bank to the company. From the bank's point of view, they are therefore a liability.

3

Royal Bank Ltd

4

Principal – Agent

5

MEL MOTOR FACTORS LTD

23 Trafford Park, Manchester MM7 6SE

The Manager
Royal Bank Ltd
18 Preston Road
Manchester MM9 0BU

15 June 19X4

Dear Sir

MEL Motor Factors Ltd – Current account number 40319442

We have today received a statement of the company's current account dated 14 June 1994. Unfortunately, two items appear to have been included in the statement in error.

On 10 June, £471.50 was paid out of the account to Western Finance by standing order under reference P/T000654ML. The standing order mandate submitted to you authorised 12 monthly payments which were to commence on 10 July 1994 and not 10 June.

On 12 June, cheque number 409662 for £240.62 was debited to the account. According to our records, we have not made a payment for this sum and in fact we cannot trace having had a cheque book containing this cheque number. Under the circumstances we can only assume that the cheque was not issued by this company.

We should be grateful if you would kindly arrange for the account to be credited with the two amounts in question and for the standing order details to be checked in your records. If you or your staff have any queries relating to these payments, then please contact me at the above address or by telephone on ....

Yours faithfully

Cathy Payne

Cathy Payne
Accountant

MEL Motor Factors Ltd, Registered Office: 23 Trafford Park, Manchester MM7 6SE
Registered in England, Number 4443561

6

A credit card

7

(a) Barclays Bank pays Lloyds Bank the sum of £2m.

(b) Adjustment of the bank's balances held at the Bank of England.

8

National Bank plc

9

The cheque must pass through the clearing system before the Mid-West Bank knows whether or not it has been paid. In the meantime, the bank may be reluctant to allow David to draw out cash against uncleared funds.

10

(a) Chang Fashions Limited

(b) Royal Bank plc

(c) K Mitchell

11

(a) Yes

(b) No

12

(a) Yes

(b) A Hallchurch has endorsed the cheque in blank which converts it into a bearer cheque. It can therefore be paid in by the holder who in this case is MEL Motor Factors Limited.

13

(a) Yes

(b) No

14

(a) Two vertical lines, drawn on a cheque with the name of a bank written between the lines.

(b) The paying bank should only pay the bank named in the crossing which therefore becomes the collecting bank.

15

The Royal Bank plc can only make a payment to the bank named in the crossing. The cheque must therefore be paid in at the Watford High Street branch of the National Bank.

16

Direct debit

17

(a) Banker's draft

(b) A banker's draft is a cheque drawn by a bank upon itself. The creditor is therefore assured of receiving the funds since there is no risk of the draft being dishonoured.

18

MEMORANDUM

To: Jane Alder Date: 1 December 19X3

From: Tony Bryant

Subject: Company bank account

I have been reviewing the company bank account details covering the last six-monthly period. Although we made use of our overdraft facility for 42 days out of 182, the account was in credit for the remaining 140 days. The balance has in fact been as high as £84,525 credit with an average across the six months of £38,640 credit.

In view of the interest that could be earned by holding surplus funds in a deposit account rather than the current account, I would suggest that we arrange for such an account to be opened. If you are in agreement, could I please have your authorisation to instruct the bank to make the necessary arrangements.

19

FUTURE ELECTRICAL LIMITED

31 Watford Way, Banbury BN7 021

Mr B Travers
Managing Director
Curran Stores Limited
14 Woolford Road
Lanchaster L14 8QS

1 June 19X3

Dear Mr Travers

Curran Stores Limited – Balance of account

I refer to our telephone conversation of today concerning the current balance of your company account with ourselves. You will recall that the statement you received had a closing balance of £10,325 whilst your own records showed a balance of only £7,325.

The £3,000 difference relates to the unpaid cheque you were querying which had been included as an item on the statement. The cheque is enclosed and you will note that the words have been written as three pounds instead of three thousand pounds. Your bankers have therefore returned the cheque unpaid and we have consequently had to debit your account.

We should be grateful if you would kindly arrange for the cheque to be corrected and returned to us or, alternatively, for a replacement cheque to be issued.

We look forward to hearing from you.

Yours sincerely

Accounts Department

Chapter 5

1

(a) Cheque not paid by drawer's bank; probably because insufficient funds in drawer's account.

(b) Debtors' ledger control; cash at bank.

2

No

3

Credit entry

4

Debit entry

5

Credit entry

6

Debit entry

7

Credit entry

8

(a) £104

(b) £89

9

(a) £3,683

(b) None

Note. The bank reconciliation would appear as follows.

		£
Balance per cash book		4,892
Add:	Dividend	104
Less:	Direct debit	(89)
Adjusted balance		4,907
Balance per bank statement		8,590
Less:	Unpresented cheque (416)	(3,683)
Balance per cash book		4,907

10

£1,324 credit

11

£3,672 credit (–£184 + £30,291 – £26,435)

12

CHANG FASHIONS LIMITED

142 Regent Court, London WE4 1NN

Tel: 0181 803 6712

Mr Robert Massey
Policies Manager
Star Line Insurance Limited
23 Vicarage Road
Watford HE9 0BU

2 December 19X4

Dear Mr Massey

Motor policy no. ST9992342

I refer to your letter of 30 November advising me of the cancellation of the above policy.

We have checked our records which reveal, however, that a cheque for £526.00 made payable to Star Line Insurance Limited was issued by us on 17 November. Since the cheque was subsequently debited to our bank account on 24 November, I can only assume that it was received and banked by your company.

I should be grateful if you would kindly confirm to me as soon as possible that you have reinstated the policy and that there is therefore cover for vehicle E156 ESY.

Yours sincerely

Rahul Divan

Rahul Divan
Accountant and Company Secretary

Chang Fashions Limited, Registered Office: 142 Regent Court, London WE4 1NN
Registered in England, Number 5469971

13

(a) No

(b) £7,821 is a large sum of money and for security reasons the petty cash is normally used only for small items of expenditure.

14

Any two from the following.

(a) Should be kept securely in a locked box or safe, etc.

(b) All payments should be properly authorised.

(c) Should be the responsibility of one person.

(d) The amount of any one payment should be restricted.

15

This stops the petty cashier (or anyone else) from changing the amount to be paid to a higher figure then taking the difference.

It would be relatively easy to change numbers on their own, but it would be far more difficult to change the words and the numbers.

16

Voucher number; date; details of expenditure; authorised by; cash received by; account number.

17

£180

18

Imprest amount = Cash in hand + Value of vouchers

19

£105.59

20

MEMORANDUM

To: Phylis Cranborne Date: 29 March 19X2

From: Chris

Subject: Petty cash system

Marjorie has already notified me that she would like you to take charge of petty cash from 1 June next.

The main features of our present system are as follows:

(1) The petty cash imprest system is one in which a fixed amount of money is advanced to the cashier, sufficient to meet normal petty cash disbursements over an agreed period (in our case one month).

(2) Payments are made out of petty cash only if evidenced by properly authorised petty cash vouchers, supported by invoices or receipts.

(3) At the end of each period, the petty cashier presents a return to the cashier giving details of the total amount spent, which is repaid to the petty cashier. The amount then held is the originally agreed fixed sum.

(4) Periodically, Marjorie checks that the amount held agrees with the fixed amount, less expenditure since the last reimbursement date.

Please let me know if you have any further problems regarding the petty cash system.

Chris

Chris

Chapter 6

1

(a) No

(b) Although an offer has been made, for a contract to exist, the acceptance must be unqualified. In this case, Sally has stipulated that the radios must be delivered by the end of June.

2

(a) No

(b) Offer and acceptance are essential elements of a valid contract.

Goods advertised in catalogues are invitations to treat (ie inviting offers). The customer's letter is therefore an offer, which Hairdressing Supplies are not obliged to accept.

3

(a) No

(b) The offer to supply the discs at £7 each has been withdrawn before acceptance by ABC Music.

4

(a) Yes

(b) An agreement has been made between Future Electrical Limited and Chris consisting of both an offer to supply the Walkman and an acceptance.

(c) No

(d) Since Chris is a minor, he is not legally bound by the contract.

5

(a) No

(b) The advertisement in the magazine is not regarded legally as an offer which can be accepted. It is instead an invitation to the public to make an offer (ie an invitation to treat).

Chapter 7

1

Any six from:

- Date
- Invoice number
- Customer name and address
- Seller's name and address
- VAT details
- Terms of payment
- Purchase order number
- Number of items
- Price per item
- Description of goods

2

£31.50

Note. The answer is arrived at as follows.

	£
Sales price (10 x £25)	250.00
Less: trade discount (250 x 20%)	(50.00)
	200.00
Less: cash discount (200 x 10%)	(20.00)
	180.00
VAT @ 17.5%	31.50

3

The letters stand for the words *errors and omissions excepted* and indicate that the company reserves the right to correct, at a later date, any errors made on the invoice.

4

The price quoted does not include the cost of delivery.

5

MEMORANDUM

To:	Andrew Bolton	Date:	15 June 19X4
From:			
Subject:	Motormania		

Jim Ellis, the owner of Motormania, telephoned me today to request an increase from 8% to 10% in the trade discount given to the company. We currently allow the discount on all the company's purchases and, based on the present annual turnover of £230,910, the approximate cost to us in agreeing to this increase would be £4,600 per year.

I have told Jim Ellis that I will write to let him have your decision within the next seven days. It would therefore be helpful if I could have your reply by next Monday.

Chapter 8

1

A sequential code

2

(a) The hard disk

(b) Any one from

- to hold programmes not currently being used
- to hold the company's files (eg the various ledgers).

3

False

4

(a) Batch processing

(b) It is faster and therefore cheaper to process similar transactions together.

(c) Real–time processing.

(d) The records are always up–to–date.

5

(a) File

(b) Field

(c) Record

6

(i) Faulty goods are returned by a customer.

(ii) The overcharge of a customer needs correction.

7

(a) Credit note

(b)

Debit		*Credit*	
Sales returns	£78.30	Debtors' ledger control	£92
VAT	£13.70		

Chapter 9

1

		£		£
(a)	Creditors' control account	20	Debtor's control account	20
(b)	Bad debts	1,124	Debtors' control acocunt	1,214

2

Bad debts are an expense of the business and therefore reduce profit. The higher the bad debts figure, the smaller the profit earned.

3

(a) Transfer journal

(b) Bad debts'; debtors' ledger control

4

Yes

5

(i) To check the accuracy of the balances in the debtors' ledger.

(ii) To deter fraud in connection with debtors' ledger accounts.

(iii) To facilitate and preparation of final accounts by providing a total debtors' figure.

(iv) To enable the sub–division of ledger work.

6

(a) Yes

(b) No

(c) No

Chapter 10

1

(a) **Discount Motors – age analysis at 14 June 19X4**

Balance	*Up to 1 month*	*1–2 months*	*Over 2 months*
£	£	£	£
5,740	2,237	3,503	Nil

(b) Credit control department

2

Balance	*Up to 1 month*	*1–2 months*	*Over 2 months*
£	£	£	£
1,402	327	635	440

3

(a) Star Limited

(b) The balance has been outstanding for over three months.

4

MEMORANDUM

To: Bob Wallis   Date: 1 June 19X3

From: Joan Brookes

Subject: Moss Electrical

The balance of this account is currently £1,642 and no payments have been received since November 19X2. We have unfortunately lost touch with the owner, James Moss, and our solicitors have been unable to trace him.

Under the circumstances, I would suggest that unless Mr Moss contacts us within the next month we should then write off the debt. Could I please have your authorisation to proceed in this manner.

Chapter 11

1

Any two from:

- invoice agrees with goods received documentation
- all calculations have been correctly carried out
- price and terms are as agreed.

2

(a) A statement

(b) A credit note

(c) A purchase order

3

£2,799

Note. This answer is arrived at as follows:

	£
Goods/services ($120 \times \frac{100}{5}$)	2,400
VAT @ 17.5% x 2,400 x 95%	399
	2,799

4

(a) That the goods or services invoiced are as ordered.

(b) That the goods or services invoiced have been received or carried out respectively.

Chapter 12

1

True

2

(a) Credit note

(b) Debit note

(c) Invoice

3

(a) Sales day book

(b) Purchases day book

(c) Sales returns day book

(d) Purchases returns day book

(e) Journal

4

Sales ledger

5

Purchases ledger

6

	Debit	£	*Credit*	£
(a)	B Lowe	275	D Lowe	275
(b)	Purchases returns	9	C Dent	9
(c)	Repairs	82	Equipment	82

7

(a)	Debit	VAT		£14	
		Credit	Creditors' control account		£14
(b)	Debit	Discounts allowed		£98	
		Credit	Discounts received		£98
(c)	Debit	Purchases returns		£23	
	Debit	Sales returns		£23	
	Debit	VAT		£8	
		Credit	Creditors' control account		£27
		Credit	Debtors' control account		£27

8

Chang Fashions Limited
142 Regent Court, London WE4 1NN (Tel: 0181 803 6712)

Mr Brian Moody
Ace Imports Limited
165 Dell Trading Estate
Southampton SO10 4EP

2 December 19X4

Dear Mr Moody

Purchase order P00234

A purchase order was forwarded to your company on 12 October for the supply of two boxes of jeans priced £764.92 each. Delivery took place on 26 October but unfortunately one box contained cotton trousers instead of jeans. The cotton trousers had not been ordered under the above or any other reference number.

The company's managing director, Mary Chang, telephoned you on 27 October and at that time you promised to deliver a replacement box of jeans and to take away the unwanted trousers by 10 November. I am concerned that this has still not been carried out and must ask you to ensure that your promise is now fulfilled on receipt of this letter.

An invoice dated 16 November for the two boxes of jeans ordered was received by us on 18 November. If for any reason you are now unable to supply the second box would you please notify me immediately and issue a credit note for the £764.92 in question.

Your sincerely

Rahul Divan
Accountant and Company Secretary

Chang Fashions Limited, Registered office: 142 Regent Court, London WE4 1NN
Registered in England, number 5469971

Chapter 13

1

(a) Dr Creditors' control account
Cr Debtors' control account

(b) Dr Creditors' control account
Cr Insurance

(c) Dr Stationery
Cr Purchases

2

(a) Purchase requisition

(b) Purchase order

(c) Advice note

(d) Delivery note

(e) Goods received note

(f) Remittance advice

3

Any one from:

- to assist in the location of errors
- the total of the creditors is known at any time
- to help in the prevention of fraud.

4

(a) No

(b) No

(c) Yes

(d) No

5

	Debit	*Credit*
Purchases	18	
Creditors ledger control		18
Being correction of purchases		

Chapter 14

1

(a) (b) (c)

2

Music World Limited

51 Ashgrove Park, Birmingham BM9 7TE
Tel: 0121 963 5522

Ms Cathy Price
International Records Limited
142 Durham Road
Newcastle N12 1BE

1 December 19X3

Dear Mrs Price

Statement of account dated 30 November 19X3

We have today received a statement from your company showing the balance of Music World Limited's account to be £8,490 as at 30 November 19X3. However, according to our records the balance should be £7,160. The difference of £1,330 has been traced to two items, neither of which appears on the statement. These are a credit note for £130 received from your company and a cheque for £1,200 issued by us in favour of International Records Limited.

The credit note relates to some CDs returned on 15 November. Your company issued the note under reference number ... and it was received by us on 19 November. Please look into this matter and arrange for our account to be credited with the £130 in question.

Cheque number 000549 was issued and sent to you on 17 November by first class post. We are concerned that, if it has failed to reach you, then it may be lost in the post. Would you kindly check your records to ascertain whether or not it has now been received.

We should be grateful if you would please telephone or fax a reply as soon as possible since we will need to both contact our bankers and issue a replacement if the cheque referred to above is in fact missing.

We look forward to hearing from you.

Your sincerely

Tony Bryant
Accountant and Company Secretary

Music World Limited, Registered office: 51 Ashgrove Park, Birmingham BM9 7TE
Registered in England, number 2654379

CHAPTER 16

Practice Simulations

Unit 1 Data and Tasks

Natural Products Limited

To complete this assignment you will need:

- pen and pencil;
- calculator;
- lined A4 paper;
- dictionary.

Performance criteria covered

All 4 elements

Factfile

Business name	Natural Products Limited	
Location	Taunton, Somerset	
Personnel	Managing director	Cindy Taylor
	Sales director	Jason Taylor
	Production director	Tracy Yard
	Financial director	Steve Roberts
	Secretary to directors	Carol Evans
Business	Manufacture, wholesale and mail order sale of toiletries and cosmetics	

Business profile

The business was started in 1978 by Cindy Taylor. Early success in supplying 'natural' products to a famous retail chain led to Cindy's husband, Jason, and brother-in-law, Steve, joining the company.

The company originally based its business on products marketed under the customer's own label. Major customers continue to this day to be supermarket and drugstore chains.

Sales increased steadily throughout the 1980s. In 1989, encouraged by her staff, Cindy launched a new range of products marketed under the company's own name. These products are only available by mail order. A catalogue is produced annually.

The company hopes to be floated on the stock market soon, although the directors appreciate certain improvements will be required first in the accounting systems.

The company specialises in products which use as many natural ingredients as possible. The directors are leading campaigners against animal testing.

Sales department

The sales department is divided into two groups: the telesales staff and the sales representatives.

The telesales supervisor is Kenneth Gray and his assistant is Sheila Preston.

There are three sales representatives who cover the North and West, the Midlands and South West, and the South East and East respectively. They all report to Jason Taylor.

Production department

There are three production supervisors who supervise two purchasers, fifteen production line staff, one tester and two quality control inspectors.

Accounts department

Accounts supervisor	Caroline Everley
Ledger Clerk	Trudi Roberts
Administration and payroll	Robert Foster
Cashier and petty cashier	You

Terms of trade

The company is registered for VAT. All sales are standard-rated.

All wholesale customers are allowed settlement discounts of 25% if invoices are paid within 14 days of the date of the invoice.

Certain suppliers offer settlement discounts.

Monies received

Source	Methods of payment accepted
Wholesale customers	Cheques CHAPS
Mail Order customers	Cheques Postal orders
Telephone sales	Credit cards (Express & Global)
Staff sales (staff shop)	Cash only

Payments from wholesale customers are accompanied by a remittance advice which is part of the statement sent to customers.

Mail order sales are recorded individually on order forms. The same order form is used for telephone credit card orders.

Staff sales are recorded using a cash register in the staff shop.

Payments

Payee	*Methods of payment*
Most suppliers	Cheques
Electricity, gas, telephone	Direct debit
Sundry expenses	Petty cash

All cheques are written manually from cheque requisitions. All requisitions must be signed by Steve Roberts (FD).

All petty cash vouchers in excess of £5.00 must be accompanied by receipts. All petty cash expenditure must be authorised by Steve Roberts (FD).

Your assignment

This assessment is in three parts.

While completing this assignment, you may come across queries and discrepancies. You should do as much as possible and make a note of any problems as you go along. You will then have those queries resolved before moving on to the next part.

For instance, you should write up the petty cash book but exclude any problem items – you should make a note of these.

Whenever the assignment asks you to review or complete any documents, you will find the relevant documentation on the subsequent pages.

Part 1

This part of the assessment deals with tasks performed on 30 June 19X5.

In particular it deals with recording:

Monies received on 30 June 19X5
CHAPS advice notes received in post

Cheques written and sent on 30 June 19X5
Direct debit payments for June 19X5

Petty cash payments made on 30 June 19X5

While performing this part of the assessment, you will prepare a list of queries for a meeting with Caroline Everley.

Part 2

This part deals with the bank reconciliation performed on 6 July 19X5.

You will document any queries in a memo to Caroline Everley.

Part 3

This part deals with tasks performed on 10 July 19X5.

In particular it deals with:

Preparing journal entries

Posting entries to nominal ledger accounts

Part 1

Please read the instructions (given above) for Part 1 carefully before you start.

Today is 30 June 19X5.

A Recording and banking monies received

1 *Review payments received*

(a) Check payments received from wholesale customers against remittance advices.

(b) For each credit card telephone order, review the credit card voucher and decide whether or not to accept the payment.

Telephone authorisation must be obtained for individual orders over £50.

(c) For cheque and postal order mail order sales, review the payment and the order form and decide whether or not to accept the payment.

(d) Reconcile the daily sales reconciliation sheet with the cash in hand from the staff shop cash register. Record the takings in the cash book.

Cash in hand

£50 notes	3
£20 notes	1
£10 notes	2
£5 notes	3
£1 coins	7
50p coins	5
20p coins	4
10p coins	22
2p coins	8

2 *Bank payments received*

(a) Prepare credit card retail voucher summaries.

(b) Prepare the paying-in slip. The last paying-in slip was number 606.

B Making payments

(a) Review each cheque requisition form, ensuring it has been properly authorised.

(b) Prepare a cheque for each acceptable requisition.

C Recording receipts and payments

(a) Write up the cash book (receipts) from:

- paying-in slip and remittance advices (to identify discounts)
- CHAPS advice notes

Notes

1 Totals only are required.

2 Staff shop sales are recorded as mail order sales.

(b) Write up the cash book (payments) from:

- cheques written
- direct debit schedule (all June payments)

D Petty cash

(a) Review each petty cash voucher for authorisation and decide which payments can be made. Number vouchers for which payment is made. The last voucher was number 550.

(b) Write up the petty cash book (payments) for each payment.

(You are starting a new petty cash book, so you will have to set up your own columns).

Discrepancies and queries

Prepare a list of any problems as you discover them. You will need these for your meeting with Caroline Everley on 5 July 19X5.

Caroline has told you that she may not have enough time to complete the meeting; your notes, therefore, should be of a high enough standard to take away with her.

Documents provided

Documents received from customers and other items

- Cheque received from trade debtors 30 June 19X5
- Cheques and postal orders (mail order) received 30 June 19X5
- Complete credit card sales vouchers from 30 June 19X5
- CHAPS advice note
- Shop cash reconciliation

Blank copies of external documents

- Paying-in slips
- Credit card retail voucher summaries
- Cheques

Completed copies of internal documents

- Direct debit schedule
- Cheque requisitions
- Petty cash vouchers

Internal ledgers

- Cash book (receipts and payments)
- Petty cash book (payments)

Other internal information

- Nominal ledger listing (extract)

REMITTANCE ADVICE

Statement Date *30 May 19X5*

Acc name *COSMETIC COMPANY LIMITED* *Acc no. C0998*

Date	Trans No.	Amount	Discount	Paid
13 5 X5	INV 33477	1875.90		
18 5 X5	INV 33640	535.01		
28 5 X5	INV 33810	230.77		
		2641.68		

MONEY CITY BANK

\## - ## - ##

8/6 19 X5

Pay *Natural Products Ltd* or order

Two Thousand, six hundred &

forty-one pounds 68 pence £ *2,641.68*

For and on behalf of Cosmetic Company Limited

Tarquin Jessop

\##### ## - ## - ## #############

REMITTANCE ADVICE

Statement Date *30 May 19X5*

Acc name *CASTLE COLLECTABLES* *Acc no. CA309*

Date	Trans No.	Amount	Discount	Paid
22 4 X5	INV 33445	88.95		
24 4 X5	INV 33498	22.76		
28 5 X5	INV 33802	134.90		
		246.61		

- ## -

MONEY CITY BANK 26/6 19 X5

Pay *Natural Hair Products Ltd* or order

Two hundred & forty-six £ *246.61*

pounds 61 pence Castle Collectables

Trevor Castle

- ## - ##

FINANCIAL BANK PLC

01 - 89 - 34

26 June X5

Pay *Natural Products Ltd* or order

five pounds and ninety-eight pence only £ *5 - 98*

Miss FR Evans

Franny Evans

000267 01 - 89 - 34 47586909

ORDER FORM

Ordered by: *PLEASE USE CAPITAL LETTERS*

Name *Franny Evans*

Address *Flat 12, 16 The Parade, Bognor Regis, Sussex*

Post code

Telephone

Deliver to: *(if different to above)*

Name

Address

Post code

Have you ordered from us before Yes / No

Ref no.	Description	Qty	Price Item	Total
C24	*Egg whip*	*1*	*1 - 99*	*1 - 99*
M23	*Hair treats*	*1*	*3 - 99*	*3 - 99*

TOTAL *Free postage in UK* *£5- 98*

I enclose a cheque./postal order for
(Payable to Natural Products Limited)

NOT NEGOTIABLE

#####

£8 **BRITISH POSTAL ORDER**

SENDER MUST FILL IN PAYEE'S NAME IN INK

PLEASE PAY

Natural Products Ltd

£8

EIGHT POUNDS

AT POST OFFICE

RECEIVED/SIGNATURE

Paying Office Date Stamp

POSTAGE STAMPS

One or two postage stamps may be added to a maximum of ninety-nine pence

Paying Office Date Stamp

ORDER FORM

Ordered by: ***PLEASE USE CAPITAL LETTERS***

Name *T. J. Bilmann*

Address *3 Fountain Boulevard*

Milton Keynes **Post code** *MK5*

Telephone

Deliver to: ***(if different to above)***

Name *R. F. Bilmann*

Address *39 Grayling Gardens*

Manchester **Post code** *M20 1AE*

Have you ordered from us before **Yes / No**

Ref no.	Description	Qty	Price Item	Total
L11	*Baby Soap*	*2*	*1.50*	*3.00*
B58	*Pretty Bubbles*	*2*	*2.50*	*5.00*

TOTAL *Free postage in UK* *8.00*

I enclose a cheque./postal order for *£ 8.00*

(Payable to Natural Products Limited)

FINANCIAL BANK PLC
345 HIGH STREET DARTFORD KENT DA1 4UK

01 - 89 - 40

28/6 19 X5

Pay *Natural Products Ltd* or order

Seven pounds 89 pence only £ 7 - 89

Miss I L Cowie

I L Cowie

000196 01 - 89 - 40 34869201

ORDER FORM

Ordered by: ***PLEASE USE CAPITAL LETTERS***

Name *I L Cowie*

Address *59 Finchley Road*

BRISTOL **Post code** *BS3 9AJ*

Telephone

Deliver to: ***(if different to above)***

Name

Address

Post code

Have you ordered from us before Yes / No

Ref no.	Description Total	Qty	Price	Item
B01	Raspberry Treat	1	1-99	1-99
D80	Soapy Moloy	2	1-50	3-00
F12	Lemon & Egg	1	2-50	2-50

TOTAL *Free postage in UK* 7-49

I enclose a cheque./postal order for £ 7-49

(Payable to Natural Products Limited)

ORDER FORM

Ordered by: ***PLEASE USE CAPITAL LETTERS***

Name TRACY BERRY

Address 23 BUCKINGHAM AVENUE

EAST KILBRIDGE **Post code** G75 8EA

Telephone

Deliver to: ***(if different to above)***

Name

Address

Post code

Have you ordered from us before **Yes / No**

Ref no.	Description	Qty	Price Item	Total
M23	HAIR TREATS	1	3-99	3-99
S111	LAVENDER SHAMPOO		1	2-99 2-99
F09	SLUDGE FACE MASK1		2-50	2-50

TOTAL *Free postage in UK* 9-48

I enclose a cheque./postal order for £ 9-48

(Payable to Natural Products Limited)

3553 1120 2899 3862
12 / X5
T. BERRY
23 BUCKINGHAM AVENUE
EAST KILBRIDGE G75 8EA
NAT PROD
784330

EXPRESS

CARDHOLDER COPY

	DEPT	SALES NO	INITIALS
3 0 0 6 X 5			ANO

DESCRIPTION	AMOUNT
GOODS	9 48

9 : 4 8

CARDHOLDER'S SIGNATURE

T. Berry T.O.

CARDHOLDER'S DECLARATION: I promise to pay the total amount shown as payable together with any charges thereon subject to the rules of issue.

SALES VOUCHER
Please keep this copy for your records

ORDER FORM

Ordered by: ***PLEASE USE CAPITAL LETTERS***

Name DAWN ROSS

Address 281 FLORAL GARDENS

WATERLOOVILLE **Post code** PO7 6PY

Telephone 01705 230228

Deliver to: ***(if different to above)***

Name

Address

Post code

Have you ordered from us before ~~Yes~~ / No

Ref no.	Description	Qty	Price Item	Total
C23	UNTANGLED CONDITIONER	2	1-99	3-98
F09	SLUDGE FACE MASK	1	2-50	2-50
B53	LEMON TREAT BATH	1	1-99	1-99

TOTAL *Free postage in UK*

I enclose a cheque./postal order for £ 8-47

(Payable to Natural Products Limited)

2882 1985 6622 0088
10/X5
NATURAL PRODUCTS
556 8890

D. Ross
28 Floral Gardens
Waterlooville PO7 6PY

GLOBAL

	DEPT	SALES NO	INITIALS
3 0 0 6 2 5			ANO

DESCRIPTION	AMOUNT
GOODS	8 47

8 : 4 7

CARDHOLDER'S SIGNATURE

D Ross T.O.

CARDHOLDER'S DECLARATION: I promise to pay the total amount shown as payable together with any charges thereon subject to the rules of issue.

CARDHOLDER COPY

SALES VOUCHER
Please keep this copy for your records

SOUTHERN BANK PLC

Fundsflow Receipt Details - Customer Copy

CHAPS RECEIPT DETAILS - REF - 6744777

BRANCH	22 - 56 - 01
BANK	TAUNTON
PAYEE	NATURAL PRODUCTS LTD
A/C NO	00010990
AMOUNT	£14,776.04
PAYER	FREEMAN FOODS GROUP
S/C	11 - 67 -23
DETAILS	INV 33999

OTHER DETAILS - PAYMENT TYPE 10

PAYMENT SENT 29 05 X5 AT 14.33.23

PAYMENT RECEIVED AT 29 05 X5 AT 14.33.23

DAILY SALES RECONCILIATION

Prepared by *J. Farnborough* | Week commencing *26 June 19X5*

Reviewed by

	Total	Monday	Tuesday	Wednesday	Thursday	Friday
CASH TAKINGS	217.66	25.66	44.67	72.55	54.55	20.23
TOTAL PER TILL ROLL	217.66	25.66	44.67	72.55	54.55	20.23
DIFFERENCE	/	/	/	/	/	/

26/6/X5	27/6/X5	28/6/X5	29/6/X5	30/6/X5	30/6/X5
16:45	17:01	14:26	15:14	11:15	11:20
Total 25.66	Total 70.33X	Total 142.88X	Total 197.43X	Total 217.66X	Total 217.66Z

DIRECT DEBIT SCHEDULE

FREQUENCY	PAYEE	AMOUNT £	SPECIAL INSTRUCTIONS
Monthly	English Electricity plc	159.78	
Quarterly	English Gas plc	~~329.23~~	Jan/April/July/Oct
		299.80	Revised 3 April 19X5
Monthly	English Telecomm	~~201.39~~	Revised 5 Feb 19X5
		224.47	

CHEQUE REQUISITION

Date 29/6/X5 Voucher no 340

Amount £ 235.55 Discount £

Payee Arthur Chong Ltd.

For trade creditors, account no. C102

Purpose TC

Signed Trudi Roberts Authorised SAR

Payment date Cheque no.

CHEQUE REQUISITION

Date 29/6/X5 Voucher no 341

Amount £ 469.55 Discount £ 23.48

Payee Dwyer & Company (Import) Ltd.

For trade creditors, account no. D102

Purpose TC

Signed Trudi Roberts Authorised SAR

Payment date Cheque no.

CHEQUE REQUISITION

Date 29/6/X5 Voucher no 342

Amount £ 449.28 Discount £ 4.49

Payee Eastworld Ltd.

For trade creditors, account no. E101

Purpose TC

Signed Trudi Roberts Authorised SAR

Payment date Cheque no.

PETTY CASH VOUCHER			
Authorised by SAR	Received by	Code	No.
Date	Description		Amount
29/6/X5	Windows cleaned		8 - 90
	Total		8 - 90

A receipt is available. The window cleaner is not registered for VAT.

PETTY CASH VOUCHER			
Authorised by SAR	Received by	Code	No.
Date	Description		Amount
30/6/X5	Milk and biscuits		3 - 99
	Total		3 - 99

No receipt is available.

PETTY CASH VOUCHER			
Authorised by SAR	Received by	Code	No.

Date	Description	Amount
28/6/X5	Headlight bulb for works van	1 - 99
	Total	1 - 99

No receipt is available.

PETTY CASH VOUCHER			
Authorised by SAR	Received by	Code	No.

Date	Description	Amount
28/6/X5	Travel to station	6 - 95
	- Jason Taylor	
	- Sales conference	
	Total	6 - 95

A receipt is available from the taxi company.

PETTY CASH VOUCHER			
Authorised by SAR	Received by	Code	No.
Date	Description	Amount	
26/6/X5	Food for staff party	8 - 29	
	Total	8 - 29	

A proper VAT receipt is available, showing VAT of 89 pence.

PETTY CASH VOUCHER			
Authorised by SAR	Received by	Code	No.
Date	Description	Amount	
29/6/X5	New cashbook (blank)	12 - 98	
	Total	12 - 98	

A receipt is available but it is not a proper VAT receipt.

PETTY CASH VOUCHER			
Authorised by SAR	Received by	Code	No.

Date	Description	Amount
29/6/X5	Staff Welfare	5 - 99
	Total	5 - 99

A proper VAT receipt is available showing VAT of 50 pence.

PETTY CASH VOUCHER			
Authorised by SAR	Received by	Code	No.

Date	Description	Amount
30/6/X5	Taxi fare	2 - 80
	- Peter Fraser	
	Total	2 - 80

No receipt is available.

PETTY CASH VOUCHER			
Authorised by SAR	Received by	Code	No.

Date	Description	Amount
27/6/X5	Paint for Painting Store	10 - 45
	Paint brush set	22 - 45
	Total	32 - 90

A proper VAT receipt is available showing VAT of £4.90.

NOMINAL LEDGER LISTING (Extract)

Income

1	Wholesale sales
3	Mail order sales
143	Other income – rent
144	Discounts received

Expenditure

201	Wages and salaries
202	Rent and rates
208	Heat and light
209	Telephones
210	General insurance
211	Repairs and renewals
212	Building maintenance
220	Postage
221	Stationery
222	Travel and subsistence
230	Motor expenses
400	General expenses
401	Staff welfare
402	Cleaning materials
445	Bank interest
447	Loan interest
448	Discounts allowed

Assets

001	Fixed assets – property
002	Fixed assets – plant and machinery
003	Fixed assets – fixtures and fittings
010	Stock
011	Trade debtors
012	Cash at bank (current account)
013	Cash at bank (deposit account)
014	Cash in hand

Liabilities

020	Trade creditors
021	Hire purchase
022	VAT control account

Capital and reserves

030	Share capital
031	Share premium
032	Profit and loss account reserve

Meeting with Caroline Everley

This must take place *before* you start Part 2.

Queries and answers from meeting with Caroline Everley

Query	*Caroline's reply*
Order from IL Cowie does not agree with cheque.	We need to return to customer. This has been happening a lot recently. Please draft a standard letter to send to all such customers.
Cheque received from Castle Collectables has wrong payee.	I will deal with this. Do not include in cash book or bank.
Does the CHAPS payments have discount allowed?	Freeman Foods £256.64.

Part 2

Today is 6 July 19X5.

A Resolving queries from Part 1

Use the notes from your meeting with Caroline Everley to complete the cash book and petty cash book.

B Petty cash

(a) Reconcile the balance of petty cash in hand with the records as at 30 June 19X5.

Cash in hand is as follows:

£10	notes	10
£5	notes	2
£1	coins	3
50p	coins	3
20p	coins	3
5p	coins	1
2p	coins	3

(b) Prepare a cheque requisition form to restore the level of petty cash held to the imprest level (£200).

C Perform a bank reconciliation

Perform a bank reconciliation at 30 June 19X5.

D Letter

Draft a standard letter requested by Caroline Everley.

E Discrepancies and queries

Document any queries or differences in a memorandum to Caroline Everley.

Documents provided

Copies of external documents

- Bank statement at 30 June 19X5

Completed copies of internal documents

- Bank reconciliation as at 23 June 19X5

Blank copies of internal forms

- Petty cash reconciliation
- Cheque requisitions
- Bank reconciliation
- Memorandum

FINANCIAL BANK PLC CONFIDENTIAL

You can bank on us!

467 HIGH STREET
TAUNTON
TA1 9WE

Telephone: 01832 722098

Account CURRENT
NATURAL PRODUCTS Limited

Sheet No. 455

19X5 *Statement date:* *30 June 19X5* *Account Number 34786695*

Date	*Details*		*Withdrawals (£)*	*Deposits (£)*	*Balance (£)*
23 JUN	*Balance from sheet no. 454*				11305.11
26 JUN	MEGASTORES PLC	CHAPS		11755.25	
	COUNTER CREDIT 591			13604.01	
	COUNTER CREDIT 592			112.13	
	374		127.09		
	376		5955.80		
	ENGLISH ELECTRIC	DD	159.78		30533.83
27 JUN	COUNTER CREDIT 593			11655.24	
	COUNTER CREDIT 594			683.11	
	COUNTER CREDIT 595			112.19	
	372		87.93		
	379		368.70		
	ENGLISH TELECOMM	DD	224.47		42303.27
28 JUN	COUNTER CREDIT 596			325.11	
	COUNTER CREDIT 597			60331.90	
	380		32.98		
	382		331.80		102595.50
				14776.04	
29 JUN	FREEMAN FOODS	CHAPS		15685.23	
	GROUP			386.29	
	COUNTER CREDIT 598			89.80	
	COUNTER CREDIT 599				
	COUNTER CREDIT 600		1181.95		
	383		221.50		
	385		441.09		
	386		111.94		131576.38
	388				
30 JUN	COUNTER CREDIT 601			6650.28	
	COUNTER CREDIT 602			115.98	
	381		117.54		
	384		3785.60		
	387		785.11		
	390		683.85		
	393		1253.98		
	399		175.10		
	Balance to Sheet no. 456				131541.46

Key: *SO Standing order* *DD Direct debit* *CP Card purchase* *AC Automated cash* *OD Overdrawn*
CHAPS Clearing House Automated Payments System, BACS Bankers Automated Clearing System

BANK RECONCILIATION

Site	
Date	23/6/X5
Prepared by	A.N. Other

			£
Balance per bank statement		23/6/X5	11.305.11
Less:	Unpresented cheques (see attached list)		(13.549.03)
Plus:	Deposits-in-transit (see attached list)		86823.69
Other items (please describe)			
Balance per cash book			84.579.77

	£
Balance per cash book brought forward	55.741.27
Receipts	130.221.95
Payments	(101.383.45)
Balance per cash book carried forward	84.579.77

UNPRESENTED CHEQUES

Date	Number	£
15/6	372	87.93
16/6	374	127.09
19/6	376	5,955.80
20/6	379	368.70
21/6	380	32.98
	381	117.54
	382	331.80
23/6	383	1,181.95
	384	3,785.60
	385	221.50
	386	441.09
	387	785.11
	388	111.94
		13,549.03

DEPOSITS IN TRANSIT

Date	Paying-in slip no	£
21/6	591	13,604.01
	592	112.13
22/6	593	11,655.24
	594	683.11
	595	112.19
23/6	597	60,331.90
	596	325.11
		86,823.69

Part 3

Today is 10 July 19X5:

A Preparing journal entries

(a) Prepare journal entries to post cash book totals to the correct nominal ledger accounts.

(b) Prepare journal entries to post petty cash expenditure totals to the correct nominal ledger accounts. The last journal was number 6 –10.

B Posting entries to nominal ledger accounts

Post totals from journals to correct nominal ledger accounts.

Documents provided

Internal ledgers

- Journal
- Nominal ledger (extracts)

Blank copies of internal forms

- Memorandum

Unit 1 Answer Book

To be retained by receiving bank

For the credit of *Natural Products Ltd*

Cheques etc. for collection to be included in total credit of £ ______ paid in ______ 19 ______

	£	Brought forward	£	Brought forward	£
Carried forward	£	Carried forward	£	Total cheques etc	£

Date ______________

bank giro credit

Cashier's stamp and initials

22 - 56 - 01

SOUTHERN BANK PLC
TAUNTON HIGH STREET

£50 Notes		
£20 Notes		
£10 Notes		
£5 Notes		
£1 Coins		
50p		
20p		
Silver		
Bronze		
Total Cash		
Cheques, P.O.s, etc		
TOTAL £		

Fee	No. of chqs

Paid in by ______________

Address / Ref No. ______________

Please do not pin or staple this voucher as this will affect the machine processing

All sales vouchers must be deposited within three banking days of the dates shown on them.

If you are submitting more than 26 vouchers please enclose a separate listing.

If a voucher contravenes the terms of the retailer agreement then the amount shown on the voucher may be charged back to your bank Account, either direct or via your paying in branch.

Similarly, if the total amount shown on the Retail Voucher Summary does not balance with our total of vouchers, the difference will be credited (or debited) to your bank account.

1	£	p
1		
2		
3		
4		
5		
6		
7		
8		
9		
10		
11		
12		
13		
14		
15		
16		
17		
18		
19		
20		
21		
22		
23		
24		
25		
26		

SALES VOUCHERS TOTAL

	£	p
1		
2		
3		
4		
5		
6		

REFUND VOUCHERS

PLEASE WRITE FIRMLY WITH A BALLPOINT PEN

GLOBAL

RETAIL VOUCHER SUMMARY

RETAILER COPY 1

RETAILER NAME

DAY MONTH YEAR	RETAILER NUMBER
	AMOUNT
AUTHORISATION CODE	TOTAL POUNDS PENCE

VOUCHERS ARE ACCEPTED SUBJECT TO VERIFICATION AND TO TERMS AND CONDITIONS OF THE MERCHANT AGREEMENT

KEEP COPIES 1 & 2 AND REMIT COPIES 3 & 4 WITH YOUR SALES VOUCHERS

PLEASE COMPLETE THIS SUMMARY QUOTING YOUR CURRENT RETAILER NUMBER

RETAILER COPY

Please do not pin or staple this this will affect the machine processing

All sales vouchers must be deposited within three days of the dates shown on

If you are submitting more than 26 vouchers please a separate listing.

If a voucher contravenes the terms of the retailer agreement then the amount shown on the voucher may be charged back to your bank Account, either direct or via your paying in branch.

Similarly, if the total amount shown on the Retail Voucher Summary does not balance our total of vouchers, the difference will be credited (or debited) to your bank account.

	£	p
1		
2		
3		
4		
5		
6		
7		
8		
9		
10		
11		
12		
13		
14		
15		
16		
17		
18		
19		
20		
21		
22		
23		
24		
25		
26		
SALES VOUCHERS TOTAL		

	£	p
1		
2		
3		
4		
5		
6		
7		
REFUND VOUCHERS		

EXPRESS

PLEASE WRITE FIRMLY WITH A BALLPOINT PEN

RETAIL VOUCHER SUMMARY

RETAILER NAME

DAY MONTH YEAR

RETAILER NUMBER

AMOUNT

AUTHORISATION CODE

TOTAL POUNDS PENCE

VOUCHERS ARE ACCEPTED SUBJECT TO VERIFICATION AND TO TERMS AND CONDITIONS OF THE MERCHANT AGREEMENT

KEEP COPIES 1 & 2 AND REMIT COPIES 3 & 4 WITH YOUR SALES VOUCHERS

PLEASE COMPLETE THIS SUMMARY QUOTING YOUR CURRENT RETAILER NUMBER

RETAILER COPY

RETAILER COPY 1

SOUTHERN BANK PLC
755 HIGH STREET TAUNTON TA1 4JL

22 - 56 - 01

19

Pay

or order

£

FOR AND ON BEHALF
OF NATURAL PRODUCTS LTD

000401 22 - 56 - 01 00010990

SOUTHERN BANK PLC
755 HIGH STREET TAUNTON TA1 4JL

22 - 56 - 01

19

Pay

or order

£

FOR AND ON BEHALF
OF NATURAL PRODUCTS LTD

000402 22 - 56 - 01 00010990

SOUTHERN BANK PLC
755 HIGH STREET TAUNTON TA1 4JL

22 - 56 - 01

19

Pay

or order

£

FOR AND ON BEHALF
OF NATURAL PRODUCTS LTD

000403 22 - 56 - 01 00010990

Cash Book Receipts

Date	Narrative	Paying-in slip	Total	Debtors	Mail order	VAT control	Discount allowed
26/6	Trade debtors	598	15,685.23	15,685.23			
	Mail order (Cheque/PO)	599	386.29		328.76	57.53	
	Mail order (CC)	600	89.80		76.43	13.37	
27/6	Trade debtors	601	6,650.28	6,650.28			
	Mail order	602	115.98		98.71	17.27	
	MegaStores plc	CHAPS	11,755.25	11,755.25			204.17
28/6	Trade debtors	603	12,223.81	12,223.81			
	Mail order	604	609.22		518.49	90.73	
29/6	Trade debtors	605	5,395.40	5,395.40			
	Mail order	606	98.60		83.91	14.69	

Cash Book Payments

Date	Narrative	Cheque no	Total	Creditors	Salaries	Other	VAT control	Discount received
26/6	Blackwood Foodstuffs	389	325.99	325.99				
	Bruning & Soler	390	683.85	683.85				
	Dehlavi Kosmetatos	391	2112.16	2112.16				
	Environmentally Friendly	392	705.77	705.77				
	Greig Handling (import)	393	1253.98	1253.98				
	Halpern Freedman	394	338.11	338.11				
	Kobo Design Studio	395	500.00	500.00				
	Rayner Food Co	396	375.22	375.22				
	Year 2000 Produce Co	397	1100.68	1100.68				
27/6	HM Customs & Excise	398	23599.28				23599.28	
26/6	Petty cash	399	175.10			175.10 (P. Cash)		
28/6	Salaries - Bank Giro	400	48995.63		48995.63			

Petty Cash (payments)

		£	£	£	£	£	£	£	£	£	£

PETTY CASH RECONCILIATION

Date ____________________ Prepared by ____________________

Authorised by ____________________

	£
Cash per petty cash book	________
Balance brought forward	________
Receipts	________
Payments	________
Balance carried forward	________
Cash in hand	________
Difference	________

CHEQUE REQUISITION

Date ______________________ Voucher no ____________

Amount £ ______________________ Discount £ ____________

Payee ______________________________________

For trade creditors, account no. ______________________

Purpose ______________________________________

____

____

Signed ______________________ Authorised ____________

Payment date ______________________ Cheque no. ____________

CHEQUE REQUISITION

Date ______________________ Voucher no ____________

Amount £ ______________________ Discount £ ____________

Payee ______________________________________

For trade creditors, account no. ______________________

Purpose ______________________________________

____

____

Signed ______________________ Authorised ____________

Payment date ______________________ Cheque no. ____________

BANK RECONCILIATION

Site

Date

Prepared by

		£
Balance per bank statement		
Less:	Unpresented cheques (see attached list)	
Plus:	Deposits-in-transit (see attached list)	
Other items (please describe)		
Balance per cash book		

	£
Balance per cash book brought forward	
Receipts	
Payments	
Balance per cash book carried forward	

UNPRESENTED CHEQUES

Date	Number	£

DEPOSITS IN TRANSIT

Date	Paying-in slip no	£

MEMORANDUM

To: Date:

From:

Subject:

Journal no. ______________

Date ______________

Prepared by ______________

Code	Account	Debit		Credit	
Total					
Narrative					

Journal no. ______________

Date ______________

Prepared by ______________

Code	Account	Debit		Credit	
Total					
Narrative					

NOMINAL LEDGER

Account name *Wholesale sales* Account no. 1

Narrative	£	Narrative		£
		23/6/X5	b/f	5,115,668.90

Account name *Mail Order sales* Account no. 3

Narrative	£	Narrative		£
		23/6/X5	b/f	1,235,998.55

Account name *Discount received* Account no. 144

Narrative	£	Narrative		£
		23/6/X5	b/f	25,651.48

NOMINAL LEDGER

Account name *Wages & salaries* Account no. 201

Narrative	£	Narrative	£
31/5/X5 b/f	325,119.90		

Account name *Heat & light* Account no. 208

Narrative	£	Narrative	£
23/6/X5 b/f	12,995.65		

Account name *Telephones* Account no. 209

Narrative	£	Narrative	£
23/6/X5 b/f	3,225.91		

NOMINAL LEDGER

Account name *General insurance* Account no. 210

Narrative	£	Narrative	£
31/5/X5 b/f	2,911.55		

Account name *Repairs and renewals* Account no. 211

Narrative	£	Narrative	£
28/2/X5 b/f	2,001.68		

Account name *Building maintenance* Account no. 212

Narrative	£	Narrative	£
28/2/X5 b/f	1,500.74		

NOMINAL LEDGER

Account name *Postage* Account no. *220*

Narrative		£	Narrative	£
23/6/X5	*b/f*	*8,395.28*		

Account name *Stationery* Account no. *221*

Narrative		£	Narrative	£
23/6/X5	*b/f*	*8,020.97*		

Account name *Travel and subsistence* Account no. *222*

Narrative		£	Narrative	£
23/6/X5	*b/f*	*10,255.65*		

NOMINAL LEDGER

Account name *Motor expenses* Account no. *230*

Narrative	£	Narrative	£
16/6/X5 b/f	5,885.94		

Account name *General expenses* Account no. *400*

Narrative	£	Narrative	£
23/6/X5 b/f	3,855.01		

Account name *Staff Welfare* Account no. *401*

Narrative	£	Narrative	£
23/6/X5 b/f	4,110.28		

NOMINAL LEDGER

Account name Cleaning materials   Account no. 402

Narrative	£	Narrative	£
23/6/1X5 b/f	2.010.43		

Account name Discounts allowed   Account no. 448

Narrative	£	Narrative	£
23/6/X5 b/f	27.445.94		

Account name Trade Debtors   Account no. 011

Narrative	£	Narrative	£
23/6/X5 b/f	834.792.12		

NOMINAL LEDGER

Account name *Cash at bank (current)* Account no. *012*

Narrative	£	Narrative	£
23/6/1X5 b/f	*84,579.77*		

Account name *Cash at bank (deposit)* Account no. *013*

Narrative	£	Narrative	£
31/3X5 b/f	*250,050.00*		

Account name *Cash in hand* Account no. *014*

Narrative	£	Narrative	£
23/6/X5 b/f	*24.90*		

NOMINAL LEDGER

Account name *Trade creditors* Account no. *020*

Narrative	£	Narrative	£
		23/6/X5 b/f	367,251.44

Account name *VAT control account* Account no. *022*

Narrative	£	Narrative	£
		23/6/X5 b/f	22,987.38

Account name Account no.

Narrative	£	Narrative	£

MEMORANDUM

To: Date:

From:

Subject

Unit 1 Answers

Commentary and marking guide

Whilst for practical purposes the number of transactions involved in this simulation is limited, the tasks you are asked to perform are typical of those required in many small and medium sized businesses.

Before starting written work, be sure to read carefully through the initial fact file – to pick up information regarding the types of transactions you should be expecting to deal with (here, credit card transactions and CHAPS payments as well as cash and cheques), information regarding controls in operation that you should adhere to (eg authorisation limits) and VAT status.

Before tackling each part, look through the documents provided for that part as this may help you to understand what is required.

Some of the tasks involve checking documents against each other, or for authorisation, etc. Wherever possible, provide evidence that such checks have been carried out – use ticks or sign appropriate spaces on forms, etc.

Do not be surprised to find discrepancies or incomplete information – this happens in practice too – just list them on a separate page (in memo form if required). They will probably be cleared up later in the exercise.

Although most tasks are specifically described, watch out for 'hidden' ones – for example, the extractions of VAT on cash receipts and payments.

Finally, even if you think that some of your figures may be wrong, be consistent since it is important that all parts of the system tie up with each other. Thus amounts shown in the cash receipts book should tally with the paying in slip; cash book totals, journals and nominal ledger entries should all agree.

Marking guide

Note. Some of the tasks set within the simulation do not result in written answers (eg checking payments received against remittance advices) and thus cannot be 'marked' as such. However, there is often evidence that the task has been carried out. eg queries raised or entries elsewhere in the answer – which may help in assessing whether the task has been carried out correctly. Marks are generally allocated on the basis of the time the whole task may have been expected to take and may thus appear to be out of proportion to the actual written evidence.

Part 1

A1 (a) -(d)

Evidence that the tasks should have been correctly performed is as follows.

A query should be raised concerning the payee on the cheque received from Castle Collectibles.

Both credit card vouchers should be acceptable and thus included in the summaries.

A query should be raised with regard to IL Cowie's cheque and it should not be included on the paying-in slip.

The shop sales may be recorded separately in the cash book (the answer has these recorded on the paying-in slip and thus totalled in with other receipts in the cash book).

A1 = 6 marks

A2(a)

Check for correct completion of both documents for each credit card company – dates, amount, retailer number, etc.

A2(a) = 3 marks

A2(b)

Check for:

- cheques total and date at top
- cheque and credit card analysis
- cash analysis
- sub-total and total
- number of cheques, paid in by and reference number (607).

A2(b) = 8 marks

Part 1A = 17 marks

B (a)

All cheque requisitions acceptable, evidenced by cheques being drawn up for all and the bottom line of the requisitions being completed.

B(b)

Check for:

- date
- payee
- amount (words and numbers).

Part 1B = 6 marks

C(a)

Only the last three lines are added by the student. Check the following:

- Amounts agree to the paying-in slip.
- The analysis is correct. (*Note.* The mail order amounts (£31.93) may be shown separately from the shop cash sales (£217.66) although both should be analysed as mail-order.)
- VAT has been correctly extracted on mail-order sales.
- CHAPS receipt has been included.
- Column totals not to be included yet.

C(a) = 8 marks

C(b)

Only the last five lines are added by the student. Check that:

- amounts agree to the cheques
- the analysis is correct
- direct debits have been included
- VAT has been correctly extracted on the direct debits
- column totals not to be included yet.

C(b) = 9 marks

Part 1C = 17 marks

D(a)

All payments can be made, evidenced by all being included in the petty cash book.

D(b)

Check for:

- correct analyses columns, in accordance with NL listings on question paper
- inclusion of VAT column
- correct amounts (net of VAT)
- voucher numbers
- column totals not to be included yet.

Part 1D = 9 marks

Discrepancies and queries

These should have been identified as part of the student's checks, etc. Award marks for content, style and presentation of listing.

Queries = 3 marks

Part 1 = 52 marks

Part 2

A

Completion of cash book:

- discount of CHAPS receipt
- totalling of columns.

Completion of petty cash book:

- discount of CHAPS receipt
- totalling of columns.

Part 2A = 6 marks

B(a)

The balance brought forward (or imprest level) does not appear to be given in the notes/documents preceding this requirement. Students may arrive at this balance by a balancing figure approach or by looking in the ledger accounts given for Part 3.

Check that:

- receipt agrees with the CB
- payments agree with PCB
- balance carried forward is correct
- reconciliation is completed with date, name, etc.

B(b)

Figure to agree with student's total PC payments.

Part 2B = 5 marks

C

Check that:

- balance per bank statement is correct
- cash book shows evidence of checking off against bank statement (eg ticks)
- outstanding items correctly identified
- balance b/f on cash book correct
- receipts and payments consistent with student's cash book totals
- correct completion (date, name, totals).

Part 2C = 12 marks

D

Marks awarded for style and presentation (proper letter format).

Part 2D = 4 marks

E

No queries or differences appear to arise. If the student has any sensible relevant queries that are not answered by the information in the question, award some 'bonus' marks at discretion.

Part 2 = 27 marks

Part 3

A(a)(b)

Check for:

- appropriate journal numbers (6-11 and 6-12)
- date/name narrative
- amounts consistent with cash books
- correct ledger code numbers used
- balanced double entries.

Part 3A = 9 marks

B

Check that entries are consistent with student's journals in A, in both amount and destination account.

Part 3B = 12 marks

Part 3 = 21 marks

Summary

Part 1	52 marks
Part 2	27 marks
Part 3	21 marks
Total	100 marks

To be retained by receiving bank

For the credit of Natural Products Limited

Cheques etc for collection to be included in total credit of £ 2,671.61 paid in 30 June 19X5

	£	brought forward	£	brought forward	£
Cosmetic Co Ltd	2,641.68				
	5.98				
FR Evans	8.00				
TJ Bilmsn	9.48				
Express Global	8.47				
Carried forward	£2,673.61	carried forward	£	Total cheques etc	£

Date 20 June 19X5

Cashier's stamp and initials

22–56–01

SOUTHERN BANK PLC

TAUTON HIGH STREET

Credit Trading Company Limited

£50 Notes	150.	00
£20 Notes	20.	00
£10 Notes	20.	00
£5 Notes	15.	00
£1 Coins	7.	00
50p	2.	50
20p	.	80
Silver	2.	20
Bronze	.	16
Total Cash	217.	66
Cheques, POs etc	2,673.	61
TOTAL £	2,891.	27

Fee	No Chqs
	5

Paid in by AN Other

Address/Ref No. 607

Please do not pin or staple this voucher as this will affect the machine processing All sales vouchers must be deposited within three banking days of the dates shown on them. If you are submitting more than 26 vouchers please enclose a separate listing. If a voucher contravenes the terms of the retailer agreement then the amount shown on the voucher may be charged back to your bank account, either direct or via your paying in branch. Similarly, if the total amount shown on the Retail Voucher Summary does not balance with our total of vouchers, the difference will be credited (or debited) to your bank account.		£	p
	1	9	48
	2		
	3		
	4		
	5		
	6		
	7		
	8		
	9		
	10		
	11		
	12		
	13		
	14		
	15		
	16		
	17		
	18		
	19		
	20		
	21		
	22		
SALES VOUCHERS TOTAL		9	48
		£	p
	1		
	2		
	3		
	4		
	5		
REFUND VOUCHERS			

EXPRESS

PLEASE WRITE FIRMLY WITH A BALLPOINT PEN

RETAIL VOUCHER SUMMARY

RETAILER NAME

Natural Products Ltd

DAY		MONTH		YEAR		RETAILERS NUMBER
3	0	0	6	X	5	7843300

NO OF VOUCHERS		AMOUNT	
SALES VOUCHERS	1	9	48
REFUND VOUCHERS			

AUTHORISATION CODE

TOTAL		POUNDS		PENCE		
				9	:	4	8

VOUCHERS ARE ACCEPTED SUBJECT TO VERIFICATION AND TO TERMS AND CONDITIONS OF THE MERCHANT AGREEMENT

KEEP COPIES 1 & 2 AND REMIT COPIES 3 & 4 WITH YOUR SALES VOUCHERS

PLEASE COMPLETE THIS SUMMARY QUOTING YOUR CURRENT RETAILER NUMBER

RETAILER COPY

RETAILER COPY 1

		£	p
Please do not pin or staple this voucher as this will affect	1	8	47
the machine processing	2		
	3		
All sales vouchers must be	4		
deposited within three banking	5		
days of the dates shown on them.	6		
	7		
If you are submitting more than 26	8		
vouchers please enclose a separate listing.	9		
	10		
If a voucher contravenes the terms of	11		
the retailer agreement then the amount	12		
shown on the voucher may be charged	13		
back to your bank account, either	14		
direct or via your paying in branch.	15		
	16		
Similarly, if the total amount shown	17		
on the Retail Voucher Summary does	18		
not balance with our total of vouchers, the	19		
difference will be credited (or debited)	20		
to your bank account.	21		
	22		
SALES VOUCHERS TOTAL		8	47

		£	p
	1		
	2		
	3		
	4		
	5		
REFUND VOUCHERS			

EXPRESS

PLEASE WRITE FIRMLY WITH A BALLPOINT PEN

RETAIL VOUCHER SUMMARY

RETAILER NAME

Natural Products Ltd

DAY		MONTH		YEAR		RETAILERS NUMBER
3	0	0	6	X	5	7843300

NO OF VOUCHERS		AMOUNT	
SALES VOUCHERS	1	8	47
REFUND VOUCHERS			

AUTHORISATION CODE	TOTAL POUNDS	PENCE
	8	47

VOUCHERS ARE ACCEPTED SUBJECT TO VERIFICATION AND TO TERMS AND CONDITIONS OF THE MERCHANT AGREEMENT

KEEP COPIES 1 & 2 AND REMIT COPIES 3 & 4 WITH YOUR SALES VOUCHERS

PLEASE COMPLETE THIS SUMMARY QUOTING YOUR CURRENT RETAILER NUMBER

RETAILER COPY

RETAILER COPY 1

Cheque requisition

Date:	29 / 6 / X5	Voucher No:	340
Amount:	£235.55	Discount:	
Payee:	Arthur Chong Limited		
For trade creditors, account no:	C102		
Purpose:	TC		
Signed:	Trudi Roberts	Authorised:	SAR
Payment date:	30 / 6 / X5	Cheque No:	401

Cheque requisition

Date:	29 / 6 / X5	Voucher No:	341
Amount:	£469.55	Discount:	£23.48
Payee:	Duyer & Company (Import) Limited		
For trade creditors, account no:	D102		
Purpose:	TC		
Signed:	Trudi Roberts	Authorised:	SAR
Payment date:	30 / 6 / X5	Cheque No:	402

Cheque requisition

Date:	29 / 6 / X5	Voucher No:	342
Amount:	£449.28	Discount:	£4.49
Payee:	Earthworld Ltd		
For trade creditors, account no:	E101		
Purpose:	TC		
Signed:	Trudi Roberts	Authorised:	SAR
Payment date:	30 / 6 / X5	Cheque No:	403

SOUTHERN BANK PLC
755 HIGH STREET TAUNTON TA1 4JL

22 – 56 – 01

30 June 19 *X5*

Pay *Arthur Chong Ltd* or order

Two hundred and thirty five pounds 55 pence only

£ 235.55

FOR AND ON BEHALF OF
NATURAL PRODUCTS LTD

000401 22 – 56 – 01 00010990

SOUTHERN BANK PLC
755 HIGH STREET TAUNTON TA1 4JL

22 – 56 – 01

30 June 19 *X5*

Pay *Dwyer & Company (Import) Limited* or order

Four hundred and sixty nine pounds 55 pence only

£ 469.55

FOR AND ON BEHALF OF
NATURAL PRODUCTS LTD

000402 22 – 56 – 01 00010990

SOUTHERN BANK PLC
755 HIGH STREET TAUNTON TA1 4JL

22 – 56 – 01

30 June 19 *X5*

Pay *Earthworld Limited* or order

Four hundred and forty nine pounds 28 pence only

£ 449.28

FOR AND ON BEHALF OF
NATURAL PRODUCTS LTD

000403 22 – 56 – 01 00010990

Cash book receipts

Date	Narrative	Paying in Slip No	Total	Debtors	Mail order	VAT control	Disc allowed
			£	£	£	£	£
26/6	Trade debtors	598✓	15,685.23	15,685.23			
	Mail order (Chq/PO)	599✓	386.29		328.76	57.53	
	Mail order (CC)	600✓	89.80		76.43	13.37	
27/6	Trade debtors	601✓	6,650.28	6,650.28			
	Mail order	602✓	115.98		98.71	17.27	
	MegaStores plc	CHAPS✓	11,755.25	11,755.25			204.17
28/6	Trade debtors	603	12,223.81	12,223.81			
	Mail order	604	609.22		518.49	90.73	
29/6	Trade debtors	605	5,395.40	5,395.40			
	Mail order	606	98.60		83.91	14.69	
30/6	Trade debtors	607	2,641.68	2,641.68			
	Mail order/shop	607	249.59		212.43	37.16	
29/6	Freeman Foods Group	CHAPS✓	14,776.04	14,776.04			256.64
30/6	Totals		70,677.17	69,127.69	1,318.73	230.75	460.81

Note. As the amounts received from mail order and from the shop are being recorded for the first time, the VAT must be analysed within the cash book. VAT is charged at standard rate and is therefore calculated as 17.5/117.5 of the amount received.

Cash book payments

Date	Narrative	Cheque No	Total	Creditors	Salaries	Other	VAT control	Disc received
			£	£	£	£	£	£
26/6	Blackwood Foodstuffs	389	325.99	325.99				
	Bruning & Soler	390✓	683.85	683.85				
	Dehlavi Kosmetatos	391	2,112.16	2,112.16				
	Enviornmentally Friendly	392	705.77	705.77				
	Greig Handling (imoort)	393✓	1,253.98	1,253.98				
	Halpern Freedman	394	338.11	338.11				
	Kobo Design Studioe	395	500.00	500.00				
	Rayner Food Co	396	375.22	375.22				
	Year 2000 Produce Co	397	1,100.68	1,100.68				
27/6	HM Customes & Excise	398	23,599.28				23,599.28	
26/6	Petty cash	399✓	175.10			175.10	(P cash)	
28/6	Salaries – Bank Giro	400	48,995.63		48,995.63			
30/6	Arthur Chong Ltd	401	235.55	235.55				
	Dwyer & Co (Import)	402	469.55	469.55				23.48
	Earthworld Ltd	403	449.28	449.28				4.49
	English Electriciy	DD✓	159.78		(elec)	135.98	23.80	
	English Telecom	DD✓	224.47		(Rele)	191.04	33.43	
	Totals		81,704.40	8,550.14	48,995.63	502.12	23,656.51	27.97

Note. As the amounts paid by direct debit are being recorded for the first time, the VAT must be analysed within the cash book. VAT is charged at standard rate on electricity and telephone charges and is therefore calculated as 17.5/117.5 of the amount paid.

Petty cash book

Date	*Voucher No*	*Total*	*212 Bld Maint*	*401 Staff welfare*	*401 Motor expense*	*222 Travel & subs*	*221 Stationery*	*211 Repairs & renewals*	*022 VAT*
		£	£	£	£	£	£	£	£
30/6/X5	551	8.90	8.90						
	552	3.99		3.99					
	553	1.99			1.99				
	554	6.95				6.95			
	555	8.29		7.40					0.89
	556	12.98					12.98		
	557	5.99		5.49					0.50
	558	2.80				2.80			
	559	32.90						28.00	4.90
	Total	84.79	8.90	16.88	1.99	9.75	12.98	28.00	6.29

Petty cash reconciliation

Date: 30 / 6/ X5

Prepared by: AN other

Authorised by:

Cash per cash book

	£
Balance brought forward 23/6	24.90
Receipts	175.10
Payments	(84.79)
Balance carried forward 30/6	115.21
Cash in hand	115.21
Difference	–

Cheque requisition

Date:	6/7/X5	Voucher No:	
Amount:	£84.79	Discount:	
Payee:	Petty cash		
For trade creditors, account no:			
Purpose:	Imprest		
Signed:	AN Other	Authorised:	
Payment date:		Cheque No:	

BANK RECONCILIATION

Date : 30/6/X5

Prepared by: A N Other

	£
Balance per bank statement	131,541.46
Less: Unpresented cheques (see attached list)	(79,207.22)
Plus: Deposits-in-transit (see attached list)	21,218.30
Other items (please describe)	
Balance per cash book	73,552.54
Balance per cash book brought forward	84,579.77
Receipts	70,677.17
Payments	(81,704.40)
Balance per cash book carried forward	73,552.54

Unpresented cheques

Date	*Number*	£
26/6	389	325.99
	391	2,112.16
	392	705.77
	394	338.11
	395	500.00
	396	375.22
	397	1,100.68
	398	23,599.28
28/6	400	48,995.63
30/6	401	235.55
	402	469.55
	403	449.28
		79.207.22

Deposits in transit

Date	*Paying in slip no*	£
28/6	603	12,223.81
	604	609.22
	605	5,395.40
	606	98.60
	607	2,641.68
	607	249.59
		21,218.30

		Journal No: *Date:* *Prepared by:*	6–11 30/6/X5 AN Other
Code	*Account*	*Debit*	*Credit*
012	Cash at bank (current)	70,677.17	
011	Trade debtors		69,127.69
3	Mail order sales		1,318.73
022	VAT control		230.75
448	Discounts allowed	460.81	
011	Trade debtors		460.81
020	Trade creditors	8,550.14	
201	Wages and salaries	48,995.63	
014	Cash in hand	175.10	
208	Heat and light	135.98	
209	Telephones	191.04	
013	Deposit account		
022	VAT control	23,656.51	
012	Cash at bank (Current)		81,704.40
020	Trade creditors	27.97	
144	Discounts received		27.97
Totals		152,870.35	152,870.35
Narrative:	To record cash receipts and payments (totals)		

MEMORANDUM

To: Caroline Everley Date: 6 July 19X5

From-. A N Other

Subject: Standard letter

USING HEADED NOTEPAPER

CUSTOMER ADDRESS

DATE

Dear ....

Mail order query

Thank you very much for your order. Unfortunately your order form does not match the cheque/postal order sent to us.

I enclose both items. 1 look forward to receiving your amended order which we will send to you as soon as possible.

Yours sincerely

Caroline Everley
Accounts Supervisor

Enclosure

Nominal ledger

Account Name: Wholesale sales		Account No: 1	
Narrative	£	*Narrative*	£
		23/6/X5 b/f	5,115,668.90

Account Name: Mail order sales		Account No: 3	
Narrative	£	*Narrative*	£
		23/6/X5 b/f	1,235,998.55
		30/6/X5 6–11	1,318.73

Account Name: Discounts received		Account No: 144	
Narrative	£	*Narrative*	£
		23/6/X5 b/f	25,651.48
		30/6/X5 6–11	27.97

Account Name: Wages and salaries		Account No: 201	
Narrative	£	*Narrative*	£
31/5/X5 b/f	325,119.90		
30/6/X5 6–11	48,995.63		

Account Name: Heat and Light		Account No: 208	
Narrative	£	*Narrative*	£
23/6/X5 b/f	12,995.65		
30/6/X5 6–11	135.98		

Account Name: Telephones		Account No: 209	
Narrative	£	*Narrative*	£
23/6/X5 b/f	3,225.91		
30/6/X5 6–11	191.04		

Account Name: General insurance		Account No: 210	
Narrative	£	*Narrative*	£
31/5/X5 b/f	2,911.55		

Account Name: Repairs and renwals		Account No: 211	
Narrative	£	*Narrative*	£
28/2/x5 b/f	2,001.68		
20/6/X5 6–12	28.00		

Account Name: Building maintenance		Account No: 212	
Narrative	£	*Narrative*	£
28/2/x5 b/f	1,500.74		
20/6/X5 6–12	8.90		

Account Name: Postage		Account No: 220	
Narrative	£	*Narrative*	£
23/6/X5 b/f	8,395.28		

Account Name: Stationery		Account No: 221	
Narrative	£	*Narrative*	£
23/6/x5 b/f	8,020.97		
20/6/X5 6–12	12.98		

Account Name: Travel and subsistence		Account No: 222	
Narrative	£	*Narrative*	£
23/6/x5 b/f	10,255.65		
20/6/X5 6–12	9.75		

Account Name: Motor expenses		Account No: 230	
Narrative	£	*Narrative*	£
16/6/X5 b/f	5,885.94		
30/6/X5 6–12	1.99		

Account Name: General expenses		Account No: 400	
Narrative	£	*Narrative*	£
23/6/X5 b/f	3,855.01		

Account Name: Staff welfare		Account No: 401	
Narrative	£	*Narrative*	£
23/6/X5 b/f	4,110.28		
30/6/X5 6–12	16.88		

Account Name: Cleaning materials		Account No: 402	
Narrative	£	*Narrative*	£
23/6/X5 b/f	2,010.43		

Account Name: Discounts allowed		Account No: 448	
Narrative	£	*Narrative*	£
23/6/x5 b/f	27,445.94		
30/6/X5 6–12	460.81		

Account Name: Trade debtors		Account No: 011	
Narrative	£	*Narrative*	£
23/6/X5 b/f	834,792.12	30/6/X5 6–11	69,127.69
		30/6/X5 6–11	460.81

Account Name: Cash at bank (current)		Account No: 012	
Narrative	£	*Narrative*	£
23/6/x5 b/f	84,579.77	30/6/X5 6–11	81,704.40
30/6/X5 6–11	70,677.17		

Account Name: Cash at bank (deposit)		Account No: 013	
Narrative	£	*Narrative*	£
31/3/X5 b/f	250,050.00		

Account Name: Cash in hand		Account No: 014	
Narrative	£	*Narrative*	£
23/6/X5 b/f	24.90	30/6/X5 6-12	84.79
30/6/X5 6-11	175.10		

Account Name: Trade creditors		Account No: 020	
Narrative	£	*Narrative*	£
30/6/X5 6-11	8,550.14	23/6/X5 b/f	367,251.44
30/6/X5 6-11	27.97		

Account Name: VAT control account		Account No: 022	
Narrative	£	*Narrative*	£
30/6/X5 6-11	23,656.51	23/6/X5 b/f	22,987.38
30/6/X5 6-12	6.29	30/6/X5 6-11	230.75

Unit 2 Data and Tasks

T-S Designs Limited

To complete this assignment you will need:

- pen/pencil;
- calculator.

Factfile

Business name	T-S Designs Limited
Location	Shepherd's Bush, London
Personnel	Barry Graham – the majority shareholder and chief designer Sheila Graham – Barry's wife and assistant designer You – responsible for all aspects of the day-to-day accounting
Business	Design and printing of T-shirts

Business profile

Barry started the business working from home four years ago. Prior to that he was an art teacher. The business has recently moved to a small unit on a new industrial estate.

Barry designs logos and pictures which are then transferred onto plain T-shirts using silk-screen printing techniques.

The business currently has a large range of standard designs created by Barry. These are advertised in magazines.

Barry also accepts commissions for one-off designs, for instance for clubs and societies.

Ordering procedures

Customers place orders using the order form which accompanies the business's advert.

Standard designs

All orders for standard designs must be accompanied by the full money.

One-off designs

Orders for one-off designs must be accompanied by a deposit of £20.00.

Once a one-off design is finished the T-shirts are sent with an invoice for the balance owed. All sales invoices are recorded in the day book. All credit notes issued must be approved by Barry before recording in the day book. The business does not have a separate returns day book.

Purchasing procedures

Barry does not use purchases orders, but all goods ordered are recorded in the order book (including price agreed or expected).

All goods are recorded in the goods received log. Each delivery received is given a GRN number. Purchase invoices received from suppliers are stamped on receipt, numbered and checked for accuracy. Only accurate invoices are recorded in the day book. All others are passed to Barry who deals with queries.

Invoices for services and credit notes received are sent to Barry for his approval. They are recorded in the day book after they have been approved. The business does not have a separate returns day book.

Terms of trade

A settlement discount of 2% is offered on all invoices for the balance payable on one-off designs settled within seven days from the date of the invoice.

The company is registered for VAT.

Some suppliers offer settlement discounts.

Your assignment

Today is 5 July 19Z2. You are processing a batch of sales invoices and a batch of purchase invoices. You have been away on holiday and have discovered a backlog of invoices. Someone else has tried to process the outstanding purchase and sales invoices.

Part 1

Check the batch of sales invoices and credit notes before they are sent to customers. Finish recording them in the day book. Make postings to the nominal and debtors' ledgers.

Write off the remaining balance on J Harper's account in the debtors' ledger.

Part 2

Process the batch of purchase invoices and credit notes received and record them in the day book.

Make postings to the nominal and creditors' ledgers. (Another batch of invoices has already been posted. You may assume that you are satisfied with these.)

Part 3

Close off the accounts in the debtors' and creditors' ledger and the control accounts. Reconcile the control accounts to the ledgers. You may assume that all other accounts have nil balances.

When you are satisfied that you have solved any discrepancies reconcile First Fashions Limited's account using the statement provided. Identify any queries on the face of the statement. Adjust the ledger accounts for any errors found.

Part 4

Make a contra entry between the accounts of First Fashions Limited in the debtors' and creditors' ledgers (they have recently agreed to this).

Part 5

Produce an aged analysis of debtors and a statement to send to First Fashions Limited. Draft a covering letter to accompany the statement.

Documents provided

Completed copies of internal documents

- Sales invoices
- Credit note
- Returns notes

Documents received from suppliers

- Purchase invoices
- Credit notes
- Delivery notes
- Statement and letter

Other internal information

- Purchasing book

Answer book

- Sales day book
- Purchase day book
- Debtors' ledger
- Creditors' ledger
- Nominal ledger
- Statement of account
- Goods received log

2212X

T-S DESIGNS LTD

Unit 4 Cobbold Road Industrial Estate
Cobbold Road London W12 9RE

Sale to: First Fashions
323 King Street
Hammersmith
W6 0PJ

Tax point 29 June 19Z2

Order no. 455A

Qty	Description	Unit price £	Amount £
10	White T-shirts (small)	5.00	50.00
10	White T-shirts (medium)	6.00	60.00
10	White T-shirts (large)	7.00	70.00
15	White T-shirts (ex lge)	8.00	120.00
			300.00
Artwork			54.28
			354.28
VAT at 17.5%			60.76
			415.04
Less deposit			20.00
			395.04

Terms 2/7 n/30

REMITTANCE ADVICE

First Fashion
323 King Street
Hammersmith
W6 0PJ

Invoice no.	Date	Amount	Discount
2212X	29/6/Z2	£395.04	

Please make cheques payable to T-S Designs Ltd

2213X

T-S DESIGNS LTD

Unit 4 Cobbold Road Industrial Estate
Cobbold Road London W12 9RE

Sale to: Mr R G Smith
67 Ariel Avenue
Beckenham
BR4 8TG

Tax point 29 June 19Z2

Order no. 446A

Qty	Description	Unit price £	Amount £
20	White T-shirts (ex lge)	8.00	160.00
			160.00
Artwork			39.60
			199.60
VAT at 17.5%			34.23
			233.83
Less deposit			20.00
			213.83

Terms 2/7 n/30

REMITTANCE ADVICE

Mr R G Smith
67 Ariel Avenue
Beckenham
BR4 8TG

Invoice no.	Date	Amount	Discount
2213X	29/6/Z2	£213.83	

Please make cheques payable to T-S Designs Ltd

2214X

T-S DESIGNS LTD

Unit 4 Cobbold Road Industrial Estate
Cobbold Road London W12 9RE

Sale to: Green Lodge Garden Club
122 Morrison Road
Twickenham
TW4 8DD

Tax point 29 June 19Z2

Order no. 447A

Qty	Description	Unit price £	Amount £
24	White T-shirts (medium)	6.00	144.00
12	White T-shirts (large)	7.00	84.00
			228.00
Artwork			64.00
			292.00
VAT of 17.5%			50.08
			342.08
Less deposit			20.00
			322.08

Terms 2/7 n/30

REMITTANCE ADVICE

Green Lodge Garden Club
122 Morrison Road
Twickenham
TW4 8DD

Invoice no.	Date	Amount	Discount
2214X	29/6/Z2	£322.08	

Please make cheques payable to T-S Designs Ltd

2215X

T-S DESIGNS LTD

Unit 4 Cobbold Road Industrial Estate
Cobbold Road London W12 9RE

Sale to: Lisa Taylor
Flipper Health Club
98 Long Lane
Bicester OX6 6RE

Tax point 29 June 19Z2

Order no. 459A

Qty	Description	Unit price £	Amount £
12	Pink T-shirts (large)	7.00	84.00
12	Pink T-shirts (ex lge)	8.00	96.00
			180.00
Artwork (repeat - no charge)			0.00
			180.00
VAT at 17.5%			30.87
			210.87
Less deposit			20.00
			190.87

Terms 2/7 n/30

REMITTANCE ADVICE

Lisa Taylor
Flipper Health Club
98 Long Lane
Bicester OX6 6RE

Invoice no.	Date	Amount	Discount
2215X	29/6/Z2	£190.87	

Please make cheques payable to T-S Designs Ltd

2216X

T-S DESIGNS LTD

Unit 4 Cobbold Road Industrial Estate
Cobbold Road London W12 9RE

Sale to: Old Lane Tennis Club
Fao Sheila Walker
1 Old Lane
Sutton SM21 7TY

Tax point 29 June 19Z2

Order no. 467A

Qty	Description	Unit price £	Amount £
12	White T-shirts (small)	5.00	60.00
12	White T-shirts (medium)	6.00	72.00
12	Pink T-shirts (large)	7.00	84.00
12	Pink T-shirts (ex lge)	8.00	96.00
			312.00
Artwork			39.00
			351.00
VAT at 17.5%			60.20
			411.20
Less deposit			20.00
			391.20

Terms 2/7 n/30

REMITTANCE ADVICE

Old Lane Tennis Club
Fao Sheila Walker
1 Old Lane
Sutton SM21 7TY

Invoice no.	Date	Amount	Discount
2216X	29/6/Z2	£391.20	

Please make cheques payable to T-S Designs Ltd

2217X

T-S DESIGNS LTD

Unit 4 Cobbold Road Industrial Estate
Cobbold Road London W12 9RE

Sale to: First Fashions
323 King Street
Hammersmith
W6 0PJ

Tax point 29 June 19Z2

Order no. 456A

Qty	Description	Unit price £	Amount £
12	Red T-shirts (small)	5.00	60.00
			60.00
Artwork			43.98
			103.98
VAT at 17.5%			17.83
			121.81
Less deposit			20.00
			101.81

Terms 2/7 n/30

REMITTANCE ADVICE

First Fashion
323 King Street
Hammersmith
W6 0PJ

Invoice no.	Date	Amount	Discount
2217X	29/6/Z2	£101.81	

Please make cheques payable to T-S Designs Ltd

Credit note 187B

T-S DESIGNS LTD

Unit 4 Cobbold Road Industrial Estate
Cobbold Road London W12 9RE

Credit to: Lisa Taylor
Flipper Health Club
98 Long Lane
Bicester OX6 6RE

Date/Tax point 29 June 19Z2

Reason for credit: Incorrect no. of T-shirts charged inv. 2199X

Qty	Description	Unit price £	Amount £
5	White T-shirts (small)	5.00	25.00
			25.00
Artwork			0.00
			25.00
VAT at 17.5%			4.28
			29.28

B Graham
6/22

RETURNS NOTE		
Date 8/6/Z2	**Packed by** C Fletcher	**Number** 291
Supplier	**Details**	**Supplier ref**
First Fashions	Faulty sewing Blue T-shirts 10 × extra large	677599

RETURNS NOTE		
Date 3/6/Z2	**Packed by** C Fletcher	**Number** 292
Supplier	**Details**	**Supplier ref**
Crown Fabrics	Incorrect goods (not ordered) 24 × Green T-shirts	4222

Glad Rags Ltd

A1127

81 New Road
London
W8 5EE

Tax point 21 June 19Z2

Telephone *0181 765 8900*
Fax *0181 765 8564*

VAT Reg. No. 567 3344 82

Sale to:
T- S Design Ltd
Unit 4
Cobbold Road
Shepherd's Bush
W12 9RE

Description	*Unit price* £	*Total* £
10 black T-shirts (small)	3.40	34.00
5 black T-shirts (medium)	3.70	18.50
5 white T-shirts (large)	3.80	19.00
		71.50
Value Added Tax at 17.5%		11.89
		83.39

Invoice no. 11161	No.	
Order		
GRN		
Accuracy		
Discount		
VAT		

Trade terms

5% discount for settlement within 7 days of date of invoice

Strictly 30 days from date of invoice

REMITTANCE ADVICE

T-S Designs Ltd
Unit 4
Cobbold Road
Shepherd's Bush W12 9RE

Invoice A1127

Remittance £83.39
Discount

Glad Rags Ltd

A1046

81 New Road
London
W8 5EE

Tax point 20 June 19Z2

Telephone	*0181 765 8900*
Fax	*0181 765 8564*

VAT Reg. No. 567 3344 82

Sale to:
T-S Design Ltd
Unit 4
Cobbold Road
Shepherd's Bush
W12 9RE

Description	*Unit price* £	*Total* £
10 white T-shirts (small)	3.40	34.00
10 white T-shirts (medium)	3.70	37.00
5 white T-shirts (large)	3.80	19.00
		90.00
Value Added Tax at 17.5%		14.96
		104.96

Invoice no. 11161		
	No.	
Order		
GRN		
Accuracy		
Discount		
VAT		

Trade terms

5% discount for settlement within 7 days of date of invoice

Strictly 30 days from date of invoice

REMITTANCE ADVICE

T-S Designs Ltd
Unit 4
Cobbold Road
Shepherd's Bush W12 9RE

Invoice A1046

Remittance £104.96
Discount

Glad Rags Ltd

A1066

81 New Road
London
W8 5EE

Tax point 21 June 19Z2

Telephone *0181 765 8900*
Fax *0181 765 8564*

VAT Reg. No. 567 3344 82

Sale to:
T-S Design Ltd
Unit 4
Cobbold Road
Shepherd's Bush
W12 9RE

Description	*Unit price* £	*Total* £
5 purple T-shirts (small)	3.40	17.00
5 orange T-shirts (medium)	3.70	18.50
		35.50
Value Added Tax at 17.5%		5.90
		41.40

Invoice no. 11162		
	No.	
Order		
GRN		
Accuracy		
Discount		
VAT		

Trade terms

5% discount for settlement within 7 days of date of invoice

Strictly 30 days from date of invoice

REMITTANCE ADVICE

T-S Designs Ltd
Unit 4
Cobbold Road
Shepherd's Bush W12 9RE

Invoice A1066

Remittance £41.40
Discount

English Gas plc

English Gas plc
West London
PO Box 46
London W6 8YH

COMMERCIAL USER QUARTERLY BILLING

T-S Design Ltd
Unit 4 Ind Est
Cobbold Road
Shepherd's Bush
W12 9RE

Account reference
6785 5544 IND

Enquiries
0181 465 7654

VAT REGISTRATION NO. 567 8877 94

Meter reading Present	*Meter reading* Previous	*Gas supplied* Cubic feet (hundreds)	*Gas supplied* Therms	*Pence per therm*	£	*VAT rate*
1766	1456	310	318.99	39.8	126.96	8%
STANDING CHARGE					9.20	8%
					136.16	
Total (excl VAT)		£136.16	VAT @ 8%	£10.89	£147.05	

Date of reading	**Date of account (Tax point)**	**Calorific value**
14 6 Z2	15 6 Z2	38.4 MJ/m³ (1029 BTUs/cu.ft)

11163
B Graham
6|22

....

bank giro credit

Customer reference number
6785 5544 IND

Cashier's stamp and initials

Signature ____________________

Date ____________________

23-78-09
Southern Bank plc
Head office
collection account

Cash____________________

Cheques____________________

Total ____________________

First Fashions Ltd

567a Fulham Road London SW10 9EN

Sales inv. 677877

VAT registration number 675 8990 56

Tax point 17 6 19Z2

Sale to:

T-S Designs Ltd
Unit 4
Cobbold Road Industrial Estate
Cobbold Road
Shepherd's Bush
W12 9RE

	Unit price	
	£	£
White T-shirts 20 extra large	3.90	78.00
VAT @ 17.5%		13.65
Total		91.65

Invoice no. 11164		
Order	No.	
GRN		
Accuracy		
Discount		
VAT		

Terms: Strictly 28 days nett

First Fashions Ltd

567a Fulham Road London SW10 9EN

Sales inv. 677656

VAT registration number 675 8990 56

Tax point 10 6 19Z2

Sale to:

T-S Designs Ltd
Unit 4
Cobbold Road Industrial Estate
Cobbold Road
Shepherd's Bush
W12 9RE

	Unit price	
	£	£
Black T-shirts		
20 extra large	3.90	78.00
VAT @ 17.5%		13.65
Total		91.65

Invoice no. 11165		
	No.	
Order		
GRN		
Accuracy		
Discount		
VAT		

Terms: Strictly 28 days nett

First Fashions Ltd

567a Fulham Road London SW10 9EN

Sales inv. 677669

VAT registration number 675 8990 56

Tax point 12 6 19Z2

Sale to:

T-S Designs Ltd
Unit 4
Cobbold Road Industrial Estate
Cobbold Road
Shepherd's Bush
W12 9RE

	Unit price	
	£	£
Yellow T-shirts		
10 small	3.35	33.50
VAT @ 17.5%		5.86
Total		39.36

Terms: Strictly 28 days nett

Invoice no. 11166		
Order	No.	
GRN		
Accuracy		
Discount		
VAT		

Estate Properties Ltd

367 Riverside Way, Uxbridge, Middlesex UB8 2YF

Sales invoice no. 35702

Date 3 June 19Z2

Ref: 4cr

Rent of property *(address)*

Unit 4
Cobbold Road Industrial Estate
Cobbold Road
London
W12 9RE

Rent for the period 1 February to 30 April 19Z2
at £200 per calendar month

£600

11167
B Graham
6/22

Crown Fabrics Ltd

456 Crown Hill
Croydon CR10 1RY

VAT reg no 567 5433 17

Tel: 0181 649 6723
Fax: 0181 649 0987

Tax point 10 June 19Z2

Sale 4566

Customer

T-S Designs Ltd
Unit 4 Cobbold Road
Shepherd's Bush
London
W12 9RE

	VAT rate	
	£	£
2 dozen pink T-shirts (mixed sizes)		
@ £3.75 each		90.00
VAT	17.5%	15.75
		105.75

Invoice no. 11168		
Order	No.	
GRN		
Accuracy		
Discount		
VAT		

Our terms: Strictly 30 days from day of invoice

Crown Fabrics Ltd

456 Crown Hill
Croydon CR10 1RY

VAT reg no 567 5433 17

Tel: 0181 649 6723
Fax: 0181 649 0987

Date/Tax point 9 June 19Z2

Credit note

C567

Reason for credit

Incorrect goods delivered (Invoice 4222)

Customer

T-S Designs Ltd
Unit 4 Cobbold Road
Shepherd's Bush
London
W12 9RE

	VAT rate	
	£	£
2 dozen green T-shirts (mixed sizes) @ £3.75 each		90.00
VAT	17.5%	15.75
		105.75

C2251
B Graham
6/22

First Fashions Ltd

567a Fulham Road London SW10 9EN

Credit note 338994C

VAT registration number 675 8990 56

Date/Tax point 12 6 19Z2

Reason for credit: Faulty goods returned

T-S Designs Ltd
Unit 4
Cobbold Road Industrial Estate
Cobbold Road
Shepherd's Bush
W12 9RE

	Unit price	
	£	£
Blue T-shirts		
10 extra large	3.90	39.00
VAT @ 17.5%		6.82
Total		45.82

C2252
B Graham
6/22

First Fashions Ltd

567a Fulham Road London SW10 9EN

VAT registration number 675 8990 56

Delivery to:

Date: 9 6 19Z2

T-S Designs Ltd
Unit 4
Cobbold Road Industrial Estate
Cobbold Road
Shepherd's Bush
W12 9RE

Goods	*Quantity*
Black T-shirts (extra large)	20

Signature A Beamish

Print name A BEAMISH

Crown Fabrics Ltd

456 Crown Hill
Croydon CR10 1RY

VAT Reg. No. 567 5433 17

Tel: 0181 649 6723
Fax: 0181 649 0987

Delivery date 10 June 19Z2

Customer

T-S Designs Ltd
Unit 4
Cobbold Road Industrial Estate
Cobbold Road
Shepherd's Bush
W12 9RE

2 dozen pink T-shirts (mixed sizes)

First Fashions Ltd

567a Fulham Road London SW10 9EN

VAT registration number 675 8990 56

Delivery to:

Date: 11 6 19Z2

T-S Designs Ltd
Unit 4
Cobbold Road Industrial Estate
Cobbold Road
Shepherd's Bush
W12 9RE

Goods	*Quantity*
Yellow T-shirts (small)	10

Signature A Beamish

Print name A BEAMISH

First Fashions Ltd

567a Fulham Road London SW10 9EN

VAT registration number 675 8990 56

Delivery to: **Date:** 16 6 19Z2

T-S Designs Ltd
Unit 4
Cobbold Road Industrial Estate
Cobbold Road
Shepherd's Bush
W12 9RE

Goods	*Quantity*
White T-shirts (extra large)	20

Signature A Beamish

Print name A BEAMISH

Glad Rags Ltd

81 New Road
London
W8 5EE

Telephone *0181 765 8900*
Fax *0181 765 8564*

VAT Reg. No. 567 3344 82

Order received 2 June 19Z2

Delivery date 18 June 19Z2

Deliver to:

T-S Designs Ltd
Unit 4
Cobbold Road Industrial Estate
Cobbold Road
Shepherd's Bush
W12 9RE

Quantity	*Description*
10	White T-shirts (small)
10	White T-shirts (medium)
5	White T-shirts (large)

Received by C Fletcher

Date 18 June Z2

Glad Rags Ltd

81 New Road
London
W8 5EE

Telephone *0181 765 8900*
Fax *0181 765 8564*

VAT Reg. No. 567 3344 82

Order received 2 June 19Z2

Delivery date 19 June 19Z2

Deliver to:

T-S Designs Ltd
Unit 4
Cobbold Road Industrial Estate
Cobbold Road
Shepherd's Bush
W12 9RE

Quantity	*Description*
10	Black T-shirts (small)
5	Black T-shirts (medium)
5	Black T-shirts (large)

Received by *C Fletcher*

Date 19 June Z2

Glad Rags Ltd

81 New Road
London
W8 5EE

Telephone	*0181 765 8900*	
Fax	*0181 765 8564*	**VAT Reg. No.** 567 3344 82

Order received 3 June 19Z2 | Delivery date 20 June 19Z2

Deliver to:

T-S Designs Ltd
Unit 4
Cobbold Road Industrial Estate
Cobbold Road
Shepherd's Bush
W12 9RE

Quantity	*Description*
5	Purple T-shirts (small)
5	Orange T-shirts (medium)

Received by A Beamish | Date 20-6-Z2

First Fashions Ltd

567a Fulham Road London SW10 9EN
Tel: 0181 223 7688 Fax: 0181 223 8677

Our ref: SH/TR

3 July 19Z2

B Graham Esq
T-S Designs Ltd
Unit 4
Cobbold Road Industrial Estate
Cobbold Road
Shepherd's Bush
W12 9RE

Dear Barry

Overdue balance

It has come to my attention that invoice 676499 dated 3 May 19Z2 and shown on the statement of account dated 31 May 19Z2 has not been paid. I can only assume that this is the result of an oversight as all subsequent invoices have been paid within our normal credit period. I trust I can expect payment in full in the very near future.

I enclose a copy of the latest statement of account. If you have any queries please do not hesitate to contact me.

Yours sincerely

A.H. Jessop

A H Jessop
Credit controller

Enc

First Fashions Ltd

567a Fulham Road London SW10 9EN

STATEMENT OF ACCOUNT

Customer name T-S Designs Ltd **T40**

Customer address Unit 4 Cobbold Road Industrial Estate
Cobbold Road
Shepherd's Bush W12 9RE

Statement date	30 June 19Z2	**Dr**		**Cr**		**Balance**	
Date	**Transaction**	**£**	**p**	**£**	**p**	**£**	**p**
1/6/Z2	Balance b/f	224	34			224	34
3/6/Z2	Payment - thank you			99	80	124	54
10/6/Z2	Invoice 677656	91	65			216	19
12/6/Z2	Credit note 338994C			45	82	170	37
12/6/Z2	Invoice 677669	39	36			209	73
17/6/Z2	Invoice 677877	91	65			301	38
	Balance					301	38

Purchasing book

Date	Order no.	Supplier	Qty	Description	Unit cost £	
30/5	2212	Point Ltd	10	2 litre black	9	46
2/6	2213	Point Ltd	5	0.5 litre red	3	67
3/6	2214	Point Ltd	5	0.5 litre blue	3	67
4/6	2215	Crown Fabrics	24	Pink T-Shirts	3	75
	2216	First Fashions	20	Black T-S Ex lge	3	90
5/6	2217	First Fashions	10	Small yellow T-S	3	35
			20	White T-S Ex lge	3	90
15/6	2218	Glad Rags	10	White T-Shirts Small	3	40
			10	White T-Shirts Medium	3	70
			5	White T-Shirts Large	3	80
16/6	2219	Glad Rags	10	Black T-Shirts small	3	40
			~~10~~ 5	Black T-Shirts medium	3	70
			5	White T-Shirts large	3	80
16/6	2220	Packers Ltd	10	Dozen packs black tissue	1	80
17/6	2221	Glad Rags	5	Purple T-Shirts small	3	40
			5	Orange T-Shirts medium	3	70
28/6	2222	Point Ltd	10	2 litre orange	9	15
29/6	2223	Crown Fabrics	12	Green T-Shirts	3	75
			12	Pink T-Shirts	3	75

Unit 2 Answer Book

Sales Day Book

Date	Customer	Inv	Total	Net	VAT

PURCHASE DAY BOOK

Date	Code	Supplier	Invoice no.	Total	Purchases	Heat/light			VAT

DEBTORS' LEDGER

Account name First Fashions — Account no. 53

Narrative	£		Narrative	£	
1/6/Z2 b/f	212	60	30/6/Z2 Cash	111	09

Account name J Harper — Account no. 54

Narrative	£		Narrative	£	
31/5/Z2 Inv 2012	121	16	30/6/Z2 Cash	22	70

Account name Evergreen Tennis Club — Account no. 55

Narrative	£		Narrative	£	
30/4/Z2 Inv 1999	76	22			

DEBTORS' LEDGER

Account name Lisa Taylor Account no. 56

Narrative	£		Narrative	£	

Account name Old Lane Tennis Account no. 57

Narrative	£		Narrative	£	

Account name R G Smith Account no. 58

Narrative	£		Narrative	£	

DEBTORS' LEDGER

Account name			Account no.		
Narrative	£		Narrative	£	

Account name			Account no.		
Narrative	£		Narrative	£	

Account name			Account no.		
Narrative	£		Narrative	£	

CREDITORS' LEDGER

Account name: English Telecomm — Account no. 25

Narrative	£		Narrative	£	
30/6/Z2 Cash	381	57	30/6/Z2 Inv. 11147	158	60
			11148	222	97

Account name: Packers Ltd — Account no. 29

Narrative	£		Narrative	£	
30/6/Z2 Cash	57	48	30/6/Z2 Inv. 11149	22	23
Discount	1	00	11150	24	56
			11151	24	56
			11152	9	36

Account name: Point Ltd — Account no. 31

Narrative	£		Narrative	£	
30/6/Z2 Cash	381	64	30/6/Z2 Inv. 11153	164	03
			11154	43	12
			11155	63	33
			11156	111	16

CREDITORS' LEDGER

Account name: Crown Fabrics — Account no. 32

Narrative	£		Narrative	£	
30/5/Z2 Cash	286	00	30/5/Z2 Inv. 11103	391	75
30/5/Z2 c/f	105	75			
	391	75		391	75
			1/6/Z2 b/f	105	75

Account name: Glad Rags — Account no. 40

Narrative	£		Narrative	£	
1/6/Z2 b/f	2	03			

Account name: First Fashions — Account no. 41

Narrative	£		Narrative	£	
30/5/Z2 Cash	99	80	30/5/Z2 Inv. 11105	99	80
30/5/Z2 c/f	45	82	11108	45	82
	145	62		145	62
			1/6/Z2 b/f	45	82

CREDITORS' LEDGER

Account name	Art Supplies			Account no.	45
Narrative	**£**		**Narrative**	**£**	
30/6/Z2 Cash	9	00	30/6/Z2 Inv. 11157	6	50
			11158	3	50
			11159	2	50

Account name	English Gas plc			Account no.	50
Narrative	**£**		**Narrative**	**£**	
15/4/Z2 Cash	312	00	31/3/Z2 Inv. 110888	312	00

Account name	Estate Properties Ltd			Account no.	52
Narrative	**£**		**Narrative**	**£**	
17/4/Z2 Cash	600	00	31/3/Z2 Inv. 110892	600	00

NOMINAL LEDGER

Account name: Sales — Account no. I01

Narrative	£		Narrative	£	
			24/5/Z2 b/f	62350	90

Account name: Debtors' ledger control — Account no A05

Narrative	£		Narrative	£	
31/5/Z2 b/f	943	88	30/6/Z2 Cash	653	54
			Discount	14	15

Account name: Purchases — Account no C02

Narrative	£		Narrative	£	
24/5/Z2 b/f	24811	30			

NOMINAL LEDGER

Account name: Heat and Light — Account no. E11

Narrative	£		Narrative	£	
31/5/Z2 b/f	811	67			

Account name: Rent and rates — Account no E25

Narrative	£		Narrative	£	
31/5/Z2 b/f	1215	90			

Account name: Legal costs — Account no. E27

Narrative	£		Narrative	£	
			31/4/Z2 b/f	20	90

NOMINAL LEDGER

Account name Creditors' ledger control **Account no.** L03

Narrative	£		Narrative	£	
30/6/Z2 Cash	2829	69	31/5/Z2 b/f	2149	54
Discount	1	00	30/6/Z2 PDB	856	42

Account name VAT control **Account no.** L10

Narrative	£		Narrative	£	
			24/5/Z2 b/f	301	90

Account name **Account no.**

Narrative	£		Narrative	£	

STATEMENT OF ACCOUNT

From T-S Designs Ltd Unit 4 Cobbold Road Industrial Estate
Cobbold Road, London W12 9RE

To:

Date:

Details	Dr		Cr		Balance	
	£	p	£	p	£	p

STATEMENT OF ACCOUNT

From T-S Designs Ltd Unit 4 Cobbold Road Industrial Estate
Cobbold Road, London W12 9RE

To:

Date:

Details	Dr		Cr		Balance	
	£	p	£	p	£	p

Goods received log

Date	GRN no.	Supplier	Qty	Description	Invoice received
6/6/Z2	559-7	Point Ltd	10	0.5 litre white	11147
7/6/Z2	559-8	Point Ltd	1	0.5 litre yellow	11143
8/6/Z2	559-9	Crayon Ltd	30	Black pens	11139
9/6/Z2	559-10	First Fashions	20	Black T-Shirts	
10/6/Z2	559-11	Crown Fabrics	24	Pink T-Shirts	
11/6/Z2	559-12	First Fashions	10	Yellow T-Shirts	
16/6/Z2	559-13	First Fashions	20	White T-Shirts	
17/6/Z2	559-14	Packers Ltd	70	Plastic bags	11150
18/6/Z2	559-15	Glad Rags	10	White T-Shirts Small	
			10	White T-Shirts Medium	
			5	White T-Shirts Large	
19/6/Z2	559-16	Glad Rags	10	Black T-Shirts small	
			5	Black T-Shirts medium	
			5	White T-Shirts large	
20/6/Z2	559-17	Glad Rags	5	Purple T-Shirts small	
			5	Orange T-Shirts medium	
30/6/Z2	559-18	Point Ltd	10	2 litre orange	

Unit 2 Answers

T–S Designs Limited

Purchase invoices

First Fashions Inv 676499 omitted from accounting records

No adjustment required until copy invoice and proof of delivery received

Sales day book as at 30 June 19Z2

Customer	*Inv*	*Total*	*Net*	*VAT*
		£	£	£
First Fashions	2212	395.04	337.26	57.78
RG Smith	2213	213.83	182.58	31.25
Green Lodge Garden Clubs	2214	322.08	274.98	47.10
Lisa Taylor	2215	190.87	162.98	27.89
Old Lane Tennis Club	2216	391.20	333.98	57.22
First Fashions	2217	101.81	86.96	14.85
Lisa Taylor	187B	(29.28)	(25.00)	(4.28)
		1,585.55	1,353.74	231.81

Tutorial note

The sales day book postings have been arrived at as follows.

- The total represents the amount payable (ie. the invoice total which is net of the £20 deposit).
- The net amount takes into account the non-VAT part of the £20 deposit.
- The VAT has been calculated at 17.5% x 98% of the net invoice amount, less the VAT element of the £20 deposit (£20 x 17.5%/117.5).

Taking the first invoice (No. 2212 to First Fashions) as an example:

	Total	*Net*	*VAT*
	£	£	£
Invoice amounts	415.04	354.28	60.76
Less deposit	(20.00)	(17.02)	(2.98)
	395.04	337.26	57.78

The VAT of £60.76 which is shown on the invoice is £354.28 x 98% x 17.5%.

Purchase day book as at 30 June 19Z2

Code	*Supplier*	*Invoice no*	*Total*	*Purchase*	*Heat/ light*	*Rent / rates*	*VAT*
			£	£	£	£	£
40	Glad Rags	11160	83.39	71.50			11.89
40	Glad Rags	11161	104.96	90.00			14.96
40	Glad Rags	11162	41.40	35.50			5.90
50	English Gas plc	11163	147.05		136.16		10.89
41	First Fashions	11164	91.65	78.00			13.65
41	First Fashions	11165	91.65	78.00			13.65
41	First Fashions	11166	39.36	33.50			5.86
52	Estate Properties	11167	600.00			600.00	
32	Crown Fabrics	11168	105.75	90.00			15.75
32	Crown Fabrics	C2251	(105.75)	(90.00)			(15.75)
41	First Fashions	C2252	(45.82)	(39.00)			(6.82)
			1,153.64	347.50	136.16	600.00	69.98

DEBTORS' LEDGER

Account name: First Fashions **Account number: 53**

Narrative		£	*Narrative*		£
1/6/Z2	brought forward	212.60	30/6/Z2	Cash	111.09
30/6/22	Inv 2212	395.04			
	Inv 2217	101.81	30/6/Z2	carried forward	598.36
		709.45			709.45
30/6/Z2	brought forward	598.36	30/6/Z2	Contra	301.38
			30/6/Z2	carried forward	296.98
		598.36			598.36

Account name: J Harper **Account number: 54**

Narrative		£	*Narrative*		£
31/5/Z2	Inv 2012	121.16	30/6/Z2	Cash	22.70
			30/6/Z2	Bad debt	98.46
		121.16			121.16

Account name: Evergreen Tennis Club **Account number: 55**

Narrative		£	*Narrative*		£
30/4/22	Inv 1999	76.22			

Account name: Lisa Taylor **Account number: 56**

Narrative		£	*Narrative*		£
30/6/Z2	Inv 2215	190.87	30/6/Z2	CN 1878	29.28
			30/6/Z2	carried forward	161.59
		190.87			190.87
1/7/Z2	carried forward	161.59			

Account name: Old Lane Tennis **Account number: 57**

Narrative		£	*Narrative*		£
30/6/Z2	Inv 2216	391.20			

Account name: RG Smith **Account number: 58**

Narrative		£	*Narrative*		£
30/6/Z2	Inv 2213	213.83			

Account name: Green Lodge Garden Club **Account number: 59**

Narrative		£	*Narrative*		£
30/6/Z2	Inv 2214	322.08			

CREDITORS' LEDGER

Account name: English Telecomm **Account number:** 25

Narrative		£	*Narrative*		£
30/6/Z2	Cash	381.57	30/6/Z2	Inv 11147	158.60
				Inv 11148	222.97
		381.57			381.57

Account name: Packers Limited **Account number:** 29

Narrative		£	*Narrative*		£
30/6/Z2	Cash	57.48	30/6/Z2	Inv 11149	22.23
	Discount	1.00		Inv 11150	24.56
30/6/Z2	carried forward	22.23		Inv 11151	24.56
				Inv 11152	9.36
		80.71			80.71
			1/7/Z2	brought forward	22.23

Account name: Point Limited **Account number:** 31

Narrative		£	*Narrative*		£
30/6/Z2	Cash	381.64	30/6/Z2	Inv 11153	164.03
				Inv 11154	43.12
				Inv 11155	63.33
				Inv 11156	111.16
		381.64			381.64

Account name: Crown Fabrics **Account number:** 32

Narrative		£	*Narrative*		£
30/5/Z2	Cash	286.00	30/5/Z2	Inv 11103	391.75
30/5/Z2	carried forward	105.75			
		391.75			391.75
30/6/Z2	CR 2251	105.75	1/6/Z2	brought forward	105.75
30/6/Z2	carried forward	105.75	30/6/Z2	Inv 11168	105.75
		211.50			211.50
			1/7/Z2	brought forward	105.75

Account name: Glad Rags **Account number:** 40

Narrative		£	*Narrative*		£
1/6/Z2	brought forward	2.03	30/6/Z2	Inv 11160	83.39
30/6/Z2	carried forward	227.72		Inv 11161	104.96
				Inv 11162	41.40
		229.75			229.75
			1/7/Z2	brought forward	227.72

Account name: First Fashions **Account number:** 41

Narrative		£	*Narrative*		£
30/5/Z2	Cash	99.80	30/6/Z2	Inv 11105	99.80
30/5/Z2	carried forward	45.82		Inv 11108	45.82
		145.62			145.62
30/6/Z2	CR C2252	45.82	1/6/Z2	brought forward	45.82
			30/6/Z2	Inv 11164	91.65
				Inv 11165	91.65
30/6/Z2	carried forward	222.66		Inv 11166	39.36
		268.48			268.48
			30/6/Z2	brought forward	222.66
30/6/Z2	Contra	222.66		Adjustment	78.72

Account name: Art Supplies **Account number:** 45

Narrative		£	*Narrative*		£
30/6/Z2	Cash	9.00	30/6/Z2	Inv 11157	6.50
30/6/Z2	carried forward	3.50		Inv 11158	3.50
				Inv 11159	2.50
		12.50			12.50
			1.7.Z2	brought forward	3.50

Account name: English Gas plc **Account number:** 50

Narrative		£	*Narrative*		£
15/4/Z2	Cash	312.00	31.2.Z2	Inv 11088	312.00
			30/6/Z2	Inv 11163	147.05

Account name: Estate Properties Limited **Account number:** 52

Narrative		£	*Narrative*		£
17/4/Z2	Cash	600.00	31/3/Z2	Inv 11089	600.00
			30/6/Z2	Inv 11167	600.00

NOMINAL LEDGER

Account name: Sales **Account number:** 101

Narrative		£	*Narrative*		£
			24/5/Z2	brought forward	62,350.90
			30/6/Z2	SDB	1,353.74

Account name: Debtors' ledger control **Account number:** A05

Narrative		£	*Narrative*		£
31/5/Z2	brought forward	943.88	30/6/Z2	Cash	653.54
30/6/Z2	SDB	1,585.55		Discount	14.15
			30/6/Z2	Bad debt	98.46
			30/6/Z2	carried forward	1,763.28
30/6/Z2		2,529.43			2,529.43
		1,763.28	30/6/Z2	Contra	222.66
			30/6/Z2	carried forward	1,540.62
		1,763.28			1,763.28
1/7/Z2	brought forward	1,540.62			

Account name: Purchases **Account number:** CO2

Narrative		£	*Narrative*		£
24/5/Z2	brought forward	24,811.30			
30/6/Z2	PDB	347.50			

Account name: Heat and light **Account number:** E11

Narrative		£	*Narrative*		£
31/5/Z2	brought forward	811.67			
30/6/Z2	PDB	136.16			

Account name: Rent and rates **Account number:** E25

Narrative		£	*Narrative*		£
31/5/Z2	brought forward	1,215.90			
30/6/Z2	PDB	600.00			

Account name: Legal costs **Account number:** E27

Narrative		£	*Narrative*		£
			30/4/Z2	brought forward	20.90

Account name: Creditors' ledger control **Account number:** L03

Narrative		£	*Narrative*		£
30/6/Z2	Cash	2,829.69	31/5/Z2	brought forward	2,149.54
	Discount	1.00	30/6/Z2	PDB	856.42
30/6/Z2	Contra	222.66	30/6/Z2	PDB	1,153.64
30/6/Z2	carried forward	1,106.25			
		4,159.60			4,159.60
			1.7.Z2	brought forward	1,106.25

Account name: VAT control **Account number:** L10

Narrative		£	*Narrative*		£
30/6/Z2	PDB	69.48	24/5/Z2	brought forward	301.90
			30/6/Z2	SDB	231.82

Account name: Bad debts **Account number:** L20

Narrative		£	*Narrative*		£
30/6/Z2	Debtors' ledger control	98.46			

FIRST FASHIONS LIMITED

567a Fulham Road, London SW10 9EN

Statement of Account

Customer name: T-SDesigns Limited T40

Customer address: Unit 4 Cobbold Road Industrial Estate
Cobbold Road, Shepherd's Bush, London W12 9RE

Statement date 31 June 19Z2		*Debit*	*Credit*	*Balance*
Date	*Transaction*	£	£	£
1/6/Z2	Balance brought forward	224.34		224.34
3/6/Z2	Payment – thank you		✓ 99.80	124.54
10/6/Z2	Invoice 677656	✓ 91.65		216.19
12/6/Z2	Credit note 338994C		✓ 45.82	170.37
12/6/Z2	Invoice 677669	✓ 39.36		209.73
17/6/Z2	Invoice 677877	✓ 91.65		301.38
	Balance			301.38

Balance per statement	301.38
Missing invoice	78.72
Balance per creditors' ledger	222.66

T-S Designs Limited

Unit 4 Cobbold Road Industrial Estate, Cobbold Road, Shepherd's Bush, London W12 9RE

A H Jessop Esq
First Fashions Limited
567a Fulham Road
London SWIO 9EN

5 July 19Z2

Your ref: SHITR
Our ref: BG

Dear Arthur

Statement of account

Thank you for your letter of 3 July 19Z2. We have reviewed the statement. It appears that we have never received invoice 676499. Please send us a copy invoice and proof of delivery. We will then be happy to pay this invoice in full.

We have carried out the contra entry as agreed. Please find enclosed a statement of account updated for the contra.

Please contact me if you need any further information.

Yours sincerely

Barry Graham
Director

Statement of Account

T-S Designs Limited

Unit 4 Cobbold Road Industrial Estate, Cobbold Road, Shepherd's Bush, London W12 9RE

To: FIRST FASHIONS LIMITED
567a Fulham Road, London SW10 9EN

Date: 30/6/Z2

		Debit £	*Credit* £	*Balance* £
1/6/Z2	brought forward	212.60		212.60
30/6/Z2	Cash		111.09	101.51
30/6/Z2	Invoice 2212	395.04		496.55
	Invoice 2217	101.81		598.36
30/6/Z2	Contra		222.66	375.70

T-S Designs Limited – aged debtors' listing as at July 19Z2

No	*Account*	*Total* £	*Current* £	*30+* £	*60+* £
53	First Fashions	296.98	296.98		
54	J Harper	-			
55	Evergreen Tennis Club	76.22			76.22
56	Lisa Taylor	161.59	161.59		
57	Old Lane Tennis Club	391.20	391.20		
58	RG Smith	213.83	213.83		
59	Green Lodge Garden Club	322.08	322.08		
		1,461.90	1,385.68		76.22

A N Other 517/Z2

Date	*Grn no*	*Supplier*	*Qty*	*Description*	*Inv received*
616/Z2	559-7	Paint Limited	10	0.5 litre white	11147
716/Z2	559-8	Paint Limited	1	0.5 litre yellow	11143
816/Z2	559-9	Crayon Limited	30	Black pens	11139
916/Z2	559-10	First Fashions	20	Black T-shirts	11165
1016/Z2	559-11	Crown Fabrics	24	Pink T-shirts	11168
1116/Z2	559-12	First Fashions	10	Yellow T-shirts	11166
1616/Z2	559-13	First Fashions	20	White T-shirts	11164
1716/Z2	559-14	Packers Limited	70	Plastic bags	11150
1816/Z2	559-15	Glad Rags	10	White T-shirts – small	11161
			10	White T-shirts – medium	11161
			5	White T-shirts – large	11161
1916/Z2	559-16	Glad Rags	10	Black T-shirts – small	11160
			5	Black T-shirts – medium	11160
			5	Black T-shirts – large	11160
2016/Z2	559-17	Glad Rags	5	Purple T-shirts – small	11160
			5	Orange T-shirts – medium	11162
3016/Z2	559-18	Point Limited	10	2 litre orange	11162

Marking guide

Part 1

Sales day book	*Marks*
1 for each invoice – basic recording (date, name, number, total net of £20)	6
Principle of adjusting net/VAT amounts correctly for deposit	3
0.5 for each correctly calculated net/VAT invoice amount (consistent with student's treatment of deposit)	6
Correct recording of credit note	2
Totals	1
	18
Postings	
1 for each correct posting to debtors ledger/nominal ledger	10
Bad debt	
Writing off balance in debtors ledger and debtors control	2
	30

Part 2

Purchase day book	
1 for each invoice correctly recorded/analysed	11
Total	1
	12
Postings	
1 for each correct posting to creditors ledger/nominal ledger	16
Goods received log completion	
Entering invoice numbers	2
	30

Part 3

Closing off accounts

Deduct 1 for each incorrectly closed off a/c (even if nil balance, must be ruled off); minimum = nil	10
Reconciliation of control accounts (not shown in answer)	
Showing that balances on control accounts agree with total balances on debtors/creditors ledger accounts	4
First Fashion's reconciliation	
Evidence of checking on statement (ticks, etc)	1
Identifying discrepancy on balance brought forward (or carried forward) and tying up with 'missing invoice' letter	2
Adjusting (First Fashion's creditors) ledger ale and creditors control a/c	2
	5
	19

Part 4

Contra entry

1 for each entry in debtors/creditors ledger ales and control a/cs	4

Part 5

Aged debtors analysis

Deduct marks for incorrect analysis/amounts and poor presentation	5
Letter	
Letter format	2
Content	4
Style, presentation, etc	2
	8
Statement	
Must be consistent with student's debtors ledger account	4
	17
Total for practice simulation	**100**

Commentary

Part 1

This involves the recording of sales invoices in the day book and the subsequent posting of these to the debtors' ledger (individual invoice amounts) and to the nominal ledger account (totals).

The main problem in the day book recording is the analysis of the net and VAT amounts. Two factors complicate matters here: the deposit and the discount. These are covered in the tutorial note in the answer. When the deposit was originally received with the order, it would have been treated effectively as a cash sale: ie it would be recorded in the cash book, with the VAT analysed out, leaving the net amount as the sales figure. Thus when the balance invoice is issued, only the remaining amount payable is included in the SDB and the VAT must be reduced by the amount that has already been accounted for.

Secondly, do not forget that VAT is always calculated on the lowest amount the customer may pay – in this case, assuming the 2% settlement discount will be taken. This is why it is incorrect to calculate the VAT on the balance invoice as simply 17.5/117.5 x Balance payable. As you are given the total VAT on the invoice, which will have taken account of the discount, the easiest approach is simply to deduct the VAT included in the deposit to arrive at the VAT element for the SDB.

When writing off the bad debt, don't forget to adjust both the individual account and the control account.

Part 2

Part of the processing of purchase invoices is to check that you have actually received the goods for which you are being asked to pay. This will be done by checking them against the goods received log. Show that you have done this check by entering in the invoice number against the relevant GRN entry. You should also check the unit price quoted on the invoice against the purchasing book. If any queries arise from either of these checks, you should raise a memo as part of your answer.

Part 3

After closing off the ledger accounts, you should document your reconciliation of the control accounts to the ledgers. For example, for the debtors (remember this is before the contra on the First Fashions account):

List of debtors	
First Fashions	598.36
Evergreen Tennis Club	76.22
Lisa Taylor	161.59
Old Lane Tennis	391.20
RG Smith	213.83
Green Lodge GC	322.08
Balance on control account	1,763.28

When reconciling First Fashion's account, check off each item on the statement against the ledger account, noting down any discrepancies. The difference is in fact in the opening balance prior to the cash payment of £99.80 (£224.34 against £145.62). A letter from First Fashions throws some light on this – it would appear that an invoice (for £78.72, the difference) has been omitted from the records. In practice, you would wait for a copy invoice to check against the GRN log, etc. before adjusting the accounts. Here, you are expected to assume that it is a valid omission and adjust accordingly – as shown at the start of the answer.

Part 4

Again, do not forget to adjust both the individual accounts (in debtors' and creditors' ledgers) and the two control accounts for the contra.

Part 5

Although First Fashions is also a supplier, the statement you are required to send them is as to a customer. The only reference to the creditor side is the presence of the contra entry. However, in your covering letter it is sensible to mention the matter of the missing supplier invoice. As usual, ensure the letter is in the correct format and written in a professional style.

CHAPTER 17

Practice Central Assessment

Questions

You are reminded that competence must be achieved in each section. You should therefore attempt and aim to complete every task in each section.

All essential workings should be included within your answers, where appropriate.

You are advised to spend 60 minutes on Section 1, 75 minutes on Section 2 and 45 minutes on Section 3.

The Central Assessment is in three sections.

Section 1	Processing Exercise **Complete all four tasks**
Section 2	20 Short Answer Questions **Answer all questions**
Section 3	Communicating Accounting Information **Complete both tasks**

Sections 1, 2 and 3 all relate to the company described below.

Introduction

- Hathaway Design & Print is a family business offering printing services to industry.
- The Chief Accountant is Susan Hathaway.
- You are an Accounting Technician employed to assist Susan Hathaway.
- Double entry takes place in the nominal (general) ledger and the individual accounts of debtors and creditors are therefore regarded as memoranda accounts.

Data

Transactions

The following transactions, which occurred on 1 June 19X8, have been recorded in the Sales Day Book and the Cash Book (given below) but have not yet been entered into the ledger system. VAT has been calculated at a rate of 17.5%.

Sales day book

Date 19X8	*Details*	*Invoice No*	*Gross*	*VAT*	*Net*
			£	£	£
1 June	H Booth Limited	H01972	1,692	252	1,440
1 June	W Daiton Limited	H01973	752	112	640
1 June	The Peters Partnership	H01974	2,350	350	2,000
1 June	H Booth Limited	H01975	2,021	301	1,720
1 June	T Burbridge Limited	H01976	470	70	400
1 June	W Dalton Limited	H01977	94	14	80
			7,379	1,099	6,280

Cash book

Date 19X8	*Details*	*Disc allowed*	*Cash*	*Bank*	*Date 19X8*	*Details*	*Disc received*	*Cash*	*Bank*
		£	£	£			£	£	£
1 June	Balances b/f		120	8,392	1 June	Motor vehicle purchase			14,500
1 June	H Booth Limited	200		2,350	1 June	Loan repayment			450
1 June	T Burbridge Limited			940	1 June	Bank charges			108
1 June	W Dalton Limited			15,275	1 June	Motor insurance			317
					1 June	Balances c/f		120	11,582
		200	120	26,957				120	26,957

Balances

The following balances are available to you at the start of the day on 1 June 19X8

	£
Credit customers	
H Booth Limited	8,225
T Burbridge Limited	7,050
The Peters Partnership	5,875
W Dalton Limited	29,375
Sales	726,506
Sales (Debtors) ledger control	162,150
Bank charges	967
Discount allowed	370
VAT (credit balance)	15,365
Bank loan	15,300
Motor vehicles	17,650
Motor insurance	495

Journal entries

The following errors have been discovered and will need to be entered in Hathaway Design & Print's journal.

1. An amount of £717 has been recorded in the Office Equipment account instead of in the Electricity account.

2. A payment of £470 from a credit customer, Belton & Byng Limited, has been entered in the account of another credit customer, Belton Stationers, in error.

Section 1

Processing exercise

(Suggested time allocation: 60 minutes)

Complete all four tasks.

Task 1.1

Enter the opening balances listed on the last page into the following accounts provided in the Answer Book.

- H Booth Limited
- T Burbridge Limited
- The Peters Partnership
- W Dalton Limited
- Sales
- Sales (Debtors) Ledger Control
- Bank Charges
- Discounts Allowed
- VAT
- Bank Loan
- Motor Vehicles
- Motor Insurance

Task 1.2

Using the data shown in the sales day book and cash book, enter all the transactions into the relevant accounts.

Task 1.3

Balance off all the accounts clearly showing the balances carried down.

Taskl.4

Using the journal page provided, record the journal entries listed earlier.

Note.

- Narratives are not required in the journal.
- Journal items are **not** to be entered in the accounts.

Section 2

Short answer questions

(Suggested time allocation: 75 minutes)

Write in the space provided OR circle the correct answer in the Answer Book. Do not indicate your choice in any other way. ANSWER ALL OF THE FOLLOWING QUESTIONS.

Task 2.1

The invoice shown in the Answer Book has been prepared for a credit customer. A 2½% cash (settlement) discount is being offered. Complete the invoice by inserting the correct figures for Goods Total, VAT and Total.

Task 2.2

Should the total of the purchases day book be debited or credited to the purchases (creditors) ledger control account?

Task 2.3

List **four** books of prime (original) entry.

Task 2.4

What entries are required in the **nominal (general) ledger** to write off a bad debt of £352.50, inclusive of VAT at 17.5%? The VAT can be reclaimed.

Task 2.5

Briefly explain why a business would try to keep the amount of bad debts written off to a minimum.

Task 2.6

What is the purpose of the following documents?

(a) Delivery note

(b) Goods received note

(c) Advice note

Task 2.7

In April a local store ordered 10,000 advertising leaflets from Hathaway Design & Print to launch the opening of its new Household Department at the end of May. It was agreed that the leaflets were to be delivered on 21 May 19X8. Unfortunately, due to a printing error, the leaflets were not delivered until 1 June 19X8.

(a) Is the store within its rights to take legal action for late delivery of the leaflets?

(b) Briefly explain the reason for your answer.

Task 2.8

Hathaway Design & Print has recently issued a list of prices to its customers for its range of printed stationery. Unfortunately, an error has occurred and letterheads are listed as £5 per 1,000 instead of £50 per 1,000.

(a) Would the customers of Hathaway Design & Print be legally justified in demanding a supply of letterheads at £5 per 1,000?

(b) Briefly explain the reason for your answer.

Task 2.9

What do you understand by the term **personal account** within an accounting system.

Task 2.10

Give **three** reasons why the balance on Hathaway Design & Print's bank statement may not agree with the balance in its cash book.

Task 2.11

A cheque for £600 was received from a customer by Hathaway Design & Print but the customer's bank has now returned the cheque marked 'refer to drawer'.

What does this action usually indicate?

Task 2.12

Hathaway Design & Print has recently bought a new printing machine. Would the following be capital or revenue expenditure?

(a) Purchase of the printing machine

(b) Substantial staff training costs to operate the printing machine

(c) Ink for the printing machine

Task 2.13

Give **two** advantages of a computerised accounting system.

Task 2.14

Would you find the following accounts in the nominal (general) ledger, purchases ledger or sales ledger?

(a) Creditors control account

(b) Sales returns account

(c) B Cox Limited (a supplier)

Task 2.15

Hathaway Design & Print has recently received a quotation for industrial paper–cutting equipment for £8,000 ex works. What do you understand by the term ex works?

Task 2.16

Hathaway Design & Print keeps petty cash in a plastic bag on a shelf in the office so that it is convenient for everyone to access. Make **two** suggestions to improve security.

Task 2.17

Hathaway Design & Print is currently advertising for a Credit Controller. Describe **two** of the main functions of the person who fills this position?

Task 2.18

Hathaway Design & Print has an overdraft facility of £10,000. When its bank current account is overdrawn is the bank a creditor or debtor in the books of Hathaway Design & Print?

Task 2.19

Give **two** reasons why a credit note would be issued.

Task 2.20

With regard to the following cheque, give the name of the payee, the drawer and the drawee.

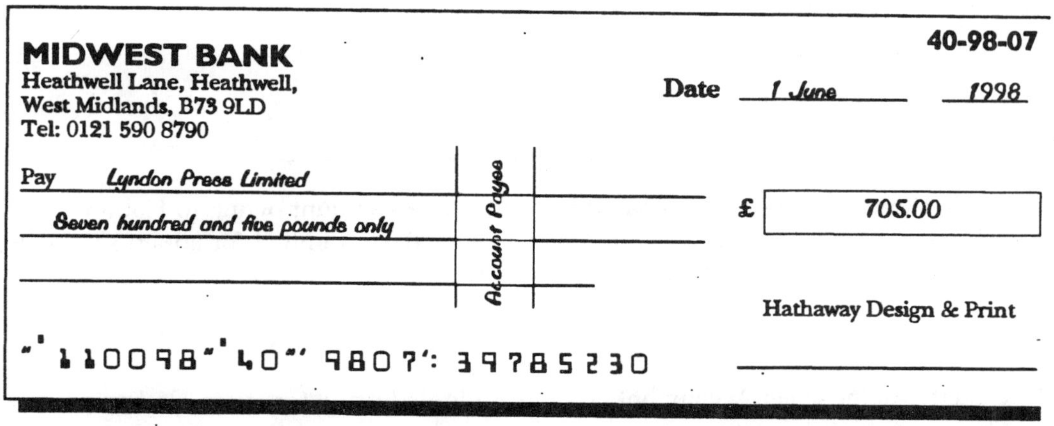

Section 3

Communicating accounting information

(Suggested time allocation: 45 minutes)

Answer both tasks.

Use the stationery provided in the Answer Book for your answers.

Data

STATEMENT

HATHAWAY DESIGN & PRINT
29 Watery Lane, Heathwell, West Midlands B71 3DQ
Telephone: 0121 590 3679 – Fax: 01 21 590 7894

To: T Baker Lirnited
Coomb Hollow
Heathwell
West Midlands 871 8ZL

31 May 19X8

Date	*Details*	*Debit*	*Credit*	*Balance*
		£	£	£
02.03.X8	Balance b/f			3,525.00
15.04.X8	Invoice H01606	1,175.00		4,700.00
27.05.X8	Invoice H01901	1,762.50		6,462.50

The above statement has been prepared in respect of an amount owing to Hathaway Design & Print. Today another order has been received from T Baker Limited for advertising leaflets, but its credit limit of £6,000 has already been exceeded.

Task 3.1

Write a letter to the Chief Accountant at T Baker Limited ready for Susan Hathaway's signature. You should enclose the statement and point out courteously but firmly that the credit limit has already been exceeded. This means that no further goods can he despatched until the amounts outstanding from March and April have been cleared.

Task 3.2

Write a memo to the Sales Department explaining the situation and informing them that no further goods should be despatched to T Baker Limited until further notice.

Answer Book

Section 1

Sales ledger

H Booth Limited

Date	*Details*	*Amount* £	*Date*	*Details*	*Amount* £

T Burbridge Limited

Date	*Details*	*Amount* £	*Date*	*Details*	*Amount* £

The Peters Partnership

Date	*Details*	*Amount* £	*Date*	*Details*	*Amount* £

W Dalton Limited

Date	Details	Amount £	Date	Details	Amount £

Nominal ledger

Sales

Date	Details	Amount £	Date	Details	Amount £

Sales (debtors) ledger control

Date	Details	Amount £	Date	Details	Amount £

Bank charges

Date	Details	Amount £	Date	Details	Amount £

Discounts allowed

Date	*Details*	*Amount* £	*Date*	*Details*	*Amount* £

VAT

Date	*Details*	*Amount* £	*Date*	*Details*	*Amount* £

Bank loan

Date	*Details*	*Amount* £	*Date*	*Details*	*Amount* £

Motor vehicles

Date	*Details*	*Amount* £	*Date*	*Details*	*Amount* £

Motor insurance

Date	*Details*	*Amount* £	*Date*	*Details*	*Amount* £

Journal

Date	*Details*	*Debit* £	*Credit* £

Section 2

Task 2.1

HATHAWAY DESIGN & PRINT

29 Watery Lane, Heathwell, West Midlands B71 3DO
Telephone: 0121 590 3679 – Fax: 0121 590 7894
Vat Reg. No. 600 1498 00

SALES INVOICE No H01978

To: C. Ridley Limited
18 St Peters Road
Heathwell
West Midlands B71 6DZ

Date and tax point: 15 June 1998

1000 Quotation sets @ £120.00 per 100 sets.

Goods Total	£__________
VAT	£__________
TOTAL	£__________

Terms: 2.5% cash discount for settlement within 7 days, otherwise net monthly

Task 2.2

Debited / Credited

Task 2.3

____

____

____

____

Task 2.4

Debit	£	*Credit*	£

Task 2.5

Task 2.6

(a) Delivery note

(b) Goods received note

(c) Advice note

Task 2.7

(a) Yes / No

(b) --

Task 2.8

(a) Yes / No

(b) --

Task 2.9

Task 2.10

Task 2.11

Task 2.12

(a) Capital / Revenue

(b) Capital / Revenue

(c) Capital / Revenue

Task 2.13

Task 2.14

(a) Creditors control account

(b) Sales returns account

(c) B Cox Limited (a supplier)

Task 2.15

Task 2.16

Task 2.17

(a) ______________________________

(b) ______________________________

Task 2.18

Creditor / Debtor

Task 2.19

____

____

____

____

Task 2.20

(a) The payee

____

(b) The drawer

____

(c) The drawee

____

Section 3

Task 3.1

HATHAWAY DESIGN & PRINT

29 Watery Lane, Heathwell, West Midlands B71 3DO
Telephone: 0121 590 3679 – Fax: 0121 590 7894

Proprietors: Donald T Hathaway, Jane Hathaway

Task 3.2

INTERNAL MEMORANDUM

To: Date:

From:

Subject:

Answers

Section 1

Sales ledger

H Booth Limited

Date	*Details*	*Amount* £	*Date*	*Details*	*Amount* £
1 June	Balance b/f	8,225	1 June	Bank	2,350
1 June	Sales	1,692	1 June	Discounts allowed	200
1 June	Sales	2,021	1 June	Balance c/d	9,388
		11,938			11,938
2 June	Balance b/d	9,388			

T Burbridge Limited

Date	*Details*	*Amount* £	*Date*	*Details*	*Amount* £
1 June	Balance brought forward	7,050	1 Jun	Bank	940
1 June	Sales	470	1 Jun	Balance c/d	6,580
		7,520			7,520
2 June	Balance b/d	6,580			

The Peters Partnership

Date	*Details*	*Amount* £	*Date*	*Details*	*Amount* £
1 June	Balance b/f	5,875	1 June	Balance c/d	8,225
1 June	Sales	2,350			
		8,225			8,225
2 June	Balance b/d	8,225			

W Dalton Limited

Date	*Details*	*Amount* £	*Date*	*Details*	*Amount* £
! June	Balance b/f	29,375	1 June	Bank	15,275
1 June	Sales	752	1 June	Balance c/d	14,946
1 June	Sales	94			
		30,221			30,221
2 June	Balance b/d	14,946			

Nominal ledger

Sales

Date	*Details*	*Amount* £	*Date*	*Details*	*Amount* £
1 June	Balance c/d	732,786	1 June	Balance b/f	726,506
			1 June	Debtors	6,280
		732,786			732,786
			2 June	Balance b/d	732,786

Sales (debtors) ledger control

Date	*Details*	*Amount* £	*Date*	*Details*	*Amount* £
1 June	Balance b/f	162,150	1 June	Bank	18,565
1 June	Sales	7,379	1 June	Discounts allowed	200
			1 June	Balance c/d	150,764
		169,529			169,529
2 June	Balance b/d	150,764			

Bank charges

Date	*Details*	*Amount* £	*Date*	*Details*	*Amount* £
1 June	Balance b/f	967	1 June	Balance c/d	1,075
1 June	Bank	108			
		1,075			1,075
2 June	Balance b/d	1,075			

Discounts allowed

Date	*Details*	*Amount* £	*Date*	*Details*	*Amount* £
1 June	Balance b/f	370	1 June	Balance c/d	570
1 June	Debtors	200			
		570			570
2 June	Balance b/d	570			

VAT

Date	*Details*	*Amount* £	*Date*	*Details*	*Amount* £
1 June	Balance c/d	16,464	1 June	Balance b/f	15,365
			1 June	Sales	1,099
		16,464			16,464
			2 June	Balance b/d	16,464

Bank loan

Date	*Details*	*Amount* £	*Date*	*Details*	*Amount* £
1 June	Bank	450	1 June	Balance b/f	15,300
1 June	Balance c/d	14,850			
		15,300			15,300
			2 June	Balance b/d	14,850

Motor vehicles

Date	*Details*	*Amount* £	*Date*	*Details*	*Amount* £
1 June	Balance b/f	17,650	1 June	Balance c/d	32,150
1 June	Bank	14,500			
		32,150			32,150
2 June	Balance b/d	32,150			

Motor insurance

Date	*Details*	*Amount* £	*Date*	*Details*	*Amount* £
1 June	Balance b/f	495	1 June	Balance c/d	812
1 June	Bank	317			
		812			812
2 June	Balance b/d	812			

Journal

Date	*Details*	*Debit* £	*Credit* £
1 June	Electricity	717	
1 June	Office equipment		717
1 June	Belton Stationers	470	
1 June	Belton & Byng Limited		470

Section 2

Task 2.1

Goods Total	£1,200.00
VAT	£204.75
Total	£1,404.75

Task 2.2

Credited

Task 2.3

Any four from:

- Purchases Day Book
- Sales Day Book
- Purchases Returns Day Book
- Sales Returns Day Book
- Cash Book
- Journal
- Petty Cash Book

Task 2.4

Dr		*Cr*	
Bad Debts account	£300.00	Sales (Debtors) Ledger Control account	£352.50
VAT	£52.50		

Task 2.5

Bad debts are an expense which reduces profit and affects cash flow.

Task 2.6

(a) Delivery note – to list and accompany a consignment of goods

(b) Goods received note – to act as an internal check confirming correct goods in correct quantities have been received.

(c) Advice note – to advise customers of an impending delivery of goods.

Task 2.7

(a) Yes

(b) The delivery date was part of the contractual agreement and, therefore, there is a clear breach of contract on the part of Hathaway Design & Print.

Task 2.8

(a) No

(b) The price list was merely an invitation to treat. No contract was formed.

Task 2.9

An account of a person or a company, for example customer or supplier.

Task 2.10

Any three from:

- Unpresented cheques
- Unrecorded deposits
- Bank charges not entered in cash book
- Interest received not entered in cash book
- Direct debits not entered in cash book
- Bank charges not yet in cash book
- Errors in cash book
- Errors in bank statement
- Dishonoured cheques

Task 2.11

The cheque has not been paid by drawer's bank, usually because of insufficient funds.

Task 2.12

(a) Capital

(b) Capital

(c) Revenue

Task 2.13

Any two from:

- Speed
- Accuracy
- Versatility
- Ease of access
- Consistency
- Space saying
- Security

Task 2.14

(a) Nominal (General) ledger

(b) Nominal (General) ledger

(c) Purchases ledger

Task 2.15

The quotation does not include the costs of delivery.

Task 2.16

Any two from:

- Provide a lockable petty cash tin.
- Keep the petty cash in a lockable drawer.
- Limit access.

Task 2.17

Any two from:

- To check creditworthiness of new customers.
- To monitor credit limits.
- To set credit terms.
- To ensure that debtors pay their accounts in accordance with the agreed terms of payment.

Task 2.18

Creditor

Task 2.19

Any two from:

- To correct an inaccurate invoice.
- To credit the return of goods.
- To credit the non-delivery of goods.

Task 2.20

(a) Lyndon Press Limited

(b) Hathaway Design & Print

(c) Midwest Bank

Section 3

Task 3.1

The letter given below is a suggested one only, and is indicative of the content and clarity expected from a competent candidate.

HATHAWAY DESIGN & PRINT

29 Watery Lane, Heathwell, West Midlands B71 3DO
Telephone: 0121 590 3679 – Fax: 0121 590 7894

Chief Accountant
T Baker Limited
Goomb Hollow
Heathwell
West Midlands B71 SZL

1 June 19X8

Dear Sir,

Overdue Account

Please find enclosed a statement of your account up to 31 May 19X8.

As you will see, payment for March and April invoices is overdue and we must ask that you let us have your cheque for £4,700 by return.

In the meantime, because the total balance outstanding of £6,462.50 exceeds your credit limit of £6,000, we regret that we will have to withhold any further deliveries until payment has been received.

Yours faithfully,

Susan Hathaway
Chief Accountant

Proprietors: Donald T Hathaway, Jane Hathaway

Task 3.2

The memorandum given below is a suggested one only, and is indicative of the content and clarity expected from a competent candidate.

INTERNAL MEMORANDUM

To:	Sales Department	Date:	1 June 19X8
From:	A Student		
Subject:	T Baker Limited		

The account of T Baker Limited is overdue and its credit limit has been exceeded. Therefore, we have today written to the Chief Accountant requesting payment of March and April invoices by return.

In the meantime, no further goods should be despatched to them until further notice.

Central Assessment Pack

CHAPTER 1

Money and Legal Tender

Revision notes

Money may be held by a business in the forms of *cash* or *bank accounts*. Cash, comprising notes and coins, is held in small quantities so as to reduce the risk of theft.

Cash can be used as:

- a method of payment; or

- to buy postal orders, a method of payment which is used when it is unsafe to use cash (for example, when mailing a remittance).

A *bank current account* is used for day to day transactions, whereas a *bank deposit account* may be opened if the business has a surplus of funds in its current account.

The deposit account will earn interest, but there are restrictions on its use.

Payments can be made from current accounts to third parties using *cheques*, and cash, cheques and postal orders may be paid in, using a *paying-in slip* to summarise the details of the deposit. *Bank statements* are received by the business regularly, showing how money has gone into or left the bank account, and the amount of money held in the account after each days' transactions.

Legal tender is any method of payment which must be accepted *by law* in settlement of a debt. *Money* is anything which is generally acceptable as a method of settling a debt. Bank of England bank notes and £1 coins issued by the Royal Mint are *unlimited legal tender* in England, whereas other coins are *limited legal tender* with limits on the amount of currency which can be used as payment.

Questions

1 Cash v cheques

Give two examples of situations where a business will find it more convenient to use coins and notes rather than cheques.

2 Bank accounts

Which of the following statements are generally true in respect of:

(a) bank current accounts and

(b) bank deposit accounts?

- (i) A bank statement is received regularly.
- (ii) Cheques may be paid in to the account.
- (iii) Cheque payments may be made from the account.
- (iv) The account is useful for day to day transactions.
- (v) The account may be used as an investment, earning interest.

3 Cheque details

List the details on a cheque which have to be filled in by the account holder making a payment.

CHAPTER 2

Receiving Money in a Retail Business

Revision notes

All cash, cheques and postal orders received by a business are at risk of being lost or stolen, so should be:

- listed on a remittance list, then;
- locked in a safe or another secure place, then;
- banked at the earliest opportunity.

Security is improved if knowledge of the combination for the safe is restricted and the person banking the money is accompanied.

Customers paying immediately by cash or cheque are given a *receipt* to show that they have paid. Credit customers are given or sent an *invoice* showing the goods and services provided and the amount they must pay. A remittance advice is a slip returned by the customer with their payment so as to identify the invoice which is being paid.

Cash or settlement discounts are sometimes offered to credit customers to encourage them to pay more quickly and thus aid the cash flow of the business. A percentage reduction in the price charged is given if the customer pays within a certain period of time.

A retailer will usually have a *till* or *cash register* which:

- stores cash for transactions and cheques, gift vouchers, book tokens and other forms of payment;
- records takings;
- issues sales receipts.

If the customer requests a VAT receipt and the transaction is below £100 including VAT at standard rate, retailers may issue a less detailed VAT receipt.

A *float* of coins and notes will be kept back when the takings in the till are banked so that change may be given to customers. Cash and cheques can be safely banked after the banks have closed by using the *night safe*; the retailer encloses two completed paying-in slips with the pouch of bankings and collects the stamped copy the next working day.

Customers paying by cheque should have a *cheque guarantee card,* guaranteeing a cheque up to the limit, usually £50 or £100, for that card. Only one cheque per transaction will be guaranteed. The retailer will check that:

- the card is valid;
- details on the card and cheque agree;
- the cheque is signed in their presence and is correctly written and then write the card number on the reverse of the cheque.

Customers may pay by *credit card.*

- This method of payment is safe and convenient as there is no need to carry cash.
- Free credit is given – payments need only be made within 25 days of receiving a monthly payment.
- Payments can be spread out.
- After repaying part of their account, the customers can purchase more goods up to their credit limit again (*revolving credit*).
- Items bought can be taken away immediately.

The retailer will have to pay commission to the credit card company for each credit card payment, but often experiences increased sales as a result of offering the facility. Retailers also receive:

- more security for payments in excess of £50; and
- immediate credit to their bank account of credit card vouchers paid in.

The credit card transaction is recorded on a *credit card sales voucher.* An *imprinter* is used to transfer the cardholder's and the retailer's details on the voucher and the transaction details are completed by the retailer.

The retailer checks that:

- the card is valid;
- the number is not on a list of stolen cards;
- if the *floor limit* set by the credit card company is exceeded, their authorisation for the transaction will be given by telephone.

Credit card vouchers are banked using a *retail voucher summary.*

Many retailers use a computerised system of accepting credit cards. The technology is known as EFTPOS (Electronic Funds Transfer at Point of Sale). This authorises transactions electronically via a direct link between the retailer's terminal and the credit card company. *Debit cards* also use EFTPOS technology. These cards make payments direct from a bank account and there is no period of credit. *Storecards* are now offered by many retailers such as Laura Ashley and Marks and Spencer for use within their shops.

Retailers will have to refund payment if:

- goods are faulty;
- goods are not as described;
- goods are not of merchantable quality;
- goods are not fit for the specific purpose for which they were sold; or
- the retailer agreed to do so in advance.

A sales receipt does not have to be produced by the customer for a refund. For credit card refunds, a *refund voucher* is completed and must be authorised by the credit card company if the original sale was authorised.

Questions

1 Cash discount

A cash discount of 3% is taken for early payment of an invoice for £84. How much cash is received in respect of this invoice?

2 Before discount

£247.94 is received in respect of invoice 14303 to Brian Brainstorm Limited. This company took advantage of a 2% settlement discount by paying within the 28-day time limit. What was the full amount of invoice 14303 before deduction of the discount?

3 Errors

List six errors that can be discovered when reviewing the remittance advices and cheques received.

4 Availability of cash discounts (AAT CA D95)

Cash discounts are only available to customers who pay immediately in cash.

True / False

5 Customer's name

Should the customer's name appear on:

(a) a completed credit card sales voucher?

(b) a VAT invoice for £350 issued by a retailer?

(c) a VAT invoice for £20 issued by a retailer?

(d) a cheque guarantee card?

6 Ron's Records

You are the proprietor of Ron's Records. One of your customers, Carl Crabbe, has written to you regarding some recent purchases. Below is an extract from the letter.

> 'One of the CDs you sold me has a big crack in it and won't play. Another one is described on the case as the London Symphony Orchestra playing 'The Nutcracker Suite', but when I opened it I found it was loud pop music by a group called The Cure. Also, I asked you for two tape cassettes suitable to play at the third birthday party of my daughter Carly. One seems suitable, but the other was a story for teenagers. I've changed my mind about these now and I'm going to show them a video, so I'd like my money back for all four items. I haven't got a receipt, but I know my rights.'

Write a letter to Mr Crabbe explaining his legal rights to a refund, referring to your policy of issuing a credit note if a refund is not legally required.

7 Accepting credit cards (AAT CA D95)

List three checks that should be made when accepting a credit card from a customer in payment for goods.

8 Accepting a cheque (AAT CA J96)

List three checks that should be carried out, in respect of the card, when a cheque supported by a cheque guarantee card is received from a customer.

CHAPTER 3

Making Payments to Credit Suppliers

Revision notes

Payment by cheque is the best way to ensure that the correct person or business is paid. Security procedures for cheque payments include the following.

- The number of people authorised to sign cheques, *cheque signatories*, should be restricted.
- There should be two signatories for large amounts ie exceeding a limit pre-set by the business.
- All payments should be supported by authorised documentation such as an invoice.
- Cheques should be used in strict numerical sequence.
- Unused (blank) cheques and cancelled cheques should be kept in a safe.
- There should be a segregation of duties between those who deal with suppliers' invoices, prepare the cheques and post the cheques.

A *remittance advice* will be sent with the cheque payment; these may be produced by the supplier with the invoice or by the business as part of a computerised cheque-printing run.

Tips and traps

Cash discounts may be received if payment is made within a time limit. If discounts are offered and VAT is included on the invoice:

- the discount is calculated on the net amount (excluding VAT)
- the VAT is calculated with reference to the discounted net amount, whether or not the discount is actually taken.

Questions

1 VAT invoice

List eight pieces of information which must appear on a full VAT invoice.

2 Aubrey Aitchinson

Aubrey Aitchinson buys six lorry tyres from Myers Tyres Limited for £250 plus VAT at 17½%. Myers Tyres Limited offers a settlement discount of 2% for payment within 28 days. How much will Aubrey Aitchinson have to pay Myers Tyres if payment is made:

(a) within 28 days

(b) after 28 days?

3 Post dated cheque (AAT CA J97)

What is a post-dated cheque?

4 Comart Supplies Limited (AAT CA J95)

Comart Supplies Limited recently purchased from Ace Imports Limited 10 printers originally priced at £200 each. A 10% trade discount was negotiated together with a 5% cash discount if payment was made within 14 days. Calculate the following.

(a) The total of the trade discount.

(b) The total of the cash discount.

(c) The total of the VAT.

5 Office equipment (AAT CA J95)

Some office equipment has been ordered from a supplier who has requested that payment should be made before the equipment has been delivered and before invoicing. You understand that a cheque can be issued against a properly completed cheque requisition form.

What system of control should exist to ensure that cheques are only issued in such circumstances for valid items of expenditure?

6 Settling debts (AAT CA J95)

Give **two** reasons why a business should avoid settling its debts by sending cash through the post.

CHAPTER 4

Banks and their Customers

Revision notes

Banks take deposits in current accounts and deposit accounts. They offer their customers money transfer services into and out of their account and can make advances in the forms of overdrafts, credit cards, loans, mortgages, business loans and credit card accounts. They also offer safe deposit boxes, night safes, foreign currency accounts, share-dealing, advice on investments, wills and insurance services.

Banks obtain payment for the customers when they pay in a cheque by crediting their account and then collecting the money from the third party. The *clearing system* takes three days and involves various physical transfers of the cheque as follows:

Day one	1	Cheques sorted at branch where paid in
	2	Sent to bank's own clearing department
Day two	3	Sent to central clearing house
	4	Sent to other bank's clearing department
Day three	5	Sent to branch of person who wrote cheque

If the accounts of the drawer and payee are at the same branch, the cheques do not need to leave the branch. If the accounts of the drawer and payee are at different branches of the same bank, steps 3 and 4 are omitted.

A *cheque* is an unconditional order in writing signed by the drawer, requiring a bank to pay on demand a sum certain in money to a named person or to the bearer.

When a cheque paid in by a customer has been accepted by a bank it must check:

- date (out of date after six months, post-dated, undated);
- payee's name;
- words and figures in agreement;
- signature present;
- crossings are obeyed;
- endorsements are consistent with the payee's name.

Endorsement of the back of a cheque by the payee allows it to be transferred to a third party.

Example

The payee is Mrs G Touchard

General	G Touchard, Mrs – payable to bearer
Specific	G Touchard, pay J Hobbs or order – payable to J Hobbs but may be reindorsed
Restrictive	G Touchard, pay to J Hobbs only

Cheque crossings mean that a cheque may be paid into a bank account only. A *special crossing* will detail the bank or branch into which the cheque must be paid. Pre-printed cheques have 'Account payee' printed on the crossing so that the cheque can only be paid into the account of the named payee and cannot be endorsed. Due to this, most forms of endorsement are now quite rare.

Other forms of payment include the following:

- *Bills of exchange* – the forerunner of cheques, today restricted mainly to trade with foreign countries.

- *Bankers draft* – a cheque drawn by a bank itself, useful when a bank's customer needs to pay a large sum of money (eg to buy a house). It is the next best thing to money as it is guaranteed by the bank.

- *Standing orders* – an instruction to the bank to make regular payments, usually for fixed amounts at fixed intervals.

- *Direct debits* – an instruction to the bank to allow a third party to collect money from the customers' account, useful if the amount or payment dates can vary.

- *Bank giro credits* (credit transfers) – a means of transferring money from one account to another, useful for paying bills such as gas, electricity etc. and for paying wages. These payments are cleared through credit clearing which is similar to the cheque clearing system.

- *BACS* (Bankers Automated Clearing Services) – a method of clearing payments in which transactions are recorded on magnetic tape or discs and then processed at the BACS bureau rather than through the clearing house. It is used by banks for standing orders and companies for direct debits and salary payments.

- *CHAPS* (Clearing House Automated Payments System) is electronic clearing for large sums only.

A *bank customer* is someone who has a current or similar account or who has agreed to open one. The bank may have a number of relationships with the customer.

- *Debtor/creditor relationship* as described below.

- *Principal* and *agent* – The bank acts as agent for the principal (customer) when dealing with third parties eg payment by direct debit.

- *Bailor* and *bailee* – The bank acts as bailee by looking after the customer's (bailor's) property.

The bank agrees to hold, receive and collect customer's money and not to close the customer's account without reasonable notice. The customer agrees to take care in writing cheques and can only ask for repayment in writing.

The bank has a number of rights:

- to charge for services;
- to reclaim losses from customers;
- to exercise a *lien* over customer's property, ie to keep goods as payment of debt;
- to use the customer's money as it wishes as long as it pays cheques written by customers; and
- to expect the customer to use reasonable care when writing cheques.

Its duties are as follows:

- to pay customer's cheques that are correctly completed by a customer who is not mentally incapacitated, bankrupt or dead!
- to obey express mandates such as standing orders
- to keep customer's details confidential
- to give reasonable notice of closure of an account
- to provide regular bank statements and to tell the customer the balance on their account on request
- to accept cash and cheques paid in by the customer
- to repay customer's money when the customer asks
- to tell the customer of any possible forgery of their signature
- to exercise proper skill and care – the customer trusts the bank and therefore the bank must act in an appropriate way (a fiduciary relationship).

The customer has a duty to use reasonable care when writing cheques and to tell the bank of any known forgery of his or her signature. The customer does *not* have to check the accuracy of his bank statement; the bank must be careful to ensure there are no mistakes.

Questions

1 M Lewis (AAT CA J95)

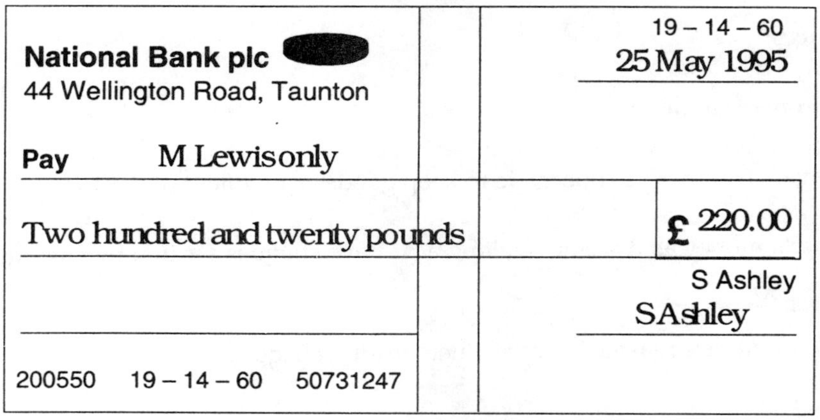

The reverse of the cheque has been signed 'M Lewis'.

(a) Could the cheque be paid into Comart Supplies Limited's bank account?

(b) Briefly explain the reason for your answer.

2 Cheque (AAT CA J95)

The cheque shown in question 1 has two vertical lines printed on it to form a crossing. However, since there are no instructions between the lines, such as 'not negotiable' or 'account payee only', the crossing has no effect and the cheque can be cashed by the payee.

True or false?

3 Wendy Roberts (AAT CA J95)

Wendy Roberts checks her bank statement and realises that she only has £120 left in her account with bills to pay totalling £200. Her salary is due in two weeks' time and she does not foresee similar problems occurring again in the near future. Which bank service would seem the most appropriate to meet her needs – a bank overdraft or a bank loan?

4 Summit Glazing Limited (AAT CA D95)

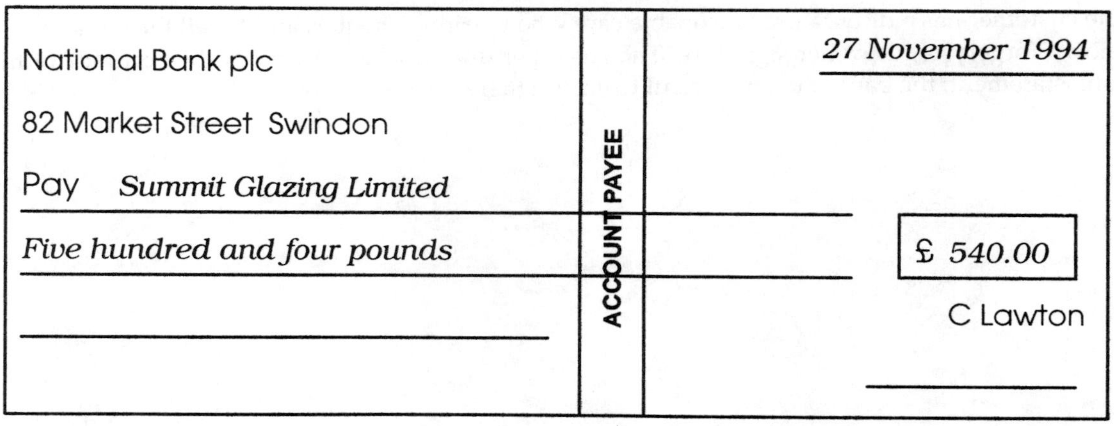

The above cheque has been received from a customer. Give two reasons why it would not be accepted for payment if it was presented to National Bank Plc.

5 A Jones 1 (AAT CA J96)

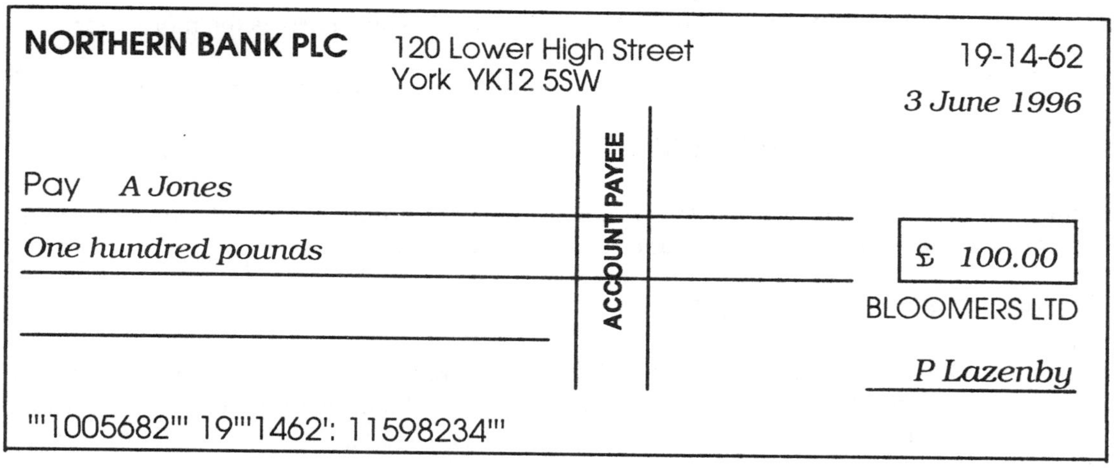

Briefly explain the effect of the crossing on the above cheque.

6 A Jones 2 (AAT CA J96)

Referring to the cheque given in question 5, give the name of:

(a) the drawer

(b) the drawee

(c) the payee

7 Bloomers (AAT CA J96)

Bloomers has agreed to make regular monthly payments to Apollo Communications plc. The amount of the payment varies from month to month. Which service provided by the banks would appear to be most appropriate for these payments?

8 Debit card (AAT CA J96)

A debit card allows a customer to use funds held in her bank account to make a payment without the need to issue a cheque.

True / False

9 Norwest Bank (AAT CA D96)

Norwest Bank has arranged the insurance of all the company's assets. In this transaction what is the banker/customer relationship?

Principal and agent / Mortgagor and mortgagee

10 Comart Supplies Limited (AAT CA J95)

In taking out a bank loan, Comart Supplies Limited was required by the bank to give a mortgage over its premises.

(a) In the mortgagor/mortgagee relationship described, which party is the mortgagor?

(b) Explain briefly the reason why the bank would normally ask for the mortgage.

11 Summit Glazing (AAT CA D95)

Summit Glazing has an overdraft facility of £20,000. When Summit Glazing's current account is overdrawn is the bank a debtor or creditor in Summit Glazing's accounts?

12 JLW Limited (AAT CA J97)

JLW Limited has taken out a bank loan, which is to be repaid over a two year period by eight equal quarterly repayments. Which service provided by the banks would seem most appropriate for these payments?

13 Bank statement (AAT CA J96)

The bank statement received on 1 June showed that the Northern Bank plc had charged Bloomers Limited £70 for its services. Bloomers Limited's monthly bank charges do not normally exceed £50. Paul Lazenby, the Accountant, is concerned about this significant increase in charges as there has not been any noticeable increase in banking transactions.

Prepare a letter to the bank manager, David Williams, which is to be signed by Paul Lazenby. The bank's address is Northern Bank plc, 120 Lower High Street, York YK12 5SW. Your letter should express concern over the increase in charges and request an explanation. When drafting the letter you should bear in mind that Bloomers has a good relationship with its bankers and has always been satisfied with the service provided by the Lower High Street branch.

CHAPTER 5

Maintaining a Cash Book and Petty Cash

Revision notes

A *cash book* records the receipts and payments into and out of the business' bank account, analysing each receipt and payment by type (an *analysed* cash book). The totals of each type of receipt and payment are *posted* each month to the general ledger by means of a journal entry, for example, if the cash book is purely a *book of prime entry*.

			£	£
Dr	Cash at bank (receipts)		800	
	Cr	Cash sales		300
	Cr	Debtors		447
	Cr	VAT		53
Dr	Creditors		530	
Dr	Rent		80	
Dr	Wages and salaries		100	
Dr	Insurance		40	
	Cr	Cash at bank (payments)		750
			1,550	1,550

Sometimes the cash book itself will be part of the double entry.

Cash discounts allowed or received are recorded in *memorandum columns* as a reminder to make the double entry in respect of discounts. The *actual amount paid or received* is recorded in the total and analysis columns.

A *bank reconciliation* is a control which is performed each month to ensure that the cash book has been correctly written up.

Tips and traps

Cash sales must have VAT analysed as this is the first time the sale has been recorded. Cash from debtors does **not** need to have VAT analysed as this is not the first time the sale has been recorded.

A credit in the cash book means a reduction in the bank balance. A credit on the bank statement means an increase in the bank balance as the statement of account is prepared from the bank's point of view. If you increase your bank balance, the bank is holding more of your money (ie it owes you more), so their creditor is increased.

Petty cash

Petty cash is used to make small cash payments. The cash is obtained by cashing a cheque at the bank or from cash sales. Payments are recorded on a numbered voucher and require authorisation prior to the money being paid. Receipts are attached to the voucher.

Payments are also recorded in the petty cash book which analyses the expenses paid for and VAT if the business can reclaim it.

An *imprest system* is often used as it reduces the risk of theft or fraud. This operates by topping up the petty cash to a pre-set level each week. This level will be based on the requirements of the business. As each petty cash payment is made, a voucher for that value will be completed such that:

cash + vouchers = original amount of cash

At the end of the week, the petty cashier is reimbursed for the value of the vouchers which are filed.

Questions

1 Cheque 302462 – 1 (AAT CA J95)

Midwest Bank plc

Comart Supplies Limited

Statement of Account Account No: 80148762

Date	*Details*	*Debit* £	*Credit* £	*Balance* £
1 June	Balance forward			3,465 O/D
1 June	Silicon World BGC		1,000	2,465 O/D
1 June	Loan repayment TR	400		2,865 O/D
1 June	Cheque no. 302462	1,205		4,070 O/D

O/D Overdrawn *BGC Bank giro credit* *TR Transfer*

If cheque number 302462 had been presented to the bank prior to 1 June, what would have been the opening balance of the bank statement shown above?

2 Cheque 302462 – 2 (AAT CA J95)

The bank giro credit and transfer shown on the bank statement were used to update the cash book. Explain briefly why it was not necessary to include cheque number 302462 in the updating process.

3 Bank reconciliation (AAT CA J95)

In preparing a bank reconciliation statement to agree the balance of the updated cash book with the balance of the bank statement:

(a) Would a cheque for £3,240 payable to ITC Computers Limited be added to or subtracted from the cash book balance?

(b) Would receipts totalling £15,356 be added to or subtracted from the cash book balance?

4 Unpaid entry (AAT CA J95)

If a cheque received from a customer was subsequently returned unpaid by that customer's bank, would the unpaid entry appear as a debit or a credit on Comart Suppliers Limited's bank statement?

5 Dishonoured cheque (AAT CA D95)

What book-keeping entries are required in the general ledger to record a dishonoured cheque which has been received from a customer and paid into Summit Glazing's bank account?

6 Cash refund (AAT CA D95)

What book-keeping entries would be necessary to record a cash refund of £94 (inclusive of VAT) to a customer?

7 Journal (AAT CA D95)

Give two uses of the Journal as a book of original entry.

8 Discounts allowed column (AAT CA J96)

Should the total of the discounts allowed column in the cash book be debited or credited to the discounts allowed account?

9 MMS Textiles (AAT CA D96)

Give **three** reasons why the balance shown on MMS Textiles' bank statement may not agree with the balance on its bank account in the cash book.

10 VAT column (AAT CA J95)

Should the total of the VAT column in a petty cash book be debited or credited to the VAT account?

11 Summit Glazing (AAT CA D95)

Summit Glazing operates an imprest petty cash system. The imprest amount is £150.00. At the end of the period the totals of the four analysis columns in the petty cash book were as follows

Column 1	23.12
Column 2	6.74
Column 3	12.90
Column 4	28.50

How much cash is required to restore the imprest amount?

12 Bloomers Limited (AAT CA J96)

At present Bloomers Limited's petty cash is kept in a fabric cash bag in an unlocked drawer. When the petty cash book is balanced and the petty cash is counted there is frequently a shortfall of cash for which there is no obvious explanation. As you are to be given responsibility for petty cash, Paul Lazenby (the Accountant) has asked you to recommend measures which can be introduced to improve the security of the petty cash.

Prepare a memorandum to Paul Lazenby detailing your recommendations.

CHAPTER 6

Legal Relationship of Buyer and Seller

Revision notes

A *contract* is a legally binding agreement which can be enforced by the courts under civil law. A contract has seven fundamental requirements in order to be valid:

- agreement (= offer and acceptance);
- the intention to create legal relations;
- consideration;
- written formalities (some contracts only);
- capacity to contract;
- genuine consent; and
- the contract must be legal and possible.

A contract declared *void* means that neither party may enforce any rights under the contract and money or goods handed over must be returned. This could occur, for example, if some fundamental mistake concerning the contract has been made.

If one of the parties may avoid the contract at their option (for example, if some fact relating to the contract was misrepresented to him) it is *voidable* and anything which happens before the contract is avoided is valid.

An unenforceable contract is valid in theory but due to the lack of some legal formality or evidence it cannot be sued upon or enforced by the court.

Agreement between the parties requires an *offer* made by the offeror to be *accepted* by the other party, the offeree. The offer is an expression of willingness to contract on certain terms with the intention that it will become binding if accepted by the other party. An offer must be communicated to the offeree and may be:

- made to a specific person or the world at large;
- conditional, but it must be certain; and
- express or implied.

An offer should not be confused with an *invitation to treat* which is an invitation made by the first party to a second party to make an offer to the first party. Acceptance should be made whilst the offer is still in force and be absolute and unqualified, otherwise a counter offer will be made. Acceptance must be communicated to the offeror where notification is specifically or tacitly required.

Once an offer *lapses*, it cannot be accepted. An offer may be *revoked* (or withdrawn) by the offeror at any time before it has been accepted. The offeree may notify the offeror that he does not wish to accept the offer. Rejection may be express or implied.

There should be an intention to create legal relations if an agreement is to become a contract. This is presumed in commercial agreements, but not in domestic or social arrangements.

Contracts may be made informally, even verbally, except in cases where they must be:

- made by deed, eg where there is no consideration as in a 'deed of gift' to charity, contracts for the transfer of a British registered ship or aeroplane and legal conveyances of land or leases of land for more than three years;

- in writing, eg transfer of company shares, bills of exchange and cheques, hire purchase contracts, contracts of marine insurance and contracts for the future sale of interests in land; or

- evidenced in writing, eg money-lending agreements and contracts of guarantee.

Minors (persons under 18) do not have the capacity to enter into any contract that they wish. They may enter into contracts for 'necessaries' or contracts which benefit them (eg contracts for education). Most contracts other than these are *unenforceable* by the third party against the minor, but enforceable by the minor against the third party.

The parties to a contract must have genuinely consented to its terms. The genuineness of the consent will be affected if *mistake* or *misrepresentation* has occurred.

Questions

1 Wendy Roberts (AAT CA J97)

Wendy Roberts, one of Comart Supplies Limited's sales staff, offers to sell a second-hand colour printer to Robert Ford for £175. Robert wants time to think about it and Wendy tells him that she will leave the offer open until the end of the day. At 2.00 pm Robert calls back to say that he is willing to buy the printer for £160. At 3.00 pm Wendy sells the printer to Caroline Brown for £175 and arranges delivery for the following day. At 4.30 pm Robert returns and tells Wendy that he is now willing to buy the printer for £175.

(a) Can Robert claim that he has a contract with the company and insist that the printer is sold to him?

(b) Briefly explain the reason for your answer.

2 Comart Supplies Limited (AAT CA J95)

On 15 May, Comart Supplies Limited received some new software from County Computers Limited. A letter which was enclosed acknowledged that the software had not been ordered and pointed out that it was being offered at a special price of £265. The letter also stated that, unless County Computers Limited had heard from Comart Supplies Limited within 10 days, it would be assumed that the purchase was to be concluded and an invoice would be issued. By 25 May Comart Supplies Limited had not responded to the letter.

(a) Does a contract to purchase the software exist between the two companies?

(b) Briefly explain the reason for your answer.

3 Summit Glazing (AAT CA D95)

Summit Glazing received an enquiry from Stanhope Builders to purchase a Viceroy conservatory. A quotation was sent out offering to supply a Viceroy for £5,600. The next day Mary Owen realised a mistake had been made as the price quoted should have been £6,500. Mary immediately wrote to Stanhope Builders informing them that the quoted price was incorrect and that the conservatory could not therefore be supplied as offered. The following day Karl Hope from Stanhope Builders telephoned to say that although he had received Mary's letter he wanted to accept the original offer, insisting that the conservatory should be supplied for £5,600.

(a) Does a valid contract exist between Summit Glazing and Stanhope Builders?

(b) Explain briefly the reason for your answer.

4 Mr Green (AAT CA D95)

On 18 November a customer, Mr Green, had a double glazed replacement window fitted by Summit Glazing. He telephoned the next day complaining that one of the toplights would not open. The Summit Glazing employee who inspected the window said it appeared to be a manufacturing fault and advised Mr Green to contact the manufacturer to have the fault corrected.

(a) Was the employee legally justified in advising Mr Green to contact the manufacturer?

(b) Explain briefly the reason for your answer.

5 Carriage paid (AAT CA D95)

What does it mean if goods are sold 'carriage paid'?

6 Gift Box (AAT CA J96)

Gift Box is both a supplier to and a customer of Bloomers Limited. It has been agreed that a debt of £75 owing to Gift Box is to be set-off against the balance of £300 owed by Gift Box.

What entries would be required in the **general ledger** to record this set-off?

7 Dried flowers (AAT CA J96)

An arrangement of dried flowers has been displayed with a £5 price ticket. A customer wanting to purchase the arrangement was told that an incorrect price ticket had been used and that the price was in fact £25.

(a) Can the customer insist on purchasing the arrangement for £5?

(b) Explain briefly the reason for your answer

8 Bloomers Limited (AAT CA J96)

Bloomers Limited has been asked to give a quotation for supplying flowers for an international conference, which is to be organised by CMP plc. The quotation was sent by post on 22 May 19X6 and received by CMP plc the next day. CMP plc posted a letter accepting Bloomer's quotation on 29 May 19X6. This letter was received by Bloomers on 30 May 19X6.

(a) On which date was the contract made?

(i) 23 May 19X6

(ii) 29 May 19X6

(iii) 30 May 19X6

(b) Explain briefly the reason for your answer

9 JLW Limited (AAT CA J97)

A supplier offered JLW Limited 125 grammes of scrap gold at the price of £2.85 per gramme. The company offered to buy the gold for £2.75 per gramme. The supplier refused to sell at this price. JLW Limited then said it would be prepared to buy the gold at the original offer price of £2.85 per gramme.

(a) At this point does a contract for the sale of the scrap gold exist?

(b) Explain briefly the reasons for your answer.

CHAPTER 7

Trading on Credit Terms

Revision notes

It is important for a business to operate controls over credit sales to ensure that they will receive cash from their customers in the period of credit agreed in their contract. With *new* customers, *trade references, bank references* and references from *agencies* such as Dun and Bradstreet will be investigated to establish their creditworthiness. A *credit limit* will then be set for that customer. Established customers will constantly be reviewed to ensure that they are paying outstanding invoices on a timely basis and that their credit limit will not be exceeded by new orders. Credit limits should be reviewed regularly and a *stop list* used to prevent goods and services from being supplied to customers identified as risky.

The customer will initiate a credit transaction by sending a *purchase order* for the goods they require. The business will confirm this order by raising a *sales order* which also serves to prompt the purchase or manufacture of the goods. A sequentially-numbered *delivery note* or *despatch note,* signed by the customer, advises them of the goods delivered and is used internally to update stock records and initiate invoicing. A *sales invoice* showing the quantity of goods supplied and the amount to be paid is sent to the customer. Sales invoices should be:

- sequentially-numbered;
- used in order, keeping spoiled copies;
- checked to ensure that all deliveries and only proper deliveries are invoiced;
- authorised before being sent to customers; and
- correctly coded as to customer account and product type to ensure correct recording in the ledgers.

Trade or bulk discounts may be given to certain customers depending on the level of goods or services they guarantee to buy. VAT is calculated *after* deduction of the discount which is shown on the invoice.

Questions

1 James' Games Limited

For all orders of 1,000 items, James' Games Limited offers a discount of 1%, thereafter increasing by 0.5% for every 250.

If 1,750 items are ordered at £1 each plus VAT at 17½%, what will be the total invoice value?

2 Stop list

What is a stop list?

3 Advice note (AAT CA J95)

An advice note is a document sent to a customer advising the customer or acknowledging that an order has been received.

True / False

4 Remittance advice (AAT CA J96)

A remittance advice is a document sent by a supplier to a customer to advise the customer that goods ordered have been dispatched to the customer.

True / False

5 Proforma invoice (AAT CA J97)

What is the purpose of a proforma invoice?

CHAPTER 8

Maintaining the Sales Day Book

Revision notes

The *sales day book* is a diary of all credit sales invoices in numerical and date order, prepared from the invoices and recording customer code and product code. The invoice totals are analysed by product and the VAT element is separated out to give the true sales value to the business of each product.

There are several different systems of coding:

- sequential
- block (allocates bands of numbers to particular categories)
- significant digit (individual digits and letters used to represent features of the coded item)

decimal/hierarchical (eg 3 = social science, 37 = education, etc).

Accounting systems may be manual or computerised. They basically work in the same way.

There are two methods of processing:

- batch processing (large numbers of transactions are grouped together and processed at the same time)
- on-line, real-time processing (transactions are input as they occur)

A *file* is an organised collection of individual *records* which share a common structure. A *field* is a section of a *record*. Each field contains a single item of information. A *character* is a unit which is a letter, number or symbol making up a field.

Tips and traps

The totals for each product and VAT are posted to the general ledger using a journal entry.

Example

			£	£
Dr	Debtors ledger control account		X	
	Cr	Sales – product A		X
		Sales – product B		X
		VAT control account		X

Credit sales for the week ending 13 March 19X4.

Questions

1 Softsell Limited (AAT CA J95)

Software has been sold on credit to Softsell Limited, a new small business which is not registered for VAT. The invoice issued shows the cost of the software as £160 plus £28 VAT, giving a total of £188. In recording the transaction, which general ledger account(s) will be debited and which will be credited:

(a) In the books of Comart Supplies Limited?

(b) In the books of Softsell Limited?

2 Computerised accounting system (AAT CA J95)

Give two advantages of using a computerised accounting system.

3 Collectable VAT (AAT CA J95)

A manufacturer sells a product to a wholesaler for £200 plus VAT of £35. The wholesaler sells the same product to a retailer for £280 plus VAT of £49. The retailer then sells the product to a customer for £320 plus VAT of £56. What is the total amount of VAT collectable by HM Customs & Excise relating to the product?

4 Processing (AAT CA D95)

When using a computer to process accounting data there are two main systems which can be adopted.

(a) What is the system where documents or transactions for a period are grouped and processed together known as?

(b) What is the system where documents or transactions are input as they occur known as?

5 Microfiche (AAT CA D95)

Summit Glazing is considering transferring some of its records to microfiche. Give one advantage that microfiche has over paper records.

6 Updating (AAT CA J96)

What word is used to describe a computerised accounting system which automatically updates all the records involved in a financial transaction from one computer entry?

7 Sales ledger control account (AAT CA D96)

All the sales, including cash sales, are recorded in the sales ledger control account.

True / False

CHAPTER 9

Maintaining the Debtors' Ledger

Revision notes

The *debtors' ledger* or *sales ledger* is separate from the nominal ledger. It contains an account for each individual customer and shows the amounts owed by and all transactions with each customer.

The debtors' ledger is compiled mainly from:

- the sales day book which gives details of individual invoices
- the cash book which details cash received from and discounts allowed to each customer.

Other entries on accounts in the debtors' ledger include *bad debts* written off, *contras* and correction of errors.

The *debtors' ledger control account* or *sales ledger control account* is in the nominal ledger and records the total amount outstanding from debtors. A *debtors' ledger reconciliation* is a control performed regularly to ensure that the debtors ledger and debtors' ledger control account record the same total amount outstanding for debtors. The total of a list of balances compiled from the debtors ledger is compared with the balance on the debtors' ledger control account and any discrepancies are investigated and adjusted for appropriately.

Tips and traps

Individual invoices and cash receipts are recorded in the debtors' ledger which acts as a memorandum of amounts owed. **Totals** of sales and cash receipts are recorded in the debtors' ledger control account in the nominal ledger.

Debtors are recorded at the gross sales value, including VAT, as this is what they have to pay.

A *credit note* is issued by a supplier to cancel all or part of a previous sale. The customer may either have returned the goods or not received all the goods invoiced and requires a *refund*. In some cases a credit note is issued to settle a *dispute*. Credit notes cannot be issued to cancel a bad debt and thereby recover the VAT.

A *returns inwards* note will be raised to record returned goods received by the supplier and this will be used to initiate the credit note which must be authorised prior to issue. Written authorisation is required for the issue of credit notes not relating to returned goods.

Credit notes are recorded in a *sales returns day book* and this is posted in the same way as the sales day book.

Questions

1 Errors

Which of the following errors discovered during the performance of a debtors ledger reconciliation will require adjustment in the debtors' ledger?

(a) Sales day book incorrectly cast.

(b) Individual invoice amount incorrectly recorded in sales day book.

(c) Discount received not recorded anywhere in the cash book.

(d) Bad debt written off recorded only in the nominal ledger.

2 October 19X4

The following information is relevant for October 19X4

	£
Balance on debtors' ledger control account, 1 October	3,750
Invoices issued for credit sales	12,632
Invoices received for purchases	8,929
Cash received from debtors	13,004
Cash sales	2,120
Bad debts written off	1,200
Cash paid to suppliers	7,768

What is the balance on the debtors' ledger control account on 31 October 19X4?

3 Control account (AAT CA D95)

Give one reason for maintaining a sales ledger (debtors) control account.

4 Posting

When posting individual credit notes from the sales returns daybook to the debtor's ledger, two mistakes are made:

(a) a credit note for £240 is debited to the account of Gleam Cleaners Limited; and

(b) a credit note for £84 is credited to the account of Bright Lights Limited instead of Cool Shades & Co.

What action is required in respect of these errors?

5 Appropriate documents (AAT CA D95)

Complete the following sentences by inserting the name of the appropriate document.

(a) Summit Glazing sends out a .... to each credit customer on a monthly basis which summarises the transactions that have taken place and shows the amount owed by the customer.

(b) Summit Glazing sends out a .... to a credit customer in order to correct an error where the customer has been overcharged by an invoice.

(c) Summit Glazing sends out a .... with a payment to a supplier to indicate which invoices are being paid.

6 Credit notes (AAT CA J96)

Give two different circumstances which would require a credit note to be issued.

7 General ledger (AAT CA J96)

What book-keeping entries would be required in the **general ledger** to correct the following error?

A credit note for £160 plus £28 VAT issued to a customer has been treated as if it were a credit note received.

8 Bookkeeping exercise

Data

The following transactions all occurred on 1 April 19X5 and have been entered for you into summarised books of original entry.

Task

Treat 'other customers' as an individual account.

Sales day book

	Total	*VAT*	*Net*
	£	£	£
Garnett Limited	4,413	657	3,756
Wells Stores	3,447	513	2,934
Lawrence & Sons	6,377	950	5,427
Shields Limited	2,791	416	2,375
Nicolson Partnership	34,950	5,205	29,745
Grenfell Bros	11,549	1,720	9,829
Malory Homecare Limited	3,957	589	3,368
Nesbit Limited	1,000	149	851
Other customers	27,883	4,153	23,730
	96,367	14,352	82,015

Sales returns day book	*Total*	*VAT*	*NET*
Wells Stores	112	17	95
Nicolson Partnership	3,725	555	3,170
Grenfell Bros	284	42	242
	4,121	614	3,507

Journal

		Debit	*Credit*
		£	£
Dr	Office expenses	31	
	Cr Telephone		31

Being the correction of an error made on 15 March 19X5

Cash book

			£
Opening balance at start of day			2,502 (debit)
Receipts	*Discount*	*Net receipt*	
	£	£	
Wells Stores	105	5,237	
Lawrence & Sons	62	3,069	
Grenfell Bros	96	4,794	
Nesbit Limited	48	2,397	
	311		15,497
Payments			
Cash purchases (including VAT at 17.5%)		800	
Office expenses		945	
Interest		86	
Transfers to petty cash		100	
			(1,931)
Closing balance at end of day			16,068 (debit)

Petty cash book

Balance at start of day	55
Receipts – transfers from bank account	100
Payments – office expenses (including VAT at 17.5%)	(47)
Balance at end of day	108

Nominal ledger balances at the start of the day on 1 April 19X5

	£
Customers	
Garnet Limited	9,423
Wells Stores	8,077
Lawrence & Sons	6,598
Shields Limited	8,614
Nicolson Partnership	37,983
Grenfell Bros	29,514
Malory Homecare Limited	–
Nesbit Limited	1,702
Other customers	378,955
Others	
Purchases	2,647,883
Sales	3,114,304
Sales returns	6,358
Telephone	734
Office expenses	8,595
Interest	1,211
VAT	33,732 (credit)
Debtors' control account	480,866
Creditors' control account	307,332
Discounts allowed	15,898
Other debit balances	808,140
Other credit balances	516,874

Task 1

Enter the opening balances into the following accounts:

- Debtors' control account
- Office expenses
- Sales
- VAT
- Wells Stores
- Lawrence & Sons
- Grenfell Bros

Task 2

Enter all relevant transactions into the accounts shown in Task 1.

Task 3

Balance off all the accounts in which you have made entries in Task 2.

Task 4

Calculate the closing balances of the remaining customer accounts and complete the list of balances.

Task 5

Reconcile the closing balance of the debtors' control account to the total of the list of closing customer balances.

Task 6

Calculate the closing balances of the remaining accounts. Complete the list of balances by inserting the updated figures for each account in either the debit balances column or the credit balances column as appropriate. Total the two columns. The two totals should be the same. If they do not agree, try to trace and correct any errors you have made within the time you have available.

Working papers

General ledger

Debtors' control account

Date	*Details*	*Amount* £	*Date*	*Details*	*Amount* £

Office expenses

Date	*Details*	*Amount* £	*Date*	*Details*	*Amount* £

Sales

Date	*Details*	*Amount* £	*Date*	*Details*	*Amount* £

VAT

Date	*Details*	*Amount* £	*Date*	*Details*	*Amount* £

Debtors' ledger

Wells Stores

Date	*Details*	*Amount* £	*Date*	*Details*	*Amount* £

Lawrence & Sons

Date	*Details*	*Amount* £	*Date*	*Details*	*Amount* £

Grenfell Bros

Date	*Details*	*Amount* £	*Date*	*Details*	*Amount* £

	£	£
Updated debtors' control account balance		
Updated customer balances:		
Garnett Limited		
Wells Stores		
Lawrence & Sons		
Shields Limited		
Nicolson Partnership		
Grenfell Bros		
Malory Homecare Limited		
Nesbit Limited		
Other customers		
Total updated customer balances		

List of updated balances at the end of the day on 1 April 19X5:

	Debit £	Credit £
Purchases		
Sales		
Sales returns		
Telephone		
Office expenses		
Interest		
VAT		
Debtors' control account		
Creditors' control account		
Discounts allowed		
Bank		
Petty cash		
Other debit balances	808,140	
Other credit balances		516,874

CHAPTER 10

Using Information to Control Debtors

Revision notes

An *aged analysis of debtors*, prepared from the debtor's ledger, shows the age of debts. The *credit controller* uses this to identify and chase up old unpaid invoices. *Statements* of unpaid invoices are produced each month and sent to the customers. This serves as a reminder to the customer and as an internal control to the supplier as it may reveal errors in the debtor's ledger.

The credit controller chases payment by means of telephone or letter, but will resort to the courts if the customer refuses to pay and has no complaints about the goods or services received.

Questions

1 Credit

Most businesses trading on credit offer a 30-day period in which payment should be made.

(a) Why are discounts offered for payment within this period?

(b) Why are customers not taken to court immediately after the 30-day period if bills are still unpaid?

2 Bone's Phones

You have received a letter from Bone's Phones, a customer, complaining that their recent statement for 28 February 19X3 did not agree with their records. There were two discrepancies:

(a) a cheque for £430 sent by Bone's Phones on 26 February was not received by you until 1 March; and

(b) Bone's Phones insist that a disputed invoice, numbered H413, relates to goods which were never received.

The goods referred to in (b) have now been found on the premises of a different customer and a credit note authorised in respect of invoice H413.

Write a letter to Mr Bone of Bone's Phones explaining the discrepancies.

3 Champion Computers Limited (AAT CA J95)

On 30 May a statement showing a balance of £25,320 was sent to Champion Computers Limited together with a letter pointing out:

(a) Champion Computers Limited's current credit limit is only £20,000.

(b) In view of the balance of the account, Comart Supplies Limited are unable to fulfil an order received from Champion Computers Limited for six Ensign 486 computers (total cost £4,250).

On 1 June the following letter was received.

Champion Computers Limited

14 Seaview Trading Estate, Minehead, MN21 1SE (Tel: 01643 52586)

Ms Louise Ford
Company Accountant
Comart Supplies Limited
22 Trull Road
Taunton SO11 4NE

31 May 19X5

Dear Ms Ford

I refer to your letter of 30 May and the accompanying statement of our account. A cheque for £10,000 was sent to you by first class post on 1 May and this does not appear on the statement.

Although I appreciate that we have not been dealing with your company for very long, I am most concerned that you have not arranged for the delivery of the six Ensign 486 computers. These are required urgently to meet various orders received from customers.

An immediate response by return of post would be appreciated.

Yours sincerely

D Robinson

David Robinson
Accountant

You are asked by Louise Ford to investigate this matter. Your findings are listed as follows:

(1) Cheque for £10,000 referred to in the letter – received on 3 May – credited in error to Chambers Computers instead of Champion Computers Limited. You arrange for correcting entries to be made.

(2) Before correcting the above error, Chambers Computers had a balance of £32,326 and a credit limit of £40,000 – statement showing this balance sent out on 31 May.

(3) Chambers Computers' account – owned by Christine Chambers – established business with whom Comart Supplies Limited have been trading successfully for a number of years. Christine Chambers regarded as a valued customer.

(4) Chambers Computers' account – often up to or slightly above the credit limit. In view of (3) you agreed with Louise Ford that it would be sensible to raise the credit limit to £45,000.

(5) You are out of stock of Ensign 486 computers – earliest date manufacturer can deliver to you is 20 June.

(6) In stock – Wallace 486 computers – similar specification to Ensign 486 computers – same price – could deliver immediately to Champion Computers Limited.

Task 1

Draft a letter to David Robinson at Champion Computers Limited. The letter is to be signed by Louise Ford and should include the following.

(a) An apology for the error (regarding the cheque).

(b) Confirmation that the error has been corrected.

(c) Details concerning the six computers ordered and the possibility of supplying an alternative machine.

(d) A request for instructions concerning (c) above.

Task 2

Draft a letter to Christine Chambers of Chambers Computers (46 Northtown Estate, Taunton, Somerset, SO14 6PE). The letter is to be signed by Louise Ford and should include the following.

(a) Details of the error (re the cheque) and its correction.

(b) The balance of the corrected account and the current credit limit.

(c) The decision to revise the credit limit.

4 Mary Owen

During a review of overdue accounts in the sales ledger, Mary Owen, the Accountant, notes that no payment has been received from Hayden Construction since June 19X5, in spite of efforts made to recover the balance owing. Mary has heard from another creditor that the owner of Hayden Construction is now living in Australia. She feels that the debt should be written off, but the writing off of bad debts has to be sanctioned by Chris Cooper, the Managing Director. The file for Hayden Construction shows the following information.

Hayden Construction

(a) Balance £530 (Goods supplied during February 19X5).

(b) Last payment received 8 June 19X5.

(c) Recorded delivery sent 24 August 19X5 – returned marked 'premises unoccupied'.

(d) Debt collection agency report which stated that they were unable to trace the owner James Hayden.

It is now December 19X5.

Draft a suitable memorandum to Chris Cooper informing him of the facts and seeking his authorisation to write off the Hayden Construction bad debt.

5 Bad debts (AAT CA J96)

Why is it important to keep bad debts to a minimum?

CHAPTER 11

Receiving Purchase Invoices

Revision notes

A *purchase requisition* is an internal document used to request goods and services. The buying department then raises a sequentially-numbered *purchase order* to confirm an order with the supplier. This must be authorised by the relevant department head, unless the amount of the order exceeds his or her authorisation limit in which case a director should authorise it.

A goods received note is used to record all incoming goods which will be accompanied by the supplier's delivery note.

On receipt the *purchase invoice* is checked by the purchase ledger clerk:

- for accuracy of pricing, VAT and discounts;
- for clerical accuracy;
- to the purchase order; and
- to the goods received note and despatch note.

The clerk will date stamp the invoice, give it a sequential number and record it in a *purchase invoice register*. It is then sent for coding and authorisation by the relevant department head and the clerk will record it in the *purchase day book.*

VAT on purchases may be reclaimed if both the business and supplier are registered for VAT, the expenditure is not disallowable and the business has a proper VAT invoice.

Revenue expenditure (eg the payment of rent) is charged to the profit and loss account.

Capital expenditure (eg the purchase of a motor car) is not immediately charged to the profit and loss account because the benefit is spread over a considerable period of time.

Revenue expenditure is expenditure incurred in the following:

- the acquisition of assets required for conversion into cash (ie goods for resale)
- the manufacturing, selling and distribution of goods and the day-to-day administration of the business
- the maintenance of the revenue-earning capacity of the fixed assets (ie repairs, etc).

Capital expenditure is expenditure incurred in the following:

- the acquisition of fixed assets required for use in the business and not for resale
- the alteration or improvement of assets for the purpose of increasing their revenue-earning capacity.

Questions

1 Comart Supplies Limited (AAT CA J95)

Comart Supplies Limited has recently purchased five ITC computers. Would the purchase be regarded as capital expenditure or revenue expenditure if:

(a) the computers are to be used for data processing by the company?

(b) the computers are to be held as stock for sale to customers?

2 Summit Glazing Limited (AAT CA D95)

Summit Glazing Limited are planning to purchase a new van. Would the following items be capital or revenue expenditure?

(a) The purchase price of the van.

(b) Modification work to the side of the van to allow the external carriage of sheets of glass.

(c) Motor insurance for the van.

3 Ledger accounts (AAT CA D95)

Classify the following ledger accounts according to whether they represent asset/ liability/expense or revenue.

(a) Insurance

(b) Stock

(c) Discounts received

(d) Bank overdraft

4 VATable purchases (AAT CA D95)

During the quarter ended 31 October 19X5 sales amounted to £731,555 inclusive of VAT at 17.5%. On the 31 October the credit balance on the VAT account was £47,600. Calculate the value of vatable purchases made during the quarter *inclusive* of VAT.

Note. Your answer should include detailed workings.

5 Capital expenditure (AAT CA J96)

If capital expenditure is treated as revenue expenditure will the total of expenses for the period be too high / too low / unaffected?

6 Carriage (AAT CA J96)

Carriage inwards and carriage outwards are both expense accounts:

True / False

CHAPTER 12

Maintaining the Purchase Day Book

Revision notes

The *purchase day book* is a diary of all credit transactions, recording each purchase invoice. The purchases are analysed by type of product or service excluding VAT where it is recoverable; a separate VAT column is used where it is recoverable.

The purchase day book is posted at regular intervals using a journal entry such as the following.

			£	£
Debit:	Purchases	– Product 1	500.00	
		Product 2	320.00	
		Product 3	100.00	
	Electricity		85.00	
	Rent		220.00	
	Stationery		30.00	
	VAT control		181.13	
Credit:	Creditors ledger control account			1,436.13

Questions

1 Journal entry

What is the journal entry to post the following totals from the purchase day book to the general ledger?

		£
Raw materials	– steel	2,439
	– wood	751
Components		203
Sundries		76
Sub contractors		600
Electricity		185
Fixed assets – car		14,000
VAT		745
Total		18,999

2 Purchase invoice

Why does a business allocate its own number to a purchase invoice when it will already have a supplier's invoice number?

3 Primary records (AAT CA J96)

Name three primary records used for listing transactions before they are posted to the ledger accounts.

4 Bookkeeping exercise (AAT CA J96)

Introduction

The tasks and questions are based on the transactions of Bloomers Limited. The company operates a chain of flower shops. In addition to the sales made in its shops, the company also has several contracts with local hotels to supply and maintain flower displays.

The Managing Director is Alison Pallister and Paul Lazenby is the Accountant. You are employed as an Accounting Technician to assist Paul Lazenby.

Data

The following transactions all occurred on 1 June 19X6 and have yet to be entered into the ledger system. VAT has been calculated at the rate of 17.5%.

A bank statement was received on 1 June.

Sales Invoices Issued

	Total	*VAT*	*Net*
	£	£	£
York Hotels Limited	846	126	720
Deluxe Hotels plc	235	35	200
Prime Hotels Limited	376	56	320
Deluxe Hotels plc	564	84	480
	2,021	301	1,720

Purchases Invoices Received

	Total	*VAT*	*Net*	*Goods for resale*	*Heating and lighting*
	£	£	£	£	£
Exotic Blooms Limited	1,269	189	1,080	1,080	
Island Flowers Co	4,230	630	3,600	3,600	
Floristry Supplies Limited	470	70	400	400	
Yorkshire Electricity plc	423	63	360		360
	6,392	952	5,440	5,080	360

	Total	*VAT*	*Net*
	£	£	£
Credit Note Issued			
Deluxe Hotels plc	94	14	80
Credit Note Received			
Exotic Blooms Limited	235	35	200

Journal Entries

	Debit	*Credit*
	£	£
Equipment	210	
Heating and lighting		210
Heater installed – incorrectly debited to heating and lighting account		
Yorkshire Hotels plc	141	
York Hotels Limited		141
Correction of misposting of sales invoice in the sales ledger		

The following balances are available to you at the start of the day on 1 June 19X6

	£
Sales ledger (debtors) control	13,489
Purchase ledger (creditors) control	7,688
Sales	291,876
Purchases	126,934
VAT (credit balance)	6,920
Heating & lighting	11,962
Customers:	
York Hotels Limited	1,081
Deluxe Hotels plc	2,256
Prime Hotels Limited	1,739
Other customers	8,413

The following bank statement was received on 1 June 19X6

Northern Bank plc

120 Lower High Street, York, YK12 5SW

Bloomers Limited

Statement of Account

Account No. 11598234

Date	*Details*	*Debit*	*Credit*	*Balance* Credit C Debit D
19X6		£	£	
27 May	Balance brought forward			2,100C
28 May	Credit		4,000	6,100C
29 May	Bank charges	70		6,030C
30 May	Credit		2,120	8,150C
31 May	Bank Giro Credit:			
	Prime Hotels Limited		650	8,800C
31 May	Cheque No. 1005682	1,860		6,940C

Task 1.1

Enter the opening balances into the following accounts.

Sales ledger (debtors) control

Purchase ledger (creditors) control

Sales

Purchases

VAT

Heating & lighting

York Hotels Limited

Deluxe Hotels plc

Prime Hotels Limited

Task 1.2

Enter all the relevant transactions into the accounts listed in Task 1.1.

Task 1.3

Balance off all the accounts, clearly showing the balances carried down.

Task 1.4

Update the cash book using appropriate information taken from the bank statement. Balance off the bank account, clearly showing the balance carried down.

Task 1.5

Prepare a bank reconciliation statement as at 1 June 19X6.

General ledger

Sales ledger control

Date	*Details*	*Amount*	*Date*	*Details*	*Amount*
		£			£

Purchase ledger control

Date	*Details*	*Amount*	*Date*	*Details*	*Amount*
		£			£

Sales

Date	*Details*	*Amount*	*Date*	*Details*	*Amount*
		£			£

Purchases

Date	*Details*	*Amount*	*Date*	*Details*	*Amount*
		£			£

VAT

Date	*Details*	*Amount*	*Date*	*Details*	*Amount*
		£			£

Heating and lighting

Date	*Details*	*Amount*	*Date*	*Details*	*Amount*
		£			£

Sales ledger

York Hotels Limited

Date	*Details*	*Amount*	*Date*	*Details*	*Amount*
		£			£

Deluxe Hotels plc

Date	*Details*	*Amount*	*Date*	*Details*	*Amount*
		£			£

Prime Hotels Limited

Date	*Details*	*Amount* £	*Date*	*Details*	*Amount* £

Cash Book (bank columns only)

			£			£
May 27	Balance	b/d	2,100	May 27	Flora (UK) Limited	1,860
May 27	Cash sales		4,000	May 29	STD Supplies Limited	542
May 29	Cash sales		2,120	May 30	Business rates	4,320
May 31	Cash sales		1,386			

Bloomers Limited

Bank reconciliation statement as at 1 June 19X6

CHAPTER 13

Maintaining the Creditors' Ledger

Revision notes

The *creditors ledger* or *purchase ledger* is separate from the nominal ledger. It contains an account for each individual supplier and shows the amounts owed to, and all transactions with, each supplier. It is compiled mainly from:

- the purchase day book which gives details of individual invoices; and
- the cash book which details cash payments to and discounts received from each supplier.

Contras and *adjustments* for the correction of errors will also be found in the creditor's ledger accounts.

The *creditors ledger control account* or *purchase ledger control account* is in the nominal ledger and records the total amount owing to creditors. A *creditors ledger reconciliation* is a control performed regularly to ensure that the creditors ledger and creditors ledger control account record the same total amount owing to creditors. The total of a list of balances compiled from the creditors ledger is compared with the balance on the creditor's ledger control account and any differences are investigated and adjusted for appropriately.

Tips and traps

Individual invoices and cash payments are recorded in the creditors ledger which acts as a memorandum of amounts owed. **Totals** of sales and cash payments are recorded in the creditor's ledger control account in the nominal ledger.

Creditors are recorded at the gross amount, including VAT, as this is what has to be paid.

Returns of goods to suppliers may be due to faulty goods, excess goods, unauthorised goods or unsold goods purchased on a *sale or return* basis. Returns are recorded on a *returns outwards note.*

A *credit note* will be received from the supplier, checked against the returns outwards note and recorded in the *purchase returns day book.* This is analysed and posted in a similar manner to the purchase day book.

Questions

1 Errors (AAT CA J95)

Would the following errors cause a difference to occur between the balance of the creditors control account and the total of the balances in the purchases ledger?

(a) A creditor's account has been balanced off incorrectly.

(b) An invoice for £37 has been entered into the purchases day book as £39.

(c) An invoice has, in error, been omitted from the purchases day book.

2 Purchase ledger (AAT CA D95)

Which accounts are contained in the purchase ledger?

3 Balance of purchase ledger (AAT CA D95)

Would the following errors cause a difference between the balance of the purchase ledger (creditors) control account and the total of the balances in the purchase ledger?

(a) The purchase day book was overcast by £10.

(b) The value of a purchase invoice was credited to the account of ACL Limited instead of AC Lead Limited.

(c) An invoice for £47 was recorded in the purchase day book as £74.

4 Bloomers Limited (AAT CA J96)

Bloomers Limited purchases 40 glass crystal vases for £7.50 each plus VAT. The vases are then **all** sold to a hotel gift shop for £517 inclusive of VAT. How much is owed by Bloomers to HM Customs and Excise in respect of the vases?

Note. Your answer should include detailed workings.

5 Sundries Galore Limited (AAT CA J96)

Bloomers Limited has recently purchased a range of decorative ribbons from Sundries Galore Limited. The total list price of the ribbons was £340 exclusive of VAT, but Sundries Galore gave Bloomers a trade discount of 20% and, in addition, a cash discount of 5% if payment was made within 7 days. Calculate the following:

(a) The value of the trade discount

(b) The value of the cash discount available

(c) The value of VAT charged in respect of this purchase

6 Ledger (AAT CA J96)

Would the following accounts be found in the general ledger, the purchase ledger or the sales ledger?

(a) Exotic Blooms Limited (a credit supplier)

(b) Salaries and wages

(c) Motor vehicles

7 Recording returns

What is the document called which records returns to suppliers and how is each part of this document used?

8 Credit note

An invoice is found to be incorrect and a credit note is requested. Should the invoice be processed as usual or processed only when a credit note is obtained?

9 Janitorial Supplies Limited

What entry/entries would be made in respect of a credit note for purchases to the value of £100 plus VAT at 17.5% from Janitorial Supplies Limited

(a) in the creditors' ledger; and

(b) in the nominal ledger?

10 Bookkeeping exercise (AAT CA D95)

Introduction

The tasks and questions are based on the transactions of Summit Glazing Limited. The company provides a glazing service to commercial and domestic customers. It also constructs conservatories and installs replacement windows which are bought in from specialist manufacturers.

The Managing Director is Chris Cooper and Mary Owen is the Accountant/Company Secretary. You are employed as an Accounting Technician to assist Mary Owen.

Data

The following transactions all occurred on 1 December 19X5 and have yet to be entered into the ledger system. VAT has been calculated at the rate of 17.5%.

Sales Invoices Issued

	Total	*VAT*	*Net*
	£	£	£
G C J Builders Limited	8,460	1,260	7,200
Acorn Housing Association	6,063	903	5,160
Cordington Plc	2,021	301	1,720
James Building Services	799	119	680
	17,343	2,583	14,760

Purchases Invoices Received	*Total*	*VAT*	*Net*
Georgian Conservatories	705	105	600
Diamond Glass Limited	2,115	315	1,800
Russell Timber Supplies	423	63	360
Elite Windows	1,269	189	1,080
	4,512	672	3,840

Credit Note Received	*Total*	*VAT*	*Net*
Diamond Glass Limited	47	7	40

Cash Sales

Cheques	141	21	120
Notes and coins	188	28	160
	329	49	280

Cheque Received

	£
Acorn Housing Association	6,200

Cheques Issued

	£
Georgian Conservatories (Full settlement of a debt of £27,750)	27,195
Elite Windows	13,995

Journal Entry

	Debit	*Credit*
	£	£
Motor expenses	340	
Motor vehicles		340

Correction of error: Cost of repairs on delivery van debited in error to the motor vehicles account.

The following balances are available to you at the start of the day on 1 December 19X5

	£
Purchases	897,953
Sales	1,138,325
Purchase returns	4,280
Bank (debit balance)	22,723
Bank charges	1,567
VAT (credit balance)	8,136
Discounts allowed	6,340
Discounts received	2,892
Sales ledger control (debtors)	85,995
Purchase ledger control (creditors)	78,237
Wages	282,500
Rent and rates	16,225
Electricity	4,106
Telephone	1,852
Motor expenses	6,857
Insurance	5,935
Sundry expenses	2,734
Motor vehicles	56,900
Machinery and equipment	15,120
Sundry creditors	11,867
Stocks	48,930
Capital	212,000

Task 1

Enter the opening balances into the following accounts:

Bank (cash book)

Sales ledger control (debtors)

Purchase ledger control (creditors)

Purchases

Sales

VAT

Purchase returns

Discounts received

Motor vehicles

Motor expenses

Task 2

Using the balances data for 1 December 19X5 shown above, enter all the transactions into the accounts given in Task 1.

Task 3

Balance the cash book and total the discount and VAT columns, transferring the totals to the appropriate accounts.

Task 4

Balance all the remaining accounts in which you have made entries.

Note. You are not required to update any accounts other than those shown in Task 1.

Task 5

Complete the list of balances by inserting the figure for each account in either the debit column or the credit column as appropriate. Total the two columns. The two totals should be the same. If they do not agree, try to trace and correct any errors you have made within the time available. If you are still unable to make the totals balance, leave the work incomplete.

General ledger

Sales ledger control

Date	*Details*	*Amount* £	*Date*	*Details*	*Amount* £

Purchase ledger control

Date	*Details*	*Amount* £	*Date*	*Details*	*Amount* £

Purchases

Date	*Details*	*Amount* £	*Date*	*Details*	*Amount* £

Sales

Date	Details	Amount	Date	Details	Amount
		£			£

VAT

Date	Details	Amount	Date	Details	Amount
		£			£

Purchases returns

Date	Details	Amount	Date	Details	Amount
		£			£

Discounts received

Date	Details	Amount	Date	Details	Amount
		£			£

Motor vehicles

Date	*Details*	*Amount*	*Date*	*Details*	*Amount*
		£			£

Motor expenses

Date	*Details*	*Amount*	*Date*	*Details*	*Amount*
		£			£

Cash book

Date	*Details*	*Disc all*	*VAT*	*Cash*	*Bank*	*Date*	*Details*	*Disc rec'd*	*VAT*	*Cash*	*Bank*
		£	£	£	£			£	£	£	£

List of updated balances

	Debit balances £	*Credit balances* £
Purchases		
Sales		
Purchase returns		
Bank		
Bank charges		
Cash		
VAT		
Discounts allowed		
Discounts received		
Sales ledger control (debtors)		
Purchase ledger control (creditors)		
Wages		
Rent and rates		
Electricity		
Telephone		
Motor expenses		
Insurance		
Sundry expenses		
Motor vehicles		
Machinery and equipment		
Sundry creditors		
Stocks		
Capital		
Totals		

CHAPTER 14

Using Information about Creditors

Revision notes

A *suppliers' statement reconciliation* is a form of internal control. It compares the *suppliers' statements* with the individual creditors accounts in the creditors' ledger. Errors detected in this way will have to be corrected in the creditors' ledger and/or the creditors' ledger control account. Sometimes differences between a statement and the creditors' ledger control account are due to timing differences; these are not adjusted for as they reverse in a subsequent period.

Questions

1 Detachable remittance advice

Which two documents sent by the supplier to the customer often feature a detachable remittance advice?

2 Smallfry Limited

With the agreement of Smallfry Limited a contra entry has been made in the debtors and creditors ledger accounts for Smallfry Limited, but not in the nominal ledger. Would this error be discovered by performing:

(a) a suppliers' statement reconciliation?

(b) a creditors' ledger reconciliation?

(c) a trial balance?

3 Vetro Limited (AAT CA D95)

On 18 November 19X5 Summit Glazing purchased a consignment of patio doors from Vetro Limited for £4,000 plus £686 VAT (Invoice number D3472). The invoice offered a 2% cash discount for payment within 7 days. Summit Glazing paid the invoice by sending a cheque for £4,606 on 20 November. The cheque should have arrived within 7 days from the date of the invoice as it was sent by first class post. A statement dated 30 November showing a balance of £80 has now been received from Vetro Limited.

Draft a letter, to be signed by Mary Owen (the Accountant/Company Secretary), explaining the situation and requesting that the appropriate action be taken. The letter will be faxed to Edward Frazer at Vetro Limited, Unit 23 Gorse Industrial Estate, Manchester MN12 2BG.

CHAPTER 15

Processing Exercises

Processing exercise 1 (AAT CA J94)

Introduction

The tasks and questions are all centred on the activities of MEL Motor Factors Limited. The company trades in motor parts and accessories and is based in Manchester in the UK. Although customers are located entirely in the UK, goods supplied originate from both the UK and overseas.

The managing director is Andrew Bolton and Cathy Payne is the accountant. You are employed as an accounting technician to assist Cathy Payne.

Data

The following transactions all occurred on 1 June 1994 and have yet to be entered into the ledger system. VAT has been calculated to the nearest pound at a rate of 17.5% and you should continue to use this rate for any subsequent calculations. The bank statement was received on 2 June but again contains transactions relating to 1 June.

Sales invoices issued

	Total	*VAT*	*Net*
	£	£	£
Autoparts Limited	5,492	818	4,674
Salfords Stores Limited	3,396	506	2,890
Motormania	6,156	917	5,239
Other customers	22,696	3,380	19,316
	37,740	5,621	32,119

Purchases invoices received	*Total*	*VAT*	*Net*
Carmart Imports Limited	8,371	1,247	7,124
Lombard Products Limited	7,727	1,151	6,576
Lucas & Co	5,820	867	4,953
Other suppliers	12,676	1,888	10,788
	34,594	5,153	29,441

Credit note issued	*Total*	*VAT*	*Net*
Motormania	168	25	143

Journal entries

	Debit	*Credit*
	£	£
Creditors' control account	1,450	
Debtors' control account		1,450
Correction of an error made 10 May 1994		

Cheques issued

	£
Lombard Products Limited (in full repayment of a debt for £2,958)	2,817
Cash purchases (inclusive of VAT of £203)	1,363

Cheques received

Motormania (in full repayment of a debt for £1,550)	£1,472

Bank statement received

Royal Bank Limited

MEL Motor Factors Limited **Statement of account**

Account no. 40319442

Date	*Details*	*Debit*	*Credit*	*Balance*
		£	£	£
1 June	Balance forward			4,120
1 June	Bank interest		122	4,242
1 June	Bank charges	210		4,032

The following balances are available to you at the start of the day on 1 June 19X4.

	£
Customers:	
Autoparts Limited	24,617
Salfords Stores Limited	41,561
Motormania	27,124
Other customers	627,341

	£
Suppliers:	
Carmart Imports Limited	28,413
Lombard Products Limited	56,987
Lucas & Co	33,792
Other suppliers	492,853
Other:	
Purchases	2,652,194
Sales	3,122,786
Sales returns	6,225
Bank (debit balance)	4,120
Bank charges	261
Bank interest received	103
VAT (credit balance)	71,089
Discount allowed	21,408
Discount received	15,194
Debtors' control account	720,643
Creditors' control account	612,045
Various other debit balances – total	1,431,500
Various other credit balances – total	1,015,134

Tasks

Complete all of the following tasks.

Task 1

Enter the opening balances into the following accounts.

- Bank (cash book)
- Bank charges
- Bank interest received
- Debtors' control account
- Discount allowed
- Discount received
- Purchases
- VAT
- Lombard Products Limited
- Motormania

Task 2

Using the data shown above, enter all relevant transactions into the accounts shown in Task 1. Please note that the cash book has been divided into two sections, one to record receipts and the other to record payments. When making entries in the cash book, ensure that you complete the analysis columns and that you include the two items shown in the bank statement.

Task 3

Total the various columns of the cash book and clearly show the closing bank balance.

Task 4

Transfer any relevant sums from the cash book into the other accounts shown in Task 1 to complete the necessary double entry for those accounts.

Task 5

Balance off all the remaining accounts in which you have made entries.

Note. You are not required to update any accounts other than those shown in Task 1.

Processing exercise 2 (AAT CA D94)

Introduction

The tasks and questions are based on the transactions of Chang Fashions Limited. The company owns a chain of clothes shops and has its head office located in premises in London. The head office has good storage facilities for stock held, substantial sales areas for both men's and ladies' wear, and office space for the administrative staff employed within the company.

The managing director is Mary Chang and Rahul Divan is the accountant and company secretary. You are employed as an accounting technician to assist Rahul Divan.

Data

The following transactions all occurred during the week ended 2 December 19X4 and have been entered for you into summarised books of original entry. VAT has been calculated to the nearest pound at a rate of 17.5% and you should continue to use this rate for any subsequent calculations.

'Other customers' and 'other suppliers' should each be treated as individual accounts.

Purchases invoices received

	Total	*VAT*	*Net*	*Goods for resale*	*Power and heating*
	£	£	£	£	£
Style Clothes Limited	9,736	1,450	8,286	8,286	
South East Electric	3,550	529	3,021		3,021
Southern Gas	3,108	463	2,645		2,645
Trend Imports Limited	17,907	2,667	15,240	15,240	
Other suppliers	20,935	3,118	17,817	17,817	
	55,236	8,227	47,009	41,343	5,666

Purchases returns day book

	Total	*VAT*	*Net*
	£	£	£
Style Clothes Limited	256	38	218

Cash book

Opening balance at start of the week (credit)				28,619
Receipts		*Total received*	*VAT*	
		£	£	
Cash sales		52,170	7,770	
Bank interest		411		
				52,581
				23,962
Payments	*Discount*	*Total paid*	*VAT*	
	£	£	£	
Cash purchases		1,376	205	
Style Clothes Limited	160	7,420		
Southern Gas		1,204		
Shop fittings purchased		1,640	244	
Shop fittings repaired		88	13	
Refunds for returns		275	41	
Other suppliers		12,143		
				24,146
Closing balance at end of week (credit)				184

The following balances are available to you at the start of the week ended 2 December 19X4.

Suppliers:

	£
Style Clothes Limited	32,417
South East Electric	Nil
Southern Gas	1,204
Trend Imports Limited	45,862
Other suppliers	98,291
Other:	
Purchases	1,066,213
Sales	1,453,420
Purchases returns	5,741
Sales returns	6,984
Power and heating	7,122
Shop fittings	35,560
Shop fittings repairs	241
Bank interest received	319
VAT (credit balance)	38,162
Discount received	4,337
Creditors' control account	177,774
Various other debit balances – total	1,542,632
Various other credit balances – total	950,380

Tasks

Complete the following tasks

Task 1

Enter the opening balances into the following accounts.

- Creditors' control account
- Power and heating
- Purchases
- Sales returns
- Shop fittings
- VAT
- Southern Gas
- Style Clothes Limited

Task 2

Enter all relevant entries into the accounts shown in Task 1.

Task 3

Balance off all the accounts in which you have made entries in Task 2.

Task 4

Calculate the closing balances of the remaining accounts. Complete the list of updated balances by inserting the updated figure for each account in either the debit balances column or the credit balances column as appropriate. Total the two columns. The two totals should be the same. If they do not agree try to trace and correct any errors you may have made within the time you have available. If you are still unable to make the totals balance, leave the work incomplete. (In checking for errors you should take into account that the total of the suppliers' balances should be the same figure as the balance of the creditors' control account.)

Note. It is not a requirement to draw up all the individual accounts in order to calculate the closing balances for task 4. Candidates may, however, adopt that approach if they wish.

Processing Exercises (Answers)

Processing exercise 1

General ledger

Receipts cash book

Date	Details	Discount	Total received	VAT	Debtors	Other
		£	£	£	£	£
1 June	Balance b/d		4,120			
1 June	Motormania	78	1,472		1,472	
1 June	Bank interest		122			122
		78	5,714	Nil	1,472	122
			4,390			
1 June	Balance c/d		1,324			

Payments cash book

Date	Details	Discount	Total received	VAT	Debtors	Other
		£	£	£	£	£
1 June	Lombard Products Limited	141	2,817		2,817	
1 June	Purchases		1,363	203		1,160
1 June	Bank charges		210			210
		141	4,390	203	2,817	1,370

Bank charges

		£			£
1 June	Balance b/d	261	1 June	Balance c/d	471
	Bank	210			
		471			471
2 June	Balance b/d	471			

Bank interest received

		£			£
1 June	Balance c/d	225	1 June	Balance b/d	103
				Bank	122
		225			225
			2 June	Balance b/d	225

Debtors' control account

		£			£
1 June	Balance b/d	720,643	1 June	Creditors control	1,450
	Sales	37,740		Bank	1,472
				Discounts	78
				Sales returns	168
			1 June	Balance c/d	755,215
		758,383			758,383
2 June	Balance b/d	755,215			

Discounts allowed

		£			£
1 June	Balance b/d	21,408	1 June	Balance c/d	21,486
	Total for day	78			
		21,486			21,486
2 June	Balance b/d	21,486			

Discounts received

		£			£
1 June	Balance c/d	15,335	1 June	Balance b/d	15,194
				Total for day	141
		15,335			15,335
			2 June	Balance b/d	15,335

Purchases

		£			£
1 June	Balance b/d	2,652,194	1 June	Balance b/d	2,682,795
	Creditors	29,441			
	Bank	1,160			
		2,682,795			2,682,795
2 June	Balance b/d	2,682,795			

VAT

		£			£
1 June	Purchases	5,153	1 June	Balance b/d	71,089
	Sales returns	25		Sales	5,621
	Bank	203			
1 June	Balance c/d	71,329			
		76,710			76,710
			2 June	Balance b/d	71,329

Creditors' ledger

Lombard Products Limited

		£			£
1 June	Bank	2,817	1 June	Balance b/d	56,987
	Discount	141		Purchases	7,727
1 June	Balance c/d	61,756			
		64,714			64,714
			2 June	Balance b/d	61,756

Debtors' ledger

Motormania

		£			£
1 June	Balance b/d	27,124	1 June	Sales returns	168
	Sales	6,156		Bank	1,472
				Discount	78
			1 June	Balance c/d	31,562
		33,280			33,280
2 June	Balance b/d	31,562			

Processing exercise 2

General ledger

Creditors' control account

		£			£
	Purchases returns	256	26 Nov	Balance b/d	177,774
	Bank	20,767		Purchases	55,236
	Discounts	160			
2 Dec	Balance c/d	211,827			
		233,010			233,010
			3 Dec	Balance b/d	211,827

Power and heating

		£			£
27 Nov	Balance b/d	7,122	2 Dec	Balance c/d	12,788
	Purchases	5,666			
		12,788			12,788
3 Dec	Balance b/d	12,788			

Purchases

		£			£
26 Nov	Balance b/d	1,066,213	2 Dec	Balance c/d	1,108,727
	Creditors	41,343			
	Bank	1,171			
		1,108,727			1,108,727
3 Dec	Balance b/d	1,108,727			

Sales returns

		£			£
26 Nov	Balance b/d	6,984	2 Dec	Balance c/d	7,218
	Bank	234			
		7,218			7,218
3 Dec	Balance b/d	7,218			

Shop fittings

		£			£
26 Nov	Balance b/d	35,560	2 Dec	Balance c/d	36,956
	Bank	1,396			
		36,956			36,956
2 June	Balance b/d	36,956			

VAT

		£			£
	Purchases	8,227	26 Nov	Balance b/d	38,162
	Bank	503		Purchases	
2 Dec	Balance c/d	37,240		Returns	38
				Sales	7,770
		45,970			45,970
			3 Dec	Balance b/d	37,240

Creditor's ledger

Southern Gas

		£			£
	Bank	1,204	26 Nov	Balance b/d	1,204
2 Dec	Balance c/d	3,108		Purchases	3,108
		4,312			4,312
			3 Dec	Balance b/d	3,108

Style Clothes Limited

		£			£
	Purchase returns	256	26 Nov	Balance b/d	32,417
	Bank	7,420		Purchases	9,736
	Discount	160			
2 Dec	Balance c/d	34,317			
		42,153			42,153
			3 Dec	Balance b/d	34,317

List of updated balances at the end of the week

	Debit balances £	Credit balance £
Suppliers:		
Style Clothes Limited		34,317
South East Electric		3,550
Southern Gas		3,108
Trend Imports Limited		63,769
Other suppliers		107,083
Total of suppliers		211,827
Other:		
Bank		184
Purchases	1,108,727	
Sales		1,497,820
Purchases returns		5,959
Sales returns	7,218	
Power and heating	12,788	
Shop fittings	36,956	
Shop fittings repairs	316	
Bank interest received		730
VAT		37,240
Discount received		4,497
Other debit balances	1,542,632	
Other credit balances		950,380
Totals	2,708,637	2,708,637

CHAPTER 16

Answers to Chapter Questions

Chapter 1

1 Cash v cheques

Convenient use of coins and notes.

(a) To pay for small amounts such as newspapers, milk and window-cleaning

(b) To give change in cash transactions

(c) To pay wages to employees who do not have bank accounts (now rare)

2 Bank accounts

The true answers are:

(a) (i), (ii), (iii) and (iv)

Some current accounts do earn interest, but at rates much lower than those of deposit accounts.

(b) (i), (ii) and (v)

Some deposit accounts allow the use of cheque books.

3 Cheque details

The details to be filled in by the account-holder are as follows:

- date
- payee
- amount in words
- amount in numbers
- signature.

Chapter 2

1 Cash discount

		£
£81.48	Invoice amount	84.00
	Discount 3% × 84	2.52
	Cash received 97% × 84	81.48

2 Before discount

£253	Invoice amount $\frac{100}{98} \times 247.94$	253.00
	Discount $\frac{2}{98} \times 247.94$	5.06
	Cash received 98%	247.94

3 Errors

Six from:

- Discount incorrectly calculated
- Discount taken outside the time limit
- Payment disagrees with remittance advice
- Incorrectly signed cheque
- Payee incorrect on cheque
- Amount on cheque incorrect
- Words and figures on cheque disagree

4 Availability of cash discounts

False

5 Customer's name

(a) Yes

(b) Yes

(c) No

(d) Yes

6 Ron's records

Ron's Records
53 Bayview Road
Exmouth
Devon EX14 2PT

Mr C Crabbe
2 Ropers Avenue
Exmouth
Devon EX17 4SU

5 May 19X4

Dear Mr Crabbe

Refunds under the Sale of Goods Act

Thank you for your letter regarding your recent purchases from us and I apologise for any inconvenience that has been caused by the various problems you have experienced. You are correct in pointing out that you do not need a receipt to claim a refund and I shall indeed make refunds for all items qualifying under the Sale of Goods Act as detailed below.

Under the Act, your cracked CD requires a refund as it is clearly faulty. Similarly the CD which had the wrong case requires a refund as the item you bought was not as described. Also, the Act requires refunds for items which are unsuitable for the purpose specified by the customer, as is the case with the tape cassette which was unsuitable for your daughter's party. However, I am unable to give you a refund for the other tape cassette as we had no agreement that you could change your mind about this purchase. Nevertheless, it is my policy to offer a credit note in such instances as a gesture of goodwill.

If you return the purchases to the shop, I will be pleased to issue you with a refund and a credit note for the appropriate amounts. I hope this meets with your satisfaction.

Your sincerely

Ron Smith
Proprietor, Ron's Records

7 Accepting credit cards

Any three from:

- Check that the voucher signature compares with the signature on the card.
- Check that the card has not been altered or tampered with.
- Check that the card is valid.
- Check that the card is not included on the list of stolen cards.
- Check credit limit.
- Check 'floor limit'.

8 Accepting a cheque

Any three from:

- Check that the card has not been tampered with.
- Check expiry date.
- Check that the amount of the guarantee covers the value of the cheque.
- Check that the name/signature agrees with that on the cheque.
- Check that the bank details agree with those on the cheque.

Chapter 3

1 VAT invoice

Eight from:

- name of supplier
- address of supplier
- VAT registration number of supplier
- invoice number/date of sale
- name of customer
- address of customer
- nature of transaction (eg sale)
- description and quantity of goods or services

- for each item
  - VAT rate
  - amount excluding VAT (in sterling)
- total amount excluding VAT (in sterling)
- amount of VAT chargeable at each rate
- total VAT payable
- amount payable including VAT (in sterling)

2 Aubrey Aitchinson

(a)

	£
Discounted amount excluding VAT (6 × £250 × 98%)	1,470.00
Discounted VAT (17 1/2% × 1,470)	257.25
Payable to Myers Tyres Limited	1,727.25

(b)

	£
Amount excluding VAT (6 × £250)	1,500.00
Discounted VAT (17 1/2% × 1,500 × 98%)	257.25
Payable to Myers Tyres Limited	1,757.25

3 Post dated cheque

(a) The date on the cheque is later than the date the cheque was written; or

(b) a cheque dated in the future; or

(c) a cheque which will not be honoured until sometime in the future.

4 Comart Supplies Limited

(a) £200

(b) £90

(c) £299.25

5 Office equipment

The cheque requisition form should be checked against the relevant purchase order and signed by an authorised person within the company.

6 Settling debts

Any **two** from the following.

- The handling of cash would be a security risk for the sender.
- The handling of cash would be a security risk for the receiver.
- Cash may be lost or stolen in the post.
- The need for cash to be counted wastes time and can lead to errors.
- There is an absence of documentary evidence of payment.

Chapter 4

1 M Lewis

(a) No

(b) By adding the word 'only' after the payee's name, the drawer of the cheque prevents it from being endorsed or transferred to another party.

2 Cheque

False

3 Wendy Roberts

Bank overdraft

4 Summit Glazing Limited

Any two from:

- The cheque is out of date.
- The words and figures do not agree.
- The cheque has not been signed.

5 A Jones 1

It can only be paid into the bank account of the payee, A Jones – it can not be endorsed.

6 A Jones 2

(a) Bloomers Limited

(b) Northern Bank Plc

(c) A Jones

7 Bloomers

Direct debit

8 Debit card

True

9 Norwest Bank

Principal and agent

10 Comart Supplies Limited

(a) Comart Supplies Limited

(b) In the event that Comart Supplies Limited is unable or unwilling to repay the loan, the bank can sell the premises to obtain repayment from the proceeds.

11 Summit Glazing

Creditor

12 JLW Limited

Standing order

13 Bank statement

Bloomers Limited
12 Nightingale Arcade, York, YK12 3DC

Mr D Williams
Northern Bank plc
120 Lower High Street
York YK12 5SW

1 June 19X6

Dear Mr Williams

Bank charges

We have today received a bank statement dated 31 May 1996, which discloses bank charges of £70. The level of these charges has caused us some concern as they are considerably higher than normal. It is unusual for our monthly bank charges to exceed £50 and there has been no noticeable increase in our banking transactions during the last month. We would appreciate it if you could investigate the matter and provide us with an explanation of the increase.

Yours sincerely

P Lazenby

Paul Lazenby
Accountant

Bloomers Limited Registered office: 12 Nightingale Arcade, York YK12 3DC
Registered in England, number 4643757

Chapter 5

1 Cheque 302462 – 1

£4,670 debit

2 Cheque 302462 – 2

The cheque would have already been credited to the cash book at the time it was issued (ie before 1 June).

3 Bank reconciliation

(a) Added

(b) Subtracted

4 Unpaid entry

Debit

5 Dishonoured cheque

Dr Sales Ledger Control

Cr Bank

6 Cash refund

Debit	£	*Credit*	£
Sales Returns	80	Bank/Cash	94
VAT	14		

7 Journal

Any two from:

- Opening entries in a new set of books.
- The correction of errors.
- Transfers between accounts.

8 Discounts allowed column

Debited

9 MMS Textiles

Any three from:

- Unrecorded deposits.
- Unpresented cheque (s).
- Bank charges.
- Interest received.
- Dividends received.
- Direct debits not entered in cash books.
- Error in cash book.
- Error in bank statement.

10 VAT column

Debited

11 Summit Glazing

£71.26

12 Bloomers Limited

MEMORANDUM

To: Paul Lazenby   Date: 1 June 19X6

From: A Student

Subject: Petty Cash Security

As requested I have given consideration to improvements which can be made to increase the security of petty cash and make the following recommendations to restrict access to the cash held.

Firstly the cash should be kept in a secure container. I recommend that we purchase a lockable, metal cash box for this purpose. In addition the cash box should be kept in a lockable drawer, together with the petty cash book and the stock of petty cash vouchers. Access to the keys involved must be restricted. The cash box should be kept locked at all times when not in use and the drawer locked whenever the office is unoccupied.

As I am to be responsible for petty cash I should be the person who holds the keys and operates the system, but in my absence you may require access and so I recommend that you also hold a set of keys.

Chapter 6

1 Wendy Roberts

(a) No

(b) Robert's statement that he was willing to buy the printer for £160 was a counter offer and terminated the original offer. The counter offer was not accepted by Wendy. At 4.30 pm he was effectively making a new offer which could not be accepted since the printer had already been sold.

2 Comart Supplies Limited

(a) No

(b) The lack of a response cannot be taken to be an acceptance of an offer. Without an acceptance, a contract does not exist.

3 Summit Glazing

(a) No

(b) The offer was revoked before it was accepted.

4 Mr Green

(a) No

(b) Mr Green's contract is with Summit Glazing, not with the manufacturer of the window. It is therefore Summit's responsibility to correct the fault.

5 Carriage paid

The price of the goods includes delivery to the customer's premises.

6 Gift Box

Debit	£	*Credit*	£
Purchase ledger control	75	Sales ledger control	75

7 Dried flowers

(a) No

(b) The price ticket is an invitation to treat – not an offer which can be accepted to form a contract.

8 Bloomers Limited

(a) 29 May

(b) A contract is formed when an offer is accepted. Provided it is correctly addressed and postage paid, acceptance is effective when it is posted.

9 JLW Limited

(a) No

(b) JLW Limited's counter offer of £2.75 per gramme terminated the supplier's offer. JLW Limited's offer to buy at £2.85 per gramme is a new offer.

Chapter 7

1 James' Games Limited

		£
1,750 @ £1		1,750.00
Less:	Discount @ $2^1/2\%$	(43.75)
		1,706.25
Add:	VAT @ $17^1/2\%$	298.59
		2,004.84

The invoice total will be £2,004.84.

2 Stop list

A customer is put on a stop list when it is considered too risky to supply them with more goods or services, for example if they have reached their credit limit. No more goods or services are provided until they have reduced or paid their existing debts.

3 Advice note

False

4 Remittance advice

False

5 Proforma invoice

It requests payment to be made before supply.

Chapter 8

1 Softsell Limited

(a)

Debit	*Credit*
Debtors control account	Sales
VAT	

(b)

Debit	*Credit*
Purchases	Creditors control account

2 Computerised accounting system

Any **two** from the following:

- Accuracy
- Speed of processing
- Versatility (computer can be used for a variety of applications)
- Efficiency of storage (vast quantities of information can be stored in a small space)

3 Collectable VAT

£56

4 Processing

(a) Batch

(b) On line / real time.

5 Microfiche

Any one from:

- Storage space reduced.
- More durable than paper records.
- Easier to keep records secure.
- Ease of reference.

6 Updating

Integrated

7 Sales ledger control account

False

Chapter 9

1 Errors

(a) No – this only affects the totals posted to the nominal ledger.

(b) Yes

(c) No – this will affect the creditors' ledger.

(d) Yes

2 October 19X4

Debtors' ledger control account

	£		£
Balance b/f	3,750	Cash	13,004
Invoices issued	12,632	Bad debts	1,200
		Balance c/f	2,178
	16,382		16,382

The balance on debtors ledger control account on 31 October is £2,178.

3 Control account

Any one from:

- To assist in the location of errors.
- Total value owed by debtors known at any time.
- To help prevent fraud.

4 Posting

(a) Gleam Cleaners' account should be credited with £480.

(b) Dr Bright Lights Limited £84

Cr Cool Shades & Co £84

5 Appropriate documents

(a) Statement

(b) Credit note

(c) Remittance advice

6 Credit notes

Any two from

- Faulty goods returned.
- Unwanted / unordered / not as ordered goods returned.
- Invoice price charged too high.
- Invoiced goods not delivered.

7 General ledger

Debit	£	*Credit*	£
Returns outwards	160	Purchase ledger control	188
Returns inwards	160	Sales ledger control	188
VAT	28		
VAT	28		

8 Bookkeeping exercise

General ledger

Debtors' control account

Date	*Details*	*Amount*	*Date*	*Details*	*Amount*
		£			£
1/4/X5	Balance b/f	480,866	1/4/X5	Sales returns	4,121
	Sales day book	96,367		Cash received	15,497
				Discount allowed	311
				Balance c/f	557,304
		577,233			577,233
2/4/X5	Balance b/f	557,304			

Office expenses

Date	*Details*	*Amount*	*Date*	*Details*	*Amount*
		£			£
1/4/X5	Balance b/f	8,595	1/4/X5	Balance c/f	9,611
	Journal	31			
	Cash paid	945			
	Petty cash ($47 \times 100/117.5$)	40			
		9,611			9,611
2/4/X5	Balance b/f	9,611			

Sales

Date	*Details*	*Amount*	*Date*	*Details*	*Amount*
		£			£
1/4/X5	Balance b/f	3,196,319	1/4/X5	Balance b/f	3,114,304
				Sales day book	82,015
		3,196,319			3,196,319
			2/4/X5	Balance b/f	3,196,319

VAT

Date	*Details*	*Amount*	*Date*	*Details*	*Amount*
		£			£
1/4/X5	Sales returns	614	1/4/X5	Balance b/f	33,732
	Cash purchases			Sales day book	14,352
	(800 × 17.5/117.5)	119			
	Petty cash (47 × 17.5/117.5)	7			
	Balance c/f	47,344			
		48,084			48,084
			2/4/X5	Balance b/f	47,344

Debtors' ledger

Wells Stores

Date	*Details*	*Amount*	*Date*	*Details*	*Amount*
		£			£
1/4/X5	Balance b/f	8,077	1/4/X5	Sales returns	112
	Sales day book	3,447		Cash received	5,237
				Discount allowed	105
				Balance b/f	6,070
		11,524			11,524
2/4/X5	Balance b/f	6,070			

Lawrence & Sons

Date	*Details*	*Amount*	*Date*	*Details*	*Amount*
		£			£
1/4/X5	Balance b/f	6,598	1/4/X5	Cash received	3,069
	Sales day book	6,377		Discount allowed	62
				Balance c/f	9,844
		12,975			12,975
2/4/X5	Balance b/f	9,844			

Grenfell Bros

Date	*Details*	*Amount*	*Date*	*Details*	*Amount*
		£			£
1/4/X5	Balance b/f	29,514	1/4/X5	Sales returns	284
	Sales day book	11,549		Cash received	4,794
				Discount allowed	96
				Balance b/f	35,889
		41,063			41,063
2/4/X5	Balance b/f	35,889			

	£	£
Updated debtors' control account balance		557,304
Updated customer balances		
Garnett Limited (9,423 + 4,413)	13,836	
Wells Stores	6,070	
Lawrence & Sons	9,844	
Shields Limited (8,614 + 2,791)	11,405	
Nicolson Partnership (37,983 + 34,950 – 3,725)	69,208	
Grenfell Bros	35,889	
Malory Homecare Limited	3,957	
Nesbit Limited (1,702 + 1,000 – 2,397 – 48)	257	
Other customers (378,955 + 27,883)	406,838	
Total updated customer balances		557,304

List of updated balances at the end of the day on 1 April 19X5

	Debit	*Credit*
	£	£
Purchases [2,647,883 + (800 × 100/117.5)]	2,648,564	
Sales		3,196,319
Sales returns (6,358 + 3,507)	9,865	
Telephones (734 – 31)	703	
Office expenses	9,611	
Interest (1,211 + 86)	1,297	
VAT		47,344
Debtors' control account	557,304	
Creditors' control account		307,332
Discounts allowed (15,898 + 311)	16,209	
Bank	16,068	
Petty cash	108	
Other debit balances	808,140	
Other credit balances		516,874
	4,067,869	4,067,869

Chapter 10

1 Credit

(a) Discounts are used to encourage customers to pay early and thus improve the cashflow of the business. An overdraft would be reduced cutting interest charges or bank balance and interest increased by early payment.

(b) A business will allow some leeway on a credit account as a gesture of goodwill. Rigid adherence to the 30-day time limit might mean valued customers are lost. (The customer may not have paid due to dissatisfaction with the goods or services provided.)

2 Bone's Phones

Humphries Limited
2 Hanover Street
Bolton BL1 8ZA

Mr Bone
Bone's Phones
29 Park Square
Chorley CH3 1PD

15 March 19X3

Dear Mr Bone

Queries on statement of account at 28 February 19X3

With reference to your letter of 8 March 19X3 I set out below an explanation for your queries.

(1) Cheque not shown on statement

Your cheque for £430 was not received by us until 1 March and consequently did not appear on the statement at 28 February. It will, however, appear on the statement issued on 31 March.

(2) Disputed invoice H413

We accept that the goods invoiced did not reach your premises and a credit note is to be issued with due haste. I apologise for the delay in resolving this matter.

Please do not hesitate to contact me should you require any further information on these matters.

Yours sincerely

J Potter
Credit controller

3 Champion Computers Limited

Task 1

Comart Supplies Limited

22 Trull Road, Taunton, Somerset S011 4NE

Mr David Robinson
Accountant
Champion Computers Limited
14 Seaview Trading Estate
Minehead MN21 1SE

1 June 19X5

Dear Mr Robinson

Purchase order number ....

Thank you for your letter of 31 May. We have checked our records and can confirm that your cheque for £10,000 was received by us on 3 May. Unfortunately it was subsequently credited to another customer's account with a similar name to Champion Computers Limited. I should like to apologise on behalf of the company for this error which I can confirm has today been corrected to reduce the balance of your account to £15,320.

We are now anxious to meet the order placed with us but regret that we are out of stock of Ensign 486 computers. The manufacturers have been contacted and we anticipate that the earliest date for delivery would be 20 June. You might, however, want to consider the Wallace 486 machine as an alternative. We do hold these in stock and could deliver six machines to you immediately. I am enclosing full details from which you will see that they have a similar specification to the Ensign computers and can be supplied at the same price.

I should be grateful if you would kindly let me know whether or not you wish to proceed with the purchase of the Ensign computers or alternatively whether you would like to change the order to the Wallace machines.

I look forward to hearing from you and would once again like to apologise for the error made.

Yours sincerely

Louise Ford

Louise Ford
Company Accountant

Comart Supplies Limited. Registered office: 22 Trull Road, Taunton, Somerset, SO11 4NE.
Registered in England, number 2034586.

Task 2

Comart Supplies Limited

22 Trull Road, Taunton, Somerset S011 4NE

Ms Christine Chambers
Chambers Computers
46 Northtown Estate
Taunton
Somerset S014 6PE

1 June 19X5

Dear Ms Chambers

Statement of Account dated 31 May 19X5

A statement of your account was sent out on 31 May showing a balance of £32,326. Unfortunately the statement includes a receipt for £10,000 dated 3 May which in fact belongs to another of our customers with a similar name to your own. We have arranged for a correcting entry to be made today which will increase your balance to £42,326 against a credit limit of £40,000.

I have also taken the opportunity to review your account and it would seem sensible to increase the credit limit to £45,000 in view of your current volume of business with us.

I hope this action meets with your approval and that you will accept my apologies for the error made.

Yours sincerely

Louise Ford

Louise Ford
Company Accountant

Comart Supplies Limited. Registered office: 22 Trull Road, Taunton, Somerset, SO11 4NE.
Registered in England, number 2034586.

4 Mary Owen

MEMORANDUM

To: Chris Cooper — Date: 4 December 1995

From: A Student

Subject Hayden Construction

The balance on Hayden Construction's account currently stands at £530, but no payment has been received since June 1995. We have made every effort possible to recover this debt, but the firm is no longer at its premises and the debt collection agency we use has been unable to trace the firm's owner, James Hayden. We have now heard unofficially that Mr Hayden is living in Australia.

As there seems no realistic possibility of recovering this debt, I recommend that it be written-off and request your authority to do so.

5 Bad debts

Businesses exist to make a profit – bad debts reduce profits by increasing expenses.

Chapter 11

1 Comart Supplies Limited

(a) Capital

(b) Revenue

2 Summit Glazing Limited

(i) Capital

(ii) Capital

(iii) Revenue

3 Ledger accounts

(a) Expense

(b) Asset

(c) Revenue

(d) Liability

4 VATable purchases

£411,955

5 Capital expenditure

Too high

6 Carriage

True

Chapter 12

1 Journal entry

	£	£
Debit		
Raw materials – steel	2,439	
Raw materials – wood	751	
Components	203	
Sundries	76	
Subcontractors	600	
Electricity	185	
Fixed assets – car	14,000	
VAT control account	745	
Credit		
Creditor's ledger control account		18,999
	18,999	18,999

2 Purchase invoice

The allocation of a sequential number and review of the sequence ensures the completeness of recording of purchase invoices. This would not be possible if the suppliers' numbers were relied upon as they bear no relation to one another; invoices from a particular supplier will not form a complete sequence and different suppliers have different sequences of invoice numbers.

3 Primary records

Any three from:

- Sales day book
- Purchases day book
- Returns inwards day book
- Returns outwards day book
- Journal
- Cash book

4 Bookkeeping exercise

General ledger

Sales Ledger Control

Date	Details	Amount	Date	Details	Amount
		£			£
June 1	Balance b/d	13,489	June 1	Returns inwards	94
	Sales	2,021		Balance c/d	15,416
		15,510			15,510
June 2	Balance b/d	15,416			

Purchase Ledger Control

Date	Details	Amount	Date	Details	Amount
		£			£
June 1	Returns outwards	235	June 1	Balance b/d	7,688
	Balance c/d	13,845		Purchases	6,392
		14,080			14,080
			June 2	Balance b/d	13,845

Sales

Date	Details	Amount	Date	Details	Amount
		£			£
June 1	Balance c/d	293,596	June 1	Balance b/d	291,876
				Debtors	1,720
		293,596			293,596
			June 2	Balance b/d	293,596

Purchases

Date	Details	Amount	Date	Details	Amount
		£			£
June 1	Balance b/d	126,934	June 1	Balance c/d	132,014
	Creditors	5,080			
		132,014			132,014
June 2	Balance b/d	132,014			

VAT

Date	Details	Amount	Date	Details	Amount
		£			£
June 1	Purchases	952	June 1	Balance b/d	6,920
	Returns inwards	14		Sales	301
	Balance c/d	6,290		Returns outwards	35
		7,256			7,256
			June 2	Balance b/d	6,290

Heating and Lighting

Date	Details	Amount	Date	Details	Amount
		£			£
June 1	Balance b/d	11,962	June 1	Equipment	210
	Yorkshire Electricity Plc	360		Balance c/d	12,112
		12,322			12,322
June 2	Balance b/d	12,112			

Sales ledger

York Hotels Limited

Date	Details	Amount	Date	Details	Amount
		£			£
June 1	Balance b/d	1,081	June 1	Yorkshire Hotels Plc	141
	Sales	846		Balance c/d	1,786
		1,927			1,927
June 2	Balance b/d	1,786			

Deluxe Hotels Plc

Date	Details	Amount	Date	Details	Amount
		£			£
June 1	Balance b/d	2,256	June 1	Returns inwards	94
	Sales	235		Balance c/d	2,961
	Sales	564			
		3,055			3,055
June 2	Balance b/d	2,961			

Prime Hotels Limited

Date	Details	Amount	Date	Details	Amount
		£			£
June 1	Balance b/d	1,739	June 1	Returns c/d	2,115
	Sales	376			
		2,115			2,115
June 2	Balance b/d	2,115			

Cash book

Date	Details	Amount	Date	Details	Amount
		£			£
27 May	Balance b/d	2,100	27 May	Flora (UK) Limited	1,860
27 May	Cash sales	4,000	29 May	STD Supplies Limited	542
29 May	Cash sales	2,120	30 May	Business rates	4,320
31 May	Cash sales	1,386	29 May	Bank charges	70
31 May	Prime Hotels Plc	650	1 June	Balance c/d	3,464
		10,256			10,256
June 2	Balance b/d	3,464			

Bank Reconciliation Statement as at 1 June 1996

	£	£
Balance as per bank statement		6,940
Less unpresented cheques		
STD Supplies Limited	542	
Business rates	4,320	
		(4,862)
		2,078
Add unrecorded deposit 31.5.X6		1,386
Balance as per cash book		3,464

Chapter 13

1 Errors

(a) Yes

(b) No

(c) No

2 Purchase ledger

Credit suppliers

3 Balance of purchase ledger

(a) Yes

(b) No

(c) No

4 Bloomers Limited

Output = $517 \times \frac{7}{47}$	=	77.00
Input = (7.50 × 40) × 17.5%	=	52.50
VAT *owed to Customs and Excise*		24.50

5 Sundries Galore Limited

(a) £68.00

(b) £13.60

(c) £45.22

6 Ledger

(a) Purchase

(b) General

(c) General

7 Recording returns

A returns outwards note is used to record returns to suppliers.

A four-part set would be used as follows.

- Part one is sent to the supplier with the goods.
- Part two is kept in despatch.
- Part three is sent to the stores department to update their record.
- Part four is sent to the creditors' ledger department for checking with the credit note.

8 Credit note

The incorrect invoice should be processed as usual, the credit note will cancel it when processed.

9 Janitorial Supplies Limited

(a) Debit Janitorial Supplies Limited £117.50

(b)	£	£
Debit Creditors' ledger control account	117.50	
CreditPurchases		100.00
VAT control account		17.50

10 Bookkeeping exercise

General ledger

Sales ledger control

Date	*Details*	*Amount*	*Date*	*Details*	*Amount*
		£			£
Dec 1	Balance b/d	85,995	Dec 1	Bank	6,200
	Sales	17,343		Balance c/d	97,138
		103,338			103,338
Dec 2	Balance b/d	97,138			

Purchase ledger control

Date	*Details*	*Amount*	*Date*	*Details*	*Amount*
		£			£
Dec 1	Purchase returns	47	Dec 1	Balance b/d	78,237
	Bank	41,190		Purchases	4,512
	Discounts received	555			
	Balance c/d	40,957			
		82,749			82,749
			Dec 2	Balance b/d	40,957

Purchases

Date	*Details*	*Amount*	*Date*	*Details*	*Amount*
		£			£
Dec 1	Balance b/d	897,953	Dec 1	Balance c/d	901,793
	Creditors	3,840			
		901,793			901,793
Dec 2	Balance b/d	901,793			

Sales

Date	*Details*	*Amount*	*Date*	*Details*	*Amount*
		£			£
Dec 1	Balance c/d	1,153,365	Dec 1	Balance b/d	1,138,325
				Debtors	14,760
				Cash book	280
		1,153,365			1,153,365
			Dec 2	Balance c/d	1,153,365

VAT

Date	*Details*	*Amount*	*Date*	*Details*	*Amount*
		£			£
Dec 1	Purchases	672	Dec 1	Balance b/d	8,136
	Balance c/d	10,103		Sales	2,583
				Purchase returns	7
				Cash sales	49
		10,775			10,775
			Dec 2	Balance b/d	10,103

Purchase returns

Date	*Details*	*Amount*	*Date*	*Details*	*Amount*
		£			£
Dec 1	Balance c/d	4,320	Dec 1	Balance b/d	4,280
				Creditors	40
		4,320			4,320
			Dec 2	Balance b/d	4,320

Discounts received

Date	*Details*	*Amount*	*Date*	*Details*	*Amount*
		£			£
Dec 1	Balance c/d	3,447	Dec 1	Balance b/d	2,892
				Creditors	555
		3,447			3,447
			Dec 2	Balance b/d	3,447

Motor vehicles

Date	*Details*	*Amount*	*Date*	*Details*	*Amount*
		£			£
Dec 1	Balance b/d	56,900	Dec 1	Motor expenses	340
				Balance c/d	56,560
		56,900			56,900
Dec 2	Balance b/d	56,560			

Motor expenses

Date	*Details*	*Amount*	*Date*	*Details*	*Amount*
		£			£
Dec 1	Balance b/d	6,857	Dec 1	Balance c/d	7,197
	Motor vehicles	340			
		7,197			7,197
Dec 2	Balance b/d	7,197			

Cash Book

Date	Details	Disc all	VAT	Cash	Bank	Date	Details	Disc Rev	VAT	Cash	Bank
		£	£	£	£			£	£	£	£
Dec 1	Balance b/d				22,723	Dec 1	Georgian Cons	555			27,195
Dec 1	Sales		49	188	141	Dec 1	Elite Windows				13,995
Dec 1	Acorn Housing Assn				6,200	Dec 1	Balance c/d			188	
Dec 1	Balance c/d				12,126						
		–	49	188	41,190			555	–	188	41,190
Dec 2	Balance b/d			188		Dec 2	Balance b/d				12,126

Summit Glazing

List of updated balances at 1 December 19X

	Debit	*Credit*
	£	£
Purchases	901,793	
Sales		1,153,365
Purchase returns		4,320
Bank		12,126
Bank charges	1,567	
Cash	188	
VAT		10,103
Discounts allowed	6,340	
Discounts received		3,447
Sales ledger control	97,138	
Purchase ledger control		40,957
Wages	282,500	
Rent and rates	16,225	
Electricity	4,106	
Telephone	1,852	
Motor expenses	7,197	
Insurance	5,935	
Sundry expenses	2,734	
Motor vehicles	56,560	
Machinery and equipment	15,120	
Sundry creditors		11,867
Stocks	48,930	
Capital		212,000
	1,448,185	1,448,185

Chapter 14

1 Detachable remittance advice

Invoices and suppliers' statements often have a detachable remittance advice.

2 Smallfry Limited

(a) No

(b) Yes

(c) No

3 Vetro Limited

Summit Glazing Limited

14–16 Ham Lane, Swindon, SW32 7FT (Tel: 01793 635542)

Mr E Frazer
Vetro Limited
Unit 23, Gorse Industrial Estate
Manchester, MN12 2BG

4 December 1995

Dear Mr Frazer

Statement of account dated 30 November 19X5

We have today received a statement from your company showing a balance of £80 as at 30 November 1995. However according to our records our account with you should be clear.

This difference has been caused by the fact that you have not credited our account with the cash discount in respect of our payment within 7 days of Invoice no. D3472. Our cheque for £4,606 was issued and sent to you on 20 November 1995 by first class post.

Could you please confirm that our account is in fact clear.

Yours sincerely

Mary Owen

Mary Owen

Accountant/Company Secretary

Summit Glazing Limited. Registered Office: 14 – 16 Ham Lane, Swindon SW32 7FT
Registered in England (No. 1658954).

CHAPTER 17

Mock Central Assessment

Questions

You are reminded that competence must be achieved in each section. You should therefore attempt and aim to complete EVERY task in EACH section.

All essential workings should be included within your answers, where appropriate.

The central assessment is in three sections.

You are advised to spend 60 minutes on Section 1, 75 minutes on Section 2 and 45 minutes on Section 3.

Section 1	Processing Exercise
	Complete all five tasks
Section 2	20 Short Answer Questions
	Answer all questions
Section 3	Communicating Accounting Information
	Complete both tasks

Sections 1, 2 and 3 all relate to the company described below.

Introduction

- Jaz Sahota is the Managing Director of a clothing manufacturing company which trades under the name of JS Fashions Limited
- Sales are made on a cash and credit basis.
- You are employed by the company as a bookkeeper.
- Double entry takes place in the general (nominal) ledger and the individual accounts of debtors and creditors are therefore regarded as memoranda accounts.
- Assume today's date is 1 December 19X8.

Data

Transactions

The following transactions which occurred on 1 December 19X8, have been entered into the relevant books of prime entry (given below). However, no entries have yet been made into the ledger system. VAT has been calculated at a rate of 17.5%.

Sales day book

Date 19X8	*Details*	*Invoice No*	*Total* £	*VAT* £	*Net* £
1 Dec	The Clothes Shop	J304	1,269	189	1,080
1 Dec	B&B Denims	J305	5,781	861	4,920
1 Dec	O'Hara Brothers	J306	3,525	525	3,000
1 Dec	Designer Clothes Limited	J307	8,460	1,260	7,200
	Totals		19,035	2,835	16,200

Sales returns day book

Date 19X8	*Details*	*Credit Note No*	*Total* £	*VAT* £	*Net* £
1 Dec	B&B Denims	CR102	235	35	200
1 Dec	O'Hara Brothers	CR103	846	126	720
	Totals		1,081	161	920

Purchases day book

Date 19X8	*Details*	*Invoice No*	*Total* £	*VAT* £	*Purchase of fabric* £	*Telephone* £
1 Dec	Cloth Weavers Limited	10871	11,750	1,750	10,000	
1 Dec	S&L Silks	Z609	3,290	490	2,800	
1 Dec	Midland Airtine	2010	470	70		400
1 Dec	Fineweavers Limited	F5076	1,410	210	1,200	
	Totals		16,920	2,520	14,000	400

Balances

The following balances are relevant to you at the start of the day on 1 December 19X8.

	£
Credit customers	
The Clothes Shop	15,100
B & B Denims	3,250
O'Hara Brothers	8,910
Designer Clothes Limited	11,819
Sales (debtors) ledger control	169,157
Purchases (creditors) ledger control	71,306
Sales	243,810
Purchases	97,036
Sales returns	1,072
Telephone	580
Discounts allowed	320
VAT (credit balance)	15,079

Receipts and payments on 1 December 19X8

Cash Sales

	Total	*VAT*	*Net*
L Cartwright	47	7	40
M Hipkiss	141	21	120

Cheques Issued

PD Builders Limited (a creditor)	423

Cheques Received

The Clothes Shop (in full settlement of a debt of £1,800)	1,730

Section 1

Processing exercise

(Suggested time allocation: 60 minutes)

COMPLETE ALL FIVE TASKS

Task 1.1

Enter the opening balances listed above into the following accounts.

- The Clothes Shop
- B & B Denims
- O'Hara Brothers
- Designer Clothes Limited
- Sales (debtors) ledger control
- Purchases (creditors) ledger control
- Sales
- Purchases
- Sales returns
- Telephone
- Discounts Allowed
- VAT

Task 1.2

Using the data supplied, enter all the relevant transactions into the accounts in the Sales Ledger and General (Nominal) Ledger.

Task 1.3

Enter the receipts and payments shown on the previous page into the cash book.

Task 1.4

Transfer any relevant sums from the cash book into the Sales Ledger and General (Nominal) Ledger.

Task 1.5

Balance off all of the accounts and the cash book, *showing clearly the balances carried down.*

Section 2

Short answer questions

(Suggested time allocation: 75 minutes)

Write in the Answer Book provided. Do not indicate your choice in any other way.

ANSWER ALL OF THE QUESTIONS IN THIS SECTION.

Task 2.1

Complete the paying-in slip and counterfoil to bank the cash takings and cheque on 1 December 19X8, details of which are as follows:

Cash

One	£20 note	Five	50 pence coins
Twelve	£10 notes	Twenty-one	10 pence coins
Five	£5 notes	Ten	2 pence coins
Eighteen	£1 coins	Twenty	1 pence coins

Cheque

One cheque	£1,730

Task 2.2

JS Fashions Limited is a VAT registered trader. Should it charge VAT on goods supplied to a customer who is not VAT registered?

Task 2.3

Give **two** reasons why a business may offer a **trade** discount to its customers.

Task 2.4

A business will ensure that there is a cash float available in the petty cash tin. What do you understand by the term cash float?

Task 2.5

JS Fashions Limited has recently placed one of its customers on the 'stop list' which means that the customer will not be able to purchase any more goods on credit from JS Fashions Limited. Why is this action usually necessary?

Task 2.6

In what circumstances would it he more appropriate to pay bills by direct debit rather than by standing order?

Task 2.7

Should the total of the VAT amounts paid out of petty cash be debited or credited to the VAT account?

Task 2.8

JS Fashions Limited has issued a receipt for £305.50 inclusive of VAT @ 17.5%. What is the VAT amount included in this figure? (Show workings)

Task 2.9

On 16 November 19X8 JS Fashions Limited sent a quotation to a customer for the supply of denim jeans. The customer received the quotation the next day and sent a letter by post accepting the quotation on 18 November 19X8. JS Fashions Limited received the letter of acceptance on 19 November 19X8.

(a) On which date was the contract made?

(b) Briefly explain the reason for your answer.

Task 2.10

Within a computerised accounting system give **two** examples of items of hardware.

Task 2.11

JS Fashions Limited is planning to purchase a new sewing machine costing £25,000. Would the following items be classed as capital or revenue expenditure?

(a) The purchase price of the machine

(b) The cost of the initial training for staff to operate the machine (this cost is significant)

(c) The cost of future maintenance of the machine

Task 2.12

What is a post-dated cheque?

Task 2.13

A cheque which has been received from a credit customer and paid into the bank account of JS Fashions Limited has subsequently been dishonoured. What bookkeeping entries are required in the general (nominal) ledger of JS Fashions Limited to record the dishonoured cheque?

(a) Debit

(b) Credit

Task 2.14

It is common practice for businesses to produce an age analysis of debtors at the end of every month.

(a) What does this analysis show?

(b) What is the purpose of this analysis?

Task 2.15

The Sale of Goods Act 1979 requires the seller to ensure that goods must be fit for the purpose described. Name **one** other obligation the Act puts upon the seller.

Task 2.16

JS Fashions Limited does not currently offer its customers the facility to pay by credit card but is considering this method of payment

(a) Give one disadvantage to the business of accepting credit card payments.

(b) In the seller's books of account a credit card sale is treated as a cash transaction.

True / False

Task 2.17

Name **three** checks which should be made before a purchase invoice received from a supplier can be passed for payment.

Task 2.18

Carriage inwards and carriage outwards are both expense accounts.

True / False

Task 2.19

What is the meaning of the following terms:

(a) Carriage paid

(b) Terms net monthly

(c) COD

Task 2.20

List **three** classification methods for filing documents and files.

Section 3

Communicating accounting information

(Suggested time allocation: 45 minutes)

Answer BOTH TASKS.

Use the stationery provided in the Answer Book for your answers.

Data

On 1 December 19X8 the statement shown below was received from Westmid Bank plc. Jaz Sahota is concerned about the bank charges shown, as monthly bank charges do not usually exceed £70 and there has not been any significant increase in banking transactions.

Westmid Bank plc

JS Fashions Limited

Northern Parade Bradwell
Yorkshire Y017 8LA

Account No 72986321

Statement of Account

Date	*Details*	*Debit*	*Credit*	*Balance*
19X8		£	£	£
23 Nov	Balance			18,706C
24 Nov	Cheque No 100761	2,190		16,516C
25 Nov	Credit		5,000	21,516C
27 Nov	Cheque No 100764	8,108		13,408C
30 Nov	Credit		6,156	19,564C
30 Nov	Bank charges	110		19,454C

C = Credit D = Debit

Task 3.1

Draft a courteous letter, ready for Jaz Sahota's signature, expressing his concern over the increase in charges and requesting an explanation. Address the letter to the bank manager, John Goodman.

Task 3.2

The bank current account of JS Fashions Limited is always in credit by a substantial amount. You think that it would be beneficial to the company to transfer the surplus cash to an investment account where interest would he earned.

Write a memorandum to Jaz Sahota explaining the situation and suggesting he contacts the bank manager for further advice on the types of investment accounts available.

Mock Central Assessment (Answer Book)

Section 1

Sales ledger

The Clothes Shop

Date	*Details*	*Amount* £	*Date*	*Details*	*Amount* £

B&B Denims

Date	*Details*	*Amount* £	*Date*	*Details*	*Amount* £

O'Hara Brothers

Date	*Details*	*Amount* £	*Date*	*Details*	*Amount* £

Designer Clothes Limited

Date	*Details*	*Amount £*	*Date*	*Details*	*Amount £*

General (nominal) ledger

Sales (debtors) ledger control

Date	*Details*	*Amount £*	*Date*	*Details*	*Amount £*

Purchases (creditors) ledger control

Date	*Details*	*Amount £*	*Date*	*Details*	*Amount £*

Sales

Date	*Details*	*Amount £*	*Date*	*Details*	*Amount £*

Purchases

Date	*Details*	*Amount £*	*Date*	*Details*	*Amount £*

Sales returns

Date	*Details*	*Amount £*	*Date*	*Details*	*Amount £*

Telephone

Date	*Details*	*Amount £*	*Date*	*Details*	*Amount £*

Discounts Allowed

Date	*Details*	*Amount £*	*Date*	*Details*	*Amount £*

VAT

Date	Details	Amount £	Date	Details	Amount £

Cash book

Date	*Details*	*Discount allowed*	*VAT*	*Cash*	*Bank*	*Date*	*Details*	*Discount received*	*VAT*	*Cash*	*Bank*
19X8		£	£	£	£	19X8		£	£	£	£
1 Dec	Balance b/f			100	21,304						

Section 2

Task 2.1

Date: ________	**Date:** ________	£50 Notes	________
		£20 Notes	________
		£10 Notes	________
A/c 72986321		£5 Notes	________
	Bank Giro Credit	£1 Coins	________
Cash	**JS Fashions Limited**	50p	________
________	________	20p	________
		10p, 5p	________
Cheques	**WESTMID BANK PLC**	2p, 1p	________
________		Total Cash	
	70–86–96 72986321	Cheques, etc	
Total ________		POs etc	________
	:100049: 70:8696: 72986321	TOTAL £	

Task 2.2

____

____

Task 2.3

____

____

____

____

Task 2.4

Task 2.5

Task 2.6

Task 2.7

Task 2.8

Task 2.9

(a)

(b)

Task 2.10

Task 2.11

(a) Capital / Revenue

(b) Capital / Revenue

(c) Capital / Revenue

Task 2.12

Task 2.13

(a) Debit

(b) Credit

Task 2.14

(a) ____

____

(b) ____

____

Task 2.15

____

____

____

____

Task 2.16

(a) ____

____

(b) True / False

Task 2.17

____

____

____

____

Task 2.18

True / False

Task 2.19

(a) Carriage paid

(b) Terms net monthly

(c) COD

Task 2.20

(a)

(b)

(c)

Section 3

Task 3.1

JS Fashions Limited

27 Connaught Industrial Estate, Bradwell, Yorks YO17 9TD
Tel: 01874 378614 Fax: 01874 378615

Directors: J Sahota, L Sahota Company Secretary: B Smithson
Registered in England number 679801

Task 3.2

MEMORANDUM

To: Date:

From:

Subject:

Mock Central Assessment (Answers)

Section 1

Task 1. 1

Sales ledger

The Clothes Shop

Date	*Details*	*Amount* £	*Date*	*Details*	*Amount* £
1 Dec	Balance b/f	15,100	1 Dec	Bank	1,730
1 Dec	Sales	1,269	1 Dec	Discounts allowed	70
			1 Dec	Balance c/d	14,569
		16,369			16,369
2 Dec	Balance b/d	14,569			

B&B Denims

Date	*Details*	*Amount* £	*Date*	*Details*	*Amount* £
1 Dec	Balance b/f	3,250	1 Dec	Sales returns	235
1 Dec	Sales	5,781	1 Dec	Balance c/d	8,796
		9,031			9,031
2 Dec	Balance b/d	8,796			

O'Hara Brothers

Date	*Details*	*Amount* £	*Date*	*Details*	*Amount* £
1 Dec	Balance b/f	8,910	1 Dec	Sales returns	846
1 Dec	Sales	3,525	1 Dec	Balance c/d	11,589
		12,435			12,435
2 Dec	Balance b/d	11,589			

Designer Clothes Limited

Date	*Details*	*Amount* £	*Date*	*Details*	*Amount* £
1 Dec	Balance b/f	11,819	1 Dec	Balance c/d	20,279
1 Dec	Sales	8,460			
		20,279			20,279
2 Dec	Balance b/d	20,279			

General (nominal) ledger

Sales (debtors) ledger control

Date	*Details*	*Amount* £	*Date*	*Details*	*Amount* £
1 Dec	Balance brought forward	169,157	1 Dec	Sales returns	1,081
			1 Dec	Bank	1,730
1 Dec	Sales	19,035	1 Dec	Discounts allowed	70
			1 Dec	Balance c/d	185,311
		188,192			188,192
2 Dec	Balance b/d	185,311			

Purchases (creditors) ledger control

Date	*Details*	*Amount* £	*Date*	*Details*	*Amount* £
1 Dec	Bank	423	1 Dec	Balance b/f	71,306
1 Dec	Balance c/d	87,803	1 Dec	Purchases	16,920
			1 Dec		
		88,226			88,226
			2 Dec	Balance b/d	87,803

Sales

Date	Details	Amount £	Date	Details	Amount £
1 Dec	Balance c/d	260,170	1 Dec	Balance b/f	243,810
			1 Dec	Debtors	16,200
			1 Dec	Cash sales	160
		260,170			260,170
			2 Dec	Balance b/d	260,170

Purchases

Date	Details	Amount £	Date	Details	Amount £
1 Dec	Balance b/f	97,036	1 Dec	Balance c/d	111,036
1 Dec	Creditors	14,000			
		111,036			111,036
2 Dec	Balance b/d	111,036			

Sales returns

Date	Details	Amount £	Date	Details	Amount £
1 Dec	Balance b/f	1,072	1 Dec	Balance c/d	1,992
1 Dec	Debtors	920			
		1,992			1,992
2 Dec	Balance b/d	1,992			

Telephone

Date	Details	Amount £	Date	Details	Amount £
1 Dec	Balance b/f	580	1 Dec	Balance c/d	980
1 Dec	Midland Airtime	400			
		980			980
2 Dec	Balance b/d	980			

Discounts Allowed

Date	*Details*	*Amount* £	*Date*	*Details*	*Amount* £
1 Dec	Balance b/f	320	1 Dec	Balance c/d	390
1 Dec	Bank	70			
		390			390
2 Dec	Balance b/d	390			

VAT

Date	*Details*	*Amount* £	*Date*	*Details*	*Amount* £
1 Dec	Sales returns	161	1 Dec	Balance b/f	15,079
1 Dec	Purchases	2,520	1 Dec	Sales	2,835
1 Dec	Balance b/d	15,261	1 Dec	Cash sales	28
		17,942			17,942
			2 Dec	Balance c/d	15,261

Cash book

Date	*Details*	*Discount allowed*	*VAT*	*Cash*	*Bank*	*Date*	*Details*	*Discount received*	*VAT*	*Cash*	*Bank*
19X8		£	£	£	£	19X8		£	£	£	£
1 Dec	Balance b/f			100	21,304	1 Dec	PD Builders Limited				423
1 Dec	JL Cartwrifht		7	47							
1 Dec	M Hipkiss		21	141							
1 Dec	The Clothes Shop	70			1,730	1 Dec	Balance c/d			288	22,611
		70	28	288	23,034					288	23,034
2 Dec				288	22,611						
2 Dec											

Section 2

The following answers are suggested answers only and other relevant alternatives may be acceptable.

Task 2.1

Date:	01/12/X8	**Date:** 01/12/X8	£50 Notes	
			£20 Notes	20.00
			£10 Notes	120.00
A/c 72986321			£5 Notes	25.00
		Bank Giro Credit	£1 Coins	18.00
Cash	£188.00	**JS Fashions Limited**	50p	2.50
		A Student	20p	
			10p, 5p	2.10
Cheques		**WESTMID BANK PLC**	2p, 1p	.40
	£1,730.00		Total Cash	188.00
		70–86–96 72986321	Cheques, etc	1,730.00
Total	1,918.00		POs etc	
		:100049: 70:8696: 72986321	TOTAL £	1,918.00

Task 2.2

Yes

Task 2.3

Any two from:

- To encourage sales in large quantities
- To enable retailers to sell goods to the public at a profit
- To reward regular customers and attract new customers
- To match competitors' prices

Task 2.4

An amount of money put in the petty cash tin at the start of a period to enable petty cash expenses to be reimbursed. This is known as the imprest amount.

Task 2.5

The customer has usually failed to settle their account within the trading terms offered by the supplier, or has exceeded their credit limit.

Task 2.6

When the amount to be paid and/or the dates of payment vary.

Task 2.7

Debited.

Task 2.8

£305.50/1.175 = £260.00

£260.00 x 0.175 = £45.50

Task 2.9

(a) 18 November 19X8

(b) The postal rule states that the contract is effective when the acceptance is posted, provided it is correctly addressed and stamped.

Task 2.10

Any two from:

VDU	Mouse	Printer	Disks
Keyboard	CD-ROM	Central processor	

Task 2.11

(a) Capital

(b) Capital

(c) Revenue

Task 2.12

A cheque that will not be honoured until some time in the future.

Task 2.13

(a) Sales (debtors) ledger control

(b) Bank

Task 2.14

(a) It shows individual debts of customers and the amount of time each debt has been outstanding.

(b) It is used as a credit control tool to monitor and chase outstanding debts.

Task 2.15

Any one from:

- Goods should be of satisfactory quality
- Goods should fit the description
- Seller should have the right to sell (title)
- Goods should match the sample, when sale is by 'sample'

Task 2.16

(a) The retailer has to pay a percentage commission to the credit card company on credit card sales.

or

The retailer will experience a delay in payment from the credit card company.

(b) True

Task 2.17

Any three from:

- Invoice calculations are correct
- Goods received match delivery note details
- Delivery note details match purchase order
- Invoice details match goods received note
- Invoice details match delivery note
- Invoice details match purchase order
- Relevant discounts have been applied

Task 2.18

True

Task 2.19

(a) The quoted price includes the cost of delivery.

(b) *Full* payment of the invoice to be made within one month of invoice date. No settlement discount allowed

(c) Cash on Delivery

Task 2.20

(a) Alphabetical

(b) Numerical

(c) Alphanumerical

Section 3

Task 3.1

The letter given below is a suggested one only, and is indicative of the content and clarity expected from a competent candidate.

JS Fashions Limited

27 Connaught Industrial Estate, Bradwell, Yorks YO17 9TD
Tel: 01874 378614 Fax: 01874 378615

Mr John Goodman
Bank Manager
Westmid Bank plc
Northern Parade
Bradwell
Yorkshire Y017 SLA

1 December 19X8

Dear Mr Goodman,

Account No 72986321

Thank you for the latest statement of account in respect of the above numbered account.

However, we are concerned to note that the bank charges made are considerably higher than usual at £110. As you are aware our charges do not usually exceed £70 per month. As there has been no significant increase in banking transactions we are naturally concerned, and would ask you to investigate the matter and let us have an explanation of the increased charges as soon as possible.

Yours sincerely

J Sahota
Managing Director

Directors: J Sahota, L Sahota Company Secretary: B Smithson
Registered in England number 679801

Task 3.2

The memo given below is a suggested one only, and is indicative of the content and clarity expected from a competent candidate.

MEMORANDUM

To:	Jaz Sahota	Date:	1 December 19X8
From:	A Student		
Subject:	Investment		

It has come to my attention that the company bank current account is usually in credit by a substantial amount. It would, therefore, seem prudent to transfer the surplus cash to an investment account where interest would be earned.

Perhaps you would like to contact the bank manager for further advice on the types of investment accounts currently available.

Index

STUDY PACK REVIEW FORM

We hope that you have found this Study Pack stimulating and useful and that you now feel confident and well prepared for your Assessments in Units 1 and 2.

We would be grateful if you could take a few moments to complete the questionnaire below, so we can assess how well our material meets the needs of students. There's a prize for four lucky students who fill in one of these forms from across the AAT range and are lucky enough to be selected!

	Excellent	Adequate	Poor
Range of coverage by questions			
Appropriateness of coverage to Assessment once sat			
Presentation			
Level of accuracy			

Did you spot any errors or ambiguities? Please let us have the details below.

Thank you for your feedback.

Please return this form to:

AAT review forms
Profex Publishing
1 High Street
Maidenhead
Berkshire SL6 1JN

Or e-mail your comments to: profex@clara.co.uk